DISABLED PC
A Reading of Voltai _ _Contes_

FAUX TITRE

Etudes
de langue et littérature françaises
publiées

sous la direction de Keith Busby,
M.J. Freeman, Sjef Houppermans,
Paul Pelckmans et Co Vet

No. 77

Amsterdam - Atlanta, GA 1993

DISABLED POWERS:
A Reading of Voltaire's *Contes*

by

ROBIN HOWELLS

ISBN: 90-5183-583-3 (CIP)
©Editions Rodopi B.V., Amsterdam - Atlanta, GA 1993
Printed in The Netherlands

My thanks

for much salutary discussion of Voltaire's *Contes*,
to Philippe Bolusset, Llew Siddons, and especially Fée Ringham.

for generous help in preparing the manuscript, to Jenny Hawkes.

CONTENTS

INTRODUCTION:
THE CARNIVALESQUE AND THE *CONTE*

This is a study of Voltaire's *Romans et contes* under the sign of the carnivalesque. My Introduction sets out the concept of the carnivalesque, • indicating its relevance to the *conte* in the earlier Enlightenment and to Voltaire's adoption of this genre. Part I will establish a paradigm for the *Romans et contes*, using the whole corpus of twenty-six tales. In Chapter 1 the approach is principally narratological. Chapter 2 establishes a thematics of disablement. These chapters sketch in the carnivalesque dimensions of the paradigm. Part II will offer systematic carnivalesque readings of two of the *Contes*. The first is an early tale, *Le Monde comme il va*. The second is *Candide*, in every sense the *magnum opus*, from the middle period. Part III considers successively six of the later *Contes*. Along with the internal reading we shall look at how they reflect ideological changes during the age. The shift towards bourgeois realism appears not only in literary terms but in relation to the rise of materialism on the one hand, of sentiment and the patriarchal family on the other. The more limited carnivalesque of these texts, notably their uneasy treatment of corporality, provides an index of the shifts occuring. Thus we shall treat in turn the whole of the *Contes*, the single tale, and a series of tales. The Conclusion will trace the carnivalesque figure in its changing forms, from geometric to vitalist, within the *Contes* as a whole.

The carnivalesque is a concept established by Mikhail Bakhtin (1895-1975). It emerges principally in and from his book on Rabelais.[1] The term is derived from the phenomenon of carnival, which Bakhtin sees as a social event, the embodiment of a certain consciousness, and a figure of reality. The carnival is collective and dynamic. In the carnival boundaries are bridged and hierarchies are broken down. Dealing in all

---

[1] Bakhtin's study, though broadly worked out by the early 1940s, was not published until 1965. English translation *Rabelais and his World* (Cambridge Mass., 1968; Bloomington Indiana, 1984); French translation, more exactly titled, *L'Œuvre de François Rabelais et la culture populaire au moyen âge et sous la renaissance* (Paris, 1970). In the revised version of *Problems of Dostoevsky's Poetics* (1963), second English translation (Manchester, 1984), Bakhtin offers in the first half of chapter 4 a kind of summary of the carnivalesque.

forms of play, the carnival frees what seems fixed and multiplies what claims to be unique. Functioning as the comic debasement of falsehood, it declares 'the joyous relativity of all things'. Characterised by laughter and violence, by excess and disorder, it is nevertheless strongly ritualised. Though it is marked off from ordinary life, it is a time that returns (any festival) and a space re-used (any collective space). It is both repetition and renewal. It represents the 'unfinished' nature of reality and truth.

Reality's representation is in more specific terms what Bakhtin calls the grotesque body. 'Body' affirms materiality. 'Grotesque' insists on openness and incompletion. Thus the grotesque body signifies corporeal process. We can perhaps identify it at four levels. One is the human body, especially its internal processes, its centre and extremities, and its interaction with the rest of the world. The second is the collective body of the group or community, in all its manifestations and cultural practices, especially its public and popular observances. Thirdly there is the universal body of the world, heterogeneous, changing and ever-renewed. Fourth is the body by which we cognise the world and communicate with each other, the body of language. It too is shared and exchanged. Joyous debasement is offered by popular speech, mockery, parody and other kinds of double-voicing, heterogeneous discourses, all forms of play and emphasis upon the materiality of language - the body of the word.[2]

Language too is an open process. This is essentially what is meant by Bakhtin's most famous coinage, dialogism. All utterance is dialogic. It is 'in dialogue' with the language of the community, with the reality it seeks to seize, and with interlocutors real or imagined (as I am now, while writing this). Because it is always borrowed, composed of plural discourses, quotations and meanings, it is in dialogue with itself. Thus it is part of an unending transaction. Utterance which denies this aspires to monologism. It claims authority, repudiates plurality and seeks to have the last word. But it is inevitably re-opened, reworded, relativised and renewed. It is carnivalised, to reveal once more its true condition. Literature structures and stylises the innate dialogism of language. Its polyphony, as Bakhtin puts it, is orchestrated. Languages (ideologemes) are played against each other within an artistic form. For Bakhtin prose

---

[2]   The substance of the last two paragraphs can be found in Bakhtin's 'Introduction' to the *Rabelais*, though the notion of the body of language in particular is little developed.

fiction is the most capacious genre, best able to achieve the mimesis of linguistic, ideological and social interactions.[3]

Bakhtin finds the richest writing in the Renaissance, and in particular in Rabelais. The 'carnivalesque' writing of Rabelais reflects the continuing vitality of mediæval popular culture (oral, public, corporeal), and the particular intersections of the period. Latin and the vernaculars, religion and its reform, humanism and nationalism, are all in play. With the victory of nationalism in the seventeenth century comes a new state order, that of Classicism. Hierarchies become fixed and boundaries closed. The Enlightenment actually reinforces Classicism's tendency to abstraction and rationalism. It substitutes for concrete norms an atemporal and universal Reason. The literary culture is strongly normative. In literature base material is treated negatively or made acceptable to decorum. Bodily functions are euphemised; vulgar speech is neutralised. Formal structures are regular. Content is spare. Laughter is reduced to a smile. The comic is intellectualised, thematised as satire or sentimentalised. Aristocratic refinement is allied with bourgeois moralism and didacticism. Preceding the new subjective freedom of Romanticism and the concrete engagement of Realism, the Enlightenment is arguably the lowest point in the history of the carnivalesque.[4]

In every period, however, the carnivalesque is manifested. Its degree, and its particular forms, tell us about the period. This we find in the first half of the eighteenth century. The refined culture is reflected in refined forms of infraction. Parody and playfulness are perhaps the principal forms. The rococo diminishes and pluralises. Not only its aesthetics but also its politics might be characterised as 'internal freedom within external order'. Writers, or their texts, proceed by wit and indirection. They 'fail to understand' received discourses (the outsider is just one device here). They joyously transpose or fragment those discourses, sometimes inserting

---

[3] On discourses, literature and the dialogic, see especially Bakhtin's essay 'Discourse in the novel' in *The Dialogic Imagination*, ed. Michael Holquist (Austin, 1981) (French version, 'Du Discours romanesque' in *Esthétique et théorie du roman* [Paris, 1978]).

[4] See the *Rabelais*, pp.33-4, 101-120. Bakhtin is kinder to the Enlightenment - and especially to Voltaire - in chapter 4 of the revised *Dostoevsky*. He is carefully even-handed in his study, 'The Bildungsroman', in *Speech Genres and other Late Essays*, ed. Caryl Emerson and Michael Holquist (Austin, 1986), pp.29, 44-45.

alternative versions of truth. By means of multivoicing and constant irony
they resist our demand for a closed meaning. In this way the texts are
dialogic within themselves. They are in dialogue with a sophisticated
audience. The more contestatory also play a dialogic game with the censor
and the state. Through parody and playfulness they dialogue with the
received discursive order.[5]

Since the beginning of the century, the *conte* itself as a genre has stood
in this relation. Perrault's *Contes* (1691-97) - the *Mother Goose Tales* -
insert the popular matter of fairytales into the received literary order. The
diminutive tale has a diminutive hero, usually a child. The story, and
principally its moral, are gently ironised. Other fairytales, usually featuring
less juvenile and more noble protagonists, toy with the conventions of
romance and courtly love. Knowingness and literary reflexivity are typical
of this subgenre. It is soon joined by the oriental tale. Galland's *Mille et
une Nuits* (1704-17) - *The Arabian Nights* - also draw on popular material.
(In Perrault one might say that the specific counter-principle to the official
order was children; here it is women - Scheherazade and Dinarzade - and
the night.) These tales too are multiple, brief and sophisticated. Also
highly successful, they quickly spawn imitations. Such is the degree of
self-irony that it is almost impossible to distinguish pastiche from parody.
The mock-oriental tale and the mock-fairytale overlap. Both deal quite
frequently in magic, and in violence. Against Reason, they offer the oniric
and the ludic. Against realism they propose fantasy and otherness. Yet
they engage with reality through allusion and satire. Increasingly they
accommodate libertinism and the grotesque. They seem to function almost
as society's or literature's subconscious. Certainly they constitute a refined
form of the carnivalesque. Openness, hybridity and extraordinary freedom
characterise the *conte* in the first half of the eighteenth century.[6]

---

[5] On forms of cultural play in this period, see the first half of Jean Starobinski's
L'Invention de la liberté (Geneva, 1964); and the collection *Le Jeu au xviiie siècle*
(Aix-en-Provence, 1976) (especially pp.157-66, Philip Stewart, 'Le Jeu de l'amour' -
actually a wide-ranging piece). On the carnivalesque in the literature of the period, see
my 'Rococo and carnival', *Studies on Voltaire and the Eighteenth Century* 308 (1993),
pp.187-223.

[6] On parody and self-parody in the *conte* of our period, see Jean-Paul Sermain,
'La parodie dans les contes de fées (1693-1713): une loi du genre?', *Burlesque et
formes parodiques*, ed. Isabelle Landy-Houillon and Maurice Ménard

The novel at this time was still very much in the process of formation. It too was deprecated as a genre. But it had rather less freedom than the *conte*, because it was taken a little more seriously. It faced what has been called 'le dilemme du roman'. Was it to remain faithful to the romance, with which it was still widely identified (the term 'roman' still designated the romance)? Or should it represent something like everyday life? The former was unbelievable - 'roman' was widely used as a synonym for ideal falsehood. But the quotidian and the concrete were base, an unacceptable subject for art unless comic. The novel of the everyday had no artistic pedigree. Its solution was to evade the problem by denying its fictionality, claiming literal truth as the transcription of an authentic personal narrative, oral account, written memoir, letters, ... The device quickly becomes standard, and thus part of the literary system from which it claims to dissociate itself. (The 'authentic account' moreover goes back a very long way, and had been mocked in burlesque at least since *Don Quixote*.) Other attempts by the new novel to distance itself from fiction are similarly re-absorbed, taken back into the reflexive irony so characteristic of this period. The novel in its playful dimensions overlaps with the *conte*. It too is a very open genre. It too accomodates satire and libertinism. The enormous success of the *Lettres persanes* of Montesquieu (1721) is significant. That work illustrates most of the characteristics we have identified: mock-authentication, orientalism, the outsider, satire, libertinism. And, most notably, its generic hybridity accommodates 'philosophie'.

The prose narratives by Voltaire which have come to be known as his *Romans et contes* emerge from this cultural and literary context. The first to be published did not appear until the late 1740s, however, when Voltaire was over fifty. It has recently been argued that several were actually composed much earlier. *Le Crocheteur borgne* and *Cosi-Sancta* may have been created for the entertainment of the duchesse du Maine and her circle

---

(Paris-Seattle-Tübingen, 1987), pp.541-52; and Raymonde Robert, 'La parodie du conte merveilleux au xviiie siècle', *Dire la parodie: colloque de Cerisy*, ed. Clive Thomson and Alain Pagès (New York-Bern-Frankfurt-Paris, 1989), pp.183-99. On fantasy and the grotesque in the *conte*, see the extracts analysed by Henri Coulet, 'La fantaisie dans le conte français du xviiie siècle' *Burlesque et formes parodiques*, pp.503-25.

in 1715.[7] The 'Regency' character of these two roguish tales makes the
early date quite likely. Moreover it seems likely that the youthful Voltaire,
a courtier and wit adept in light verse and prose, would have attempted the
kind of exotic prose tale that was so fashionable in 1715. But, by the same
token, these two tales do not possess the full characteristics of the later
contes philosophiques. The case has also been made for dating earlier the
composition of three more strongly 'philosophical' tales. One is
Micromégas, which appeared in 1753. The revisionary view is that it was
written around 1738, reflecting the confidence in science of Voltaire's
Cirey period.[8]

The fact remains nevertheless that until the late 1740s Voltaire
published no prose tales. Why did he take so long to go into print in the
form in which he would be considered subsequently to excel? Certainly
he shared the widespread view that prose fiction was a low genre. (In the
Lettres philosophiques of 1734 his lengthy and well-informed survey of
English literature mentions no work of prose fiction. Swift is there as a
satirist - in verse as well - not a novelist.) His objection was essentially
cultural and aesthetic rather than moral: he thought novels trivial and
vulgar. He had established early his own fame, and his self-image, as a
tragic and epic poet. He then turns to prose for non-fiction works of
history, philosophy and science. The appearance of the first prose tales is
notable not only in relation to past but also to future publication. He will
continue to publish tales at fairly regular intervals until shortly before his
death thirty years later. The generic innovation of the late 1740s is
generally seen by scholars as reflecting a shift in his world-view. At this
time Voltaire is starting to lose faith in the philosophico-scientific optimism
that he had developed and argued in print during the previous twenty years.
Metaphysical and moral difficulties - notably the problem of Evil - were
becoming increasingly disturbing. Resort to the *conte* is both the index of

---

[7] The case was made by Jacqueline Hellegouarc'h, and is argued in the Pléiade
edition of the *Romans et contes*, ed. Frédéric Deloffre and Jacques Van den Heuvel
(Paris, 1979), pp.661-71, 681-85. Issues of dating apart, this is the authoritative edition
of the *Contes*, which I shall use throughout.

[8] See Jacques Van den Heuvel, *Voltaire dans ses contes* (Paris, 1967), pp.68-78.
As Van den Heuvel observes (p.70, n.14), this view was argued in detail by Ira O.
Wade in 1950 in his edition of *Micromégas*.

his dissatisfaction with the discourses of order, and the expression of it.[9]

The broader significance of the Voltairean *conte* within his life and work must include the intellectual dimension. But the generic choice is itself significant. We have noted the function of the genre in the period. For Voltaire too, the *conte* offers a relief from elevation and seriousness. It constitutes for him too a shift from official performance to more intimate pleasure. It is almost literally 'writ small'. The various kinds of oral storytelling with which it is associated - the popular 'veillée', the household nanny and childhood, the aristocratic salon or boudoir - are all suggestive. The escape from the constraints of high discourse allows a 'défoulement', a release of the repressed.[10] Voltaire's practice of anonymous publication is readily explicable by the concern to evade punishment by the state. But it is also a way of preserving his literary dignity while enjoying the freedom of having no name. To be more exact, his practice was pseudonymous. The many false names he uses are multiple masks. But, because they are unlikely names, they are calculated less to deceive than to mock. Again we return to the ludic. Through play Voltaire negotiates with his official self and the official order. The concept should be central to our understanding of the man and the writer.[11]

Play does not of course exclude structure, or seriousness. The *conte philosophique* that Voltaire creates is highly structured - as we shall see.

---

[9] The link is established by René Pomeau, *La Religion de Voltaire* (Paris, 1956; revised edition 1974), pp.240-50: 'le conte voltairien naît définitivement de la crise de 1748' (p.248). It is argued lengthily (and to some extent against himself), with particular reference to *Zadig*, *Le Monde comme il va* and *Memnon*, by Jacques Van den Heuvel, *ibid.*, pp.123-216. A more gradualist account of the intellectual shift is proposed in the judicious review of the evidence by Haydn Mason, '*Zadig* and the birth of the Voltaire *conte*', *Rousseau and the Eighteenth Century: Essays in Memory of R.A. Leigh* (Oxford, 1992), pp.283-94.

[10] See Laurence L. Bongie, 'Crisis and the birth of the Voltairian *conte*', *Modern Language Quarterly* 23 (1962), pp.53-64. Bongie includes the notion that the tales reflect a 'Voltaire dionysiaque', following the suggestive esssay by André Delattre, *Voltaire l'impétueux* (Paris, 1957).

[11] On Voltaire and play, see the remarks by René Pomeau, 'Le Jeu de Voltaire écrivain', *Le Jeu au xviii*[e] *siècle*, pp.175-76; Haydn Mason, 'Voltaire et le ludique', *Revue d'Histoire Littéraire de la France* 84 (1984), pp.539-52; and S.S.B. Taylor, 'Voltaire's humour', *SVEC* 179 (1979), pp.101-16.

It constitutes a very serious contestation. The satire is often ferocious. The didactic element is important. To reach the greatest number of readers the Voltairean *conte* harnesses an apparently frivolous genre to 'philosophical' purposes.[12] But the 'message' too is usually ironised by its context. The *conte* is also a self-contestation. It thematises its own inability to find the answer. By genre as well as by content it relativises truth. Through play and parody, laughter and violence - principles central to the carnivalesque - it celebrates the joyous relativity of all things. Disabling the discourses of order, it also disables itself.

---

[12] The most thorough study of structure, satire and didacticism - using four major *contes* - is undoubtedly Carol Sherman, *Reading Voltaire's Contes: a Semiotics of Philosophical Narration* (Chapel Hill, 1985).

PART I

Chapter 1 PARADIGM

1. TITLES

Zadig, Scarmentado, Candide, L'Ingénu, La Princesse de Babylone ....
Of Voltaire's twenty-six *Romans et contes*, over half in their titles
designate the protagonist. This principle has always been common in the
narrative (and in the dramatic) genres. Epic, romance, novel and tale all
widely employ it: the *Odyssey, L'Astrée, Madame Bovary, Cinderella*. It
was particularly commonplace in the eighteenth-century novel: *Gil Blas,
Marianne, Tom Jones, Clarissa*.

Thus Voltaire's practice is not in itself remarkable. But his names are
often odd. 'Zadig' is exotic to us, and was so for the French reader of
1750. That reader however could probably identify a work with this title
as part of the mass of 'Oriental' literature so popular in the period.[1]
'Jenni' might perhaps be perceived as English. A version of 'Johnny', it
reflects the Anglophilia and the orthography illustrated in other French
works of the time such as *Fanni Butlerd*. For the contemporary reader,
cultural and generic stereotypes were implicit in these names. With the
non-naturalistic name 'Candide' moral qualities become explicit. 'Candide'
signifies not indirectly (like 'M. de Pourceaugnac' via animal and regional
stereotypes), nor partially (like 'Gull-iver' perhaps) but (like the
seventeenth-century German 'Simplicius Simplicissimus') flatly. 'Candide'
implies some signification beyond the story, probably satirical. The names
of other titular protagonists can be added. 'L'Ingénu' is obviously

---

[1] The edition of *Zadig* by G. Ascoli, revised by J. Fabre (2 vols, Paris, 1962), lists
over two hundred French literary works 'à la couleur orientale' published between
1670 and 1749 ('Introduction'). Names beginning with 'Z' were much favoured (ii,
p.9). Voltaire's own triumph with his tragedy *Zaïre* (1732) no doubt aided the fashion.

analogous to 'Candide'.[2] 'Micromégas' can be deciphered by way of familiar Greek prefixes, and cultural conventions ('bassesse', 'maganimité'). '[E]Scarmentado' and 'Cosi-Sancta' contain more precise meanings via Spanish and Italian. From this partial survey of eponymous titles emerge several characteristics. There is a range of non-French reference: oriental, English, Spanish, Italian, classical Greek. The ease of identification however confirms cultural and generic stereotyping. The verbal gaming indicates a ludic or a satirical element. Again however this brings us back to French cultural norms of the period. The strongest norm may well be that of offering, beyond the story, a generalising discourse.

From the fuller versions of these titles two concerns are signalled strongly. One is genre. Almost all declare a generic adherence. *Cosi-Sancta ... Nouvelle africaine*; *Micromégas. Histoire philosophique*; *Zadig ... Histoire orientale*; *Histoire des voyages de Scarmentado écrite par lui-même*; *L'Ingénu. Histoire véritable tirée des manuscrits du père Quesnel.* 'Histoire', in the usage of the period, primarily designated a personal narrative, marked off (despite its supposed orality) as a separate unit within a larger work. With changing norms, its air of verisimilitude (private knowledge, immediate experience, concrete reference) led to the term being used for complete works too. 'Nouvelle', a much rarer term in the eighteenth century, also designated a verisimilar narrative. Historically and generically, both functioned in contradistinction to the category 'roman', which was almost always employed ironically in this period. The titles listed above offer various glosses upon the verisimilar term. 'Africaine', 'orientale', 'philosophique' declare subgenres by setting or theme. 'Ecrite par lui-même' affirms first-person narration, not in oral but at least in written form. 'Véritable' claims literal truth.

However the proper names we listed carry a different implication. Mainly playful, satirical or generalising, they point away from particular verisimilitude. The resultant tension in signification invites a reversed reading of the generic truth claims. They become ironic. One such claim we may find suspiciously over-emphatic anyway. 'Histoire véritable' is either a pleonasm itself or an implicit deprecation of other 'histoires'.

---

[2] An interesting attempt to differentiate the signification of the two names in relation to their textual functions can be found in Priscilla P. Clark, '"L'Ingénu": the uses and limitations of naïveté', *French Studies* 27 (1973), pp.278-86. Here our concern is to read the titles alone, within the metaliterary or metadiscursive system.

'Tirée des manuscrits du père Quesnel' repeats the authentication twice more. The attribution of a work with this title to a priest (for readers at the time, a notorious Jansenist to boot) might seem unlikely, and the allegation of a manuscript source too hackneyed to take at face value. Reflexive irony, literature disabling itself, is implicit.

The other concern is generalisation, not only in generic reference but in theme. *Cosi-Sancta* carries, along with its generic label, the subtitle 'Un petit mal pour un grand bien'. This proverbial formula invites us to expect a fable illustrating a 'moral'. Abstract categories and the promise of general wisdom are the more evident in the subtitles of other works we first noted. *Zadig* is subtitled '*la Destinée*'. In parallel we have '*Candide ou l'Optimisme*', and *Jenni*'s subtitle which personifies concepts in '*le Sage et l'Athée*'. But we observed that the supposedly proper names in the first titles also invite a thematic deciphering. One generic subtitle quite explicitly announces a generalising discourse: 'histoire philosophique'. From the folk-tale wisdom subtitling *Cosi-Sancta* to the philosophical claims made for *Micromégas*, the contract is for generalisation.

The suggestions of playfulness and satire remain present. Thus we might expect not only literature implicitly mocking the ambitions of literature. The pursuit of philosophical truth will be accompanied by the mockery of that pursuit. In both respects we might anticipate a witty and ambivalent kind of writing. Finally we can note in how many ways the titles imply a principle of duality. The obvious way is the first that we mentioned: titles implying narrative, subtitles suggesting general meaning. More exactly however we should also recognise a triplication. *Zadig/ou la Destinée/Histoire orientale* correlates with story/philosophical theme/literary genre. Three levels are marked off with equal clarity in *Cosi-Sancta/Un petit mal pour un grand bien/Nouvelle africaine*. Further though less rigorous proof for a rule of three is provided by *Candide/ou l'Optimisme/Traduit de l'allemand du docteur Ralph ...*, *L'Ingénu/Histoire véritable/tirée des manuscrits du père Quesnel* and, especially if recast, the full title of *Scarmentado*. But within the segments we are back with duality. 'Un petit mal pour un grand bien' offers rhetorical balance on either side of 'pour'. This is complemented by semantic opposition which is itself double. 'Bien' is the contrary of 'mal', 'petit' the contrary of 'grand'. (Thus we have a total of three dualities!) Opposed categories and relative proportion both reappear elsewhere too. 'Le sage et l'athée' implies another 'philosophical' opposition - however skewed - underlined by rhetorical balance. 'Micromégas' is 'little/big' within a single word, the opposition reinforced by syllabic balance and alliterative repetition. Thus duality seem to operate in every domain: from ontology to rhythm, from semantics to rhetoric, and from cognitive structure to self-referentiality.[3]

2. NARRATIVE

2.i. HERO

The hero is often designated in the title, as we have observed. Almost invariably he is presented in the first paragraph of the narrative. (The normative gender is appropriate; rarely is this chief protagonist female.) Description is authoritative and summary, typical of the tale as a genre. A few broad moral traits - 'un beau naturel', 'les moeurs les plus douces' - usually suffice. The story follows the hero and the narration is sometimes focalised through him. Naturally or culturally he is to some degree an outsider. Natural simplicity may be formally declared in his name (Candide, the Ingenu). Cultural simplicity is often connoted by youth: Candide, the Ingenu; 'Jenni n'avait pas encore vingt ans' (*Jenni*, i, p.597). Simplicity may be signalled through a cultural stereotype. Babouc of *Le Monde comme il va* is a Scythian, a proverbially savage breed (see *Zadig*, xii, p.89; *La Princesse de Babylone*, v, pp.381-82). The *Lettre d'un Turc* is attributed to a representative of another people known for barbarity. The Ingenu is by upbringing a Huron, another type of 'le bon sauvage'. Amabed, and Amazan in *La Princesse de Babylone*, are Hindu vegetarians. Simplicity may be marked by social or class disadvantage. The protagonist in *Candide* was born out of wedlock; in *Le Crocheteur borgne* he is a porter; in *L'Homme aux quarante écus* a peasant farmer; *Jeannot et Colin* begins as a tale of two poor provincials. Social and cultural simplicity - by convention - go together.

On the other hand, the hero may be assigned exceptional attainments. We have the philosopher Pythagoras in *Aventure indienne*, the philosopher Plato, proto-hero of *Songe de Platon*, and the anonymous philosopher-

---

[3] On 'le rythme binaire de ce monde qui cloche', see Jean Starobinski's brilliant stylistic analysis of *L'Ingénu* in *Le Remède dans le mal* (Paris, 1989), pp.144-63.

protagonists of *Les Deux consolés* and *Histoire d'un bon bramin*. He may be socially privileged. Micromégas is 'Son Excellence', Scarmentado the son of a governor and Rustan (*Le Blanc et le noir*) the son of a minor noble. The protagonists of *La Princesse de Babylone* and *Le Taureau blanc* are royal. (The alternative protagonist in the latter, Mambrès, is a magus and a counsellor of royalty.) Zadig and Memnon are wealthy and well-connected, Jenni is from the ruling classes. Thus the hero may be rich or poor, simpleton or philosopher. But this variety can be reduced to a paradigm. He is always to some degree marked off from the world. What signifies is, in every case, his explicit difference and implicit superiority in relation to the cultural norm. He is unworldly by a lack or an excess of wisdom, or of wealth. Lack or excess of wisdom makes him innocent by ignorance or idealism. Lack or excess of wealth makes him vulnerable. The former foreshadows his conflict with the norms of the world; the latter will underline its consequences as order becomes disorder.

The hero is invariably sympathetic, to us if not also to other characters. Youth and good looks (almost inseparable) are specified whenever there is to be a love interest (*Zadig, Candide, L'Ingénu, La Princesse de Babylone, Jenni*). His fuller attractiveness arises from apparently opposed qualities. He may appeal to us because he is 'un jeune homme de beaucoup d'esprit' (*Micromégas*, i, p.19) or because he has on the contrary 'l'esprit le plus simple' (*Candide*, i, p.145); because he is wealthy and privileged like the first or poor and vulnerable like the second. What the heroes have in common is 'le jugement assez droit' (*Candide*, i, p.145). This is at once an intellectual and a moral quality, implying both a logical procedure and an ethical measure. It does not mean that the judgements they make during the narrative will be right. Their understanding of the world may be quite mistaken, and their particular assessments are usually incomplete.

Sometimes the hero is highly perceptive, sometimes he is absurdly naive. Character consistency (motivation) is less important than overall meaning (function). The protagonist's mistakes, and even his wisdom, confirm his role as outsider, child, innocent or fool. They mark the literary modes of comedy and satire. And they direct us firmly towards theme. As fool the protagonist reveals, almost unawares, ironic disjunctions. His 'failure to understand' questions what we regard as normal. It also allows him to voice alternative and superior norms. He is out of step with reality - which will duly assault him. Thus he serves to show forth both a falsely ideal world-view and an incoherent real world.

2.ii. QUEST.   a. MANDATE and LAUNCH

Often the protagonist embarks on a journey. This makes him an outsider twice over. He encounters peoples or practices foreign to him. Contact, paradoxically, is rapidly established. Such contact is as essential as his innocence to his role as interrogator of reality. At the start of *Le Monde comme il va* Babouc is sent by an angel to make an absolute judgement about Persepolis.

> Va dans cette ville, examine tout ... . - Mais, Seigneur, dit humblement Babouc, je n'ai jamais été en Perse; je n'y connais personne. - Tant mieux, dit l'ange, tu ne seras point partial; tu as reçu du ciel le discernement, et j'y ajoute le don d'inspirer la confiance. (p.39)

Here the key elements are made explicit and marked off. The Hero is given his Quest by an external Mandator.[4] The Object of the quest is absolute knowledge. It is to be achieved by systematic and global examination. The hero is unfamiliar with the reality he is to engage. But precisely this will ensure a judgement free from cultural bias. His positive equipment is a natural 'discernement' ('le jugement assez droit'), and a personal empathy that draws him and the world together. Ready contact, in the *Contes*, is essential to story and theme. It is also an index of the hero's curiosity, humanity and sociability.

Here is the paradigm of the mandate. The elements of this paradigm can be identified in other tales. In *Micromégas* they are set out almost as tidily. Again the quest is undertaken consciously and deliberately. Again its object is not concrete but philosophical. The same two aspects of the quest - physical displacement and moral understanding - are made explicit, and again they coincide. Here however it is divided into two stages. First Micromégas departs his native Sirius. 'Il se mit à voyager de planète en planète, pour achever de se former *l'esprit et le coeur*, comme on dit' (i,

---

[4] The capitalised terms derive from the structural model of narrative functions first established by V. Propp in his *Morphology of the Folk-tale* (1928) (English translation: Austin Texas, 1968), and radically reworked by A.J. Greimas - in *Sémantique structurale* (Paris, 1966) and subsequently - to apply to all narrative. The 'Hero' (as in Propp) is the 'Subject' in Greimas. 'Quest' and 'Mandator' correspond to Propp's functions ix and x, while in Greimas the latter is the 'Destinateur' and the former the pursuit of an 'Object'. As an introduction to the structural analysis of narrative, I find particularly helpful J.-M. Adam, *Le Récit* (Paris, 1987).

p.20). (On this ironic double-voicing of the object of the quest, see §3, below.) He encounters and converses with the Saturnian. Then, 'après avoir raisonné pendant une révolution du soleil, ils résolurent de faire ensemble un petit voyage philosophique' (ii, p.24).

Itinerary and purpose are less precisely defined here, at both stages, than in *Le Monde comme il va*. The mandating function, at both stages, is also a little different. Babouc's quest was mandated by an angel. Micromégas sets off from Sirius because he is banished from the court; at the second stage the decision to travel is made freely. The object, at both stages, he defines for himself. Or rather, at the second stage journey and purpose are agreed jointly by him and the Saturnian companion. Structurally, the hero is doubled. (Through incompetence his double will serve as a comic foil.) Thematically he is supplied with a regular interlocutor for his question. Humanely, he and we are gladdened by companionship. The gifts required to carry out the project are noted. The Saturnian too will be equipped with the means to interrogate those whom they meet. 'Il avait le don des langues, aussi bien que le Sirien' (vi, p.30) (Babouc had 'le don d'inspirer la confiance'). The hero alone however is 'un bon observateur' (i, p.21) (Babouc possessed 'le discernement' in order to 'examine[r]').

Closely parallel again is the *Lettre d'un Turc*. The work begins:

> Lorsque j'étais dans la ville de Bénarès, ..., je tâchai de m'instruire. J'entendais passablement l'indien; j'écoutais beaucoup et remarquais tout. (p.131)

The reality and the project are identified in the first sentence. The linguistic means along with the cognitive method - global examination - are noted in the second. As in *Micromégas*, the hero is doubled. 'J'étais logé chez mon correspondant Omri'. But here the two are in harmony. 'Jamais nous n'avons eu une parole plus haute que l'autre'. Moslem and Hindu, they lived nevertheless 'comme deux frères'. The first paragraph has established the mandate. Now comes what I am calling the launch. A new paragraph begins: 'Un jour, nous allâmes ensemble à la pagode de Gavani'. The shift from dominant imperfect to preterite tense reflects the start of the sequential narrative. The 'continuous' project is engaged by 'punctual' events.

'Memnon conçut un jour le projet insensé d'être parfaitement sage' is the incipit of *Memnon* (p.125). The project, more specific this time, is again declared in the first sentence. (Here a preterite and the temporal marker 'un jour' are assigned to the project itself. But the *Lettre d'un Turc* also began with a temporal marker - 'lorsque' - and a preterite assigned to the invention of the project.) It is not clear whether 'parfaitement' is Memnon's voice insisting that the project is absolute, or the narrator's commentary ironising upon it. 'Insensé' belongs to the latter, but goes beyond irony or even inversion prompted by semantic wit. It declares directly and authoritatively, in advance, that the project is insane. Memnon then reviews its three elements: 'Je n'aimerai jamais de femme ...'; 'je serai toujours sobre'; 'mon bien est solidement placé ...'. Mandate established, protagonist and events can start off. The launch is marked as in the previous case by a new paragraph and a modal shift. Again physical movement accompanies the temporal movement. The 'journey' is still more modest than previously, but it is admirably emblematic. 'Ayant fait ainsi son petit plan de sagesse dans sa chambre, Memnon mit la tête à la fenêtre' (p.126). Theory comes out into the world. Head as abstract thought becomes head as part of the body, soon to be damaged by engagement with the rest of reality.

Zadig is a much longer work than any whose preliminaries we have examined so far. We can however once more identify and develop the paradigm of mandate and launch. Zadig and his situation are presented in the first paragraph of the first chapter. The second paragraph begins with the project. 'Zadig ... crut qu'il pouvait être heureux' (i, p.58) ('Memnon conçut un jour le projet ...'). Two sentences tell us of his projected mariage to Sémire, and then comes the launch. 'Se promenant ensemble vers une porte de Babylone, ... ils virent venir à eux des hommes armés de sabres et de flèches' (p.58). Here are in fact the first verbs of physical movement in the tale, which underlines the shift to the tense of narration. The couple are leaving their state of theoretical harmony ('se promenant ensemble' parallels the 'nous allâmes ensemble' and 'ils résolurent de faire ensemble' that we noted previously.) They are heading towards an emblematic 'porte' (in parallel, 'Memnon mit la tête à la fenêtre'). This time the world also comes to them ('venir à eux'), and it is armed to the teeth. It begins to wreak on them its carnivalising violence. It intends to kidnap Sémire. Thus the primal unity represented by the couple (we recall again the initial ensembles of the *Lettre d'un Turc* and *Micromégas*) is about to be sundered. It wounds Zadig in the eye (which recalls Memnon, converted in the same way to a grotesque body). The latter is not only a brutally ironic invitation to see more clearly, but another version of the sundering. Ideal symmetry is destroyed by the kidnapping of half the couple, as by the damaging of one eye.

'Etre heureux' is the project, the world the resistant reality. (With *Memnon* in mind, we note that Zadig exclaims after one episode 'Qu'il est dangereux de se mettre à la fenêtre! et qu'il est difficile d'être heureux dans cette vie!': iii, p.65.) The tale's subtitle however promised a more abstract or philosophical theme. The question of 'la destinée' is raised in the narrative. *Micromégas* too established a second project. But there it appeared arbitrarily and separately. In *Zadig* it can appear for a reason, emerging from the more personal and affective first project of happiness. (Tale and 'philosophique' narrative are edging towards novel.) It is however established not by the protagonist but by the impersonal narrator. (The novel is some way off.) The problem of Providential order is raised when narration glosses an event as 'une bizarrerie ordinaire de la fortune' (iii, p.63). Only some pages later is it voiced through the protagonist, when Zadig generalises from perception of his own unstable 'bonheur' to the universal: 'Voilà donc de quoi dépendent les destins des hommes!' (vi, p.70). For his 'journey' in the usual or literal sense of the term we must wait longer. It is motivated as flight from the court and pursuit of a love interest, which were also linked respectively with the two journeys of Micromégas. Again however we can observe a difference (moving relatively closer to novel). In *Zadig* diegetic situations are much more fully established; the motives for flight form a single plot; the beloved will remain in the protagonist's mind and duly reappear later in the narrative.

Candide once more reproduces and modifies the paradigm. The question is declared in the subtitle. But in the narrative the presentation of protagonist and situation comes first. The couple of lovers are sundered, violently, and the male banished. (Comparing *Candide* with *Zadig*, we observe that the Baron combines Orcan's assault and Moabdar's authority [*Zadig*, i, viii], likewise Cunégonde combines Sémire the original beloved and Astarté the constant beloved [*Zadig*, i, viiff].) This occurs at the end of the first chapter. A new chapter marks the launch: 'Candide, chassé du paradis terrestre, marcha ...'. The allusion to the Garden of Eden, we can now see, is significant not just within *Candide*. It signifies that state of innocent order in which all the protagonists, and *Contes*, begin. To seek order is the philosophical project, and narrative itinerary, given to the protagonist. In *Candide* this is of course the verification of the 'meilleur des mondes possibles'.

The theorist of the best order, mandating the protagonist, is Pangloss. The external mandator we met in angelic form at the start of *Le Monde comme il va*. Here however he is no angel. Rather, he is the diminishing double or human parody, a domestic pedagogue, 'le précepteur et l'oracle de la maison'. He is no angel either in his dealings with Paquette: abstract theory is promptly confronted with his own corporeal reality. The phrase we cited as marking the launch of Candide's journey contained the preterite 'marcha'. But the first verbs of narration occur earlier, immediately after the protagonist's state of order is summarised. ('Candide ... croyait innocemment ...' as 'Zadig crut ...'.) A new paragraph begins:

> Un jour Cunégonde, en se promenant auprès du château, dans le petit bois qu'on appelait *parc*, vit entre des broussailles le docteur Pangloss qui donnait une leçon de physique expérimentale à la femme de chambre de sa mère, petite brune très jolie et très docile. (i, p.146)

Here, strictly, is the launch. We have not only the first preterite but what we should now recognise as its usual transitional antecedents - 'un jour' ('punctual' when *within* a narrative rather than at the start), a verb of movement, and a participle. The whole scientific conceit, centred on the phrase 'physique expérimentale', juxtaposes the elevated periphrases of theory with the implied reality of down-to-earth activity. (Likewise 'appelait' foregrounds the sign and 'parc' denotes cultural pretension, juxtaposed with the reductive reality of '*petit* bois' and '*petite* brune'.) This initial action is indeed linked to the launch of Candide into the world. The bond is both metaphorical (the first embrace foreshadows the second which is then reversed by sundering) and metonymic (the ricochet of lust from Pangloss to Paquette to Cunégonde to Candide which causes his battery and banishment). Pangloss the mandator will periodically reappear as companion and interlocutor. (The angel Ituriel, plus the Saturnian or Omri, are the paler avatars.) But so will almost all of this initial cast. Our preference for *Candide* over the other *contes* is surely due in part to the irrepressible interaction of desires and bodies which begins here.

One might expect to find considerable affinities between *Candide* and *L'Ingénu*. The names of the protagonists seem to denote the same moral quality. The former appellation was attributed by the narrator to the hero's 'esprit le plus simple'; the latter was explained by the Huron himself by the fact that 'je dis toujours naïvement ce que je pense' (i, p.288). The former had 'le jugement assez droit'; of the latter we are unambiguously told 'il voyait les choses comme elles sont' (xiv, p.325). To the Ingenu is attributed, on his first appearance in the narrative, 'un air si simple et si naturel' (i, p.287). Nature is the ideal order or theory: 'L'Ingénu se défendit sur les privilèges de la loi naturelle, qu'il connaissait parfaitement' (vi, p.303). Less ironised, 'il n'écoute que la simple nature' (xi, p.318).

But the Ingenu also gives 'nature' a new bias.   'Je suis assez accoutumé à dire ce que je pense, ou plutôt ce que je sens. ... . J'ai parlé d'après la nature: il se peut que chez moi la nature soit très imparfaite; mais il se peut aussi qu'elle soit quelquefois peu consultée par la plupart des hommes' (xii, p.320).   Nature is beginning to connote not received classical reason but immediate proto-romantic feeling.   However, the narrator continues 'Alors il récita des vers d'*Iphigénie*, dont il était plein'! The heart and received rhetoric are as one.   The old or the new revelation may be implied in the Ingenu's affirmation that he will present the truth, and 'il est impossible qu'on ne se rende pas à cette vérité quand on la sent' (viii, p.309).   Here we move a little from the patterns of the earlier *contes*. The presentation of protagonist and theory is much more diffuse.   It is literally scattered, as the references here show.   It is both less and more authoritative: less in that the protagonist is not presented first by the narrator but, using internal focalisation, through the eyes of the Kerkabons; more in the categorical claims made by narrator and protagonist.   Theory is more complex, reference and issues more concrete.   Voltaire seems to be looking for a synthesis, which integrates theory and reality.

Does the start of *L'Ingénu* show traces of our paradigm?   The tale begins not with the eponymous protagonist but with the strange visit of St Dunstan.   We can say that this belongs to myth time (pre-reality); and that it anticipates the surprising arrival on the same spot of the Ingenu.   The second paragraph links mythical past with present ('lui donna le nom ... qu'il porte encore').   The dominant tense is the preterite.   The third paragraph begins:

> En l'année 1689, le 15 juillet au soir, l'abbé de Kerkabon, prieur de Notre-Dame de la Montagne, se promenait sur le bord de la mer avec Mlle de Kerkabon, sa soeur ...   (p.285)

This very precise time contrasts the more pointedly with the initial myth time.   We have once more the couple and the walk.   This begins however a three-paragraph presentation of the Prior and his sister - entirely in the imperfect tense. They refer sadly to the fact that their lost brother and his wife (another couple) sailed from the same spot for Canada (a departure to balance the Ingenu's coming arrival, repeating the arrival/departure of Dunstan) where they were killed. Then - next paragraph - 'Comme ils s'attendrissaient l'un et l'autre à ce souvenir, ils virent entrer dans la baie de Rance un petit bâtiment ...'. The imperfect tense (and memory) switches to the preterite of punctual action. The little ship brings the Ingenu (as 'la petite montagne' brought Dunstan). The protagonist now is not one of the couple; and they are now a family couple. The new arrival comes not to sunder them but to complete them as a member of the family, and to complete cultural reality with his positive - no longer simply unreal - natural order.

The last of the 'classic' narratives is the *Histoire de Jenni*. Here we have once more a male protagonist, young ('Jenni n'avait pas encore vingt ans') and most attractive ('on ne pouvait le voir sans l'aimer'). He is presented in the first chapter, through the eyes of other characters. He is in a sense naive, and in a sense he is led astray by a theory - that of atheism. But this theory does not emerge until chapter iv. More important, it is not a theory in the sense of our paradigm, for it is presented as negative and cynical. The theory that we have identified is idealist and innocent, like the protagonist who bears it into the world. Jenni indeed, unlike all protagonists till now, does not function as an outsider or eiron. We do however seem to begin with another original couple. As in *L'Ingénu* it is familial. But now it is father and son. The first sentence of the first chapter undertakes to tell us about 'le respectable Freind et ... son étrange fils'. Is the father now more important? In *Jenni*, as in *L'Ingénu*, there are significant shifts away from our paradigm. We shall look at them more fully in Chapter 5.

The united couple as the emblem of original order we first met in the *Lettre d'un Turc*. It appeared too in the four classic narratives: *Zadig, Candide, L'Ingénu* and *Jenni*. We find it also in a number of more minor *contes*. In several of these it is clearly thematised. *Jeannot et Colin* implies it in the title. It becomes explicit when the eponymous couple are first presented to us 'à l'école'. The second paragraph runs thus:

> Jeannot et Colin étaient fort jolis pour des Auvergnats; ils s'aimaient beaucoup; et ils avaient ensemble de petites privautés, de petites familiarités, dont on se ressouvient toujours avec agrément quand on se rencontre ensuite dans le monde. (p.269)

Strongly connoted are youth, innocence and harmony (the 'comme deux frères' of the *Lettre d'un Turc*) anterior to entering the world. The third paragraph gives us the separation:

> Le temps de leurs études était sur le point de finir, quand un tailleur apporta à Jeannot un habit de velours à trois couleurs .... . Jeannot prit un air de supériorité.

We note the usual mark of the launch: the shift from continuous tenses to the preterite, by way of 'sur le point de' (in effect a participle). 'Le temps de leurs études' is thus indeed the non-time or pre-time. What intrudes to separate them is the world: concretely a gift from Paris, morally vanity. The separation is figured as two becoming three: the tailor is a *tiers* and he brings a tricoloured garment.   It is figured too in Jeannot's new '*supér*iorité', a dead metaphor that comes alive if we recall that the Turk's image of primal fraternity was 'jamais ... une parole plus *haute* que l'autre' (p.131).

Youth, study, innocence are all marks of the ideal order which is theory. Another mark is dream. The *Songe de Platon* is set in the youth of the world, and consists mainly of a set of dreams (non-time) about harmony (pre-world). The text begins thus:

> Platon rêvait beaucoup, et on n'a pas moins rêvé depuis. Il avait songé que la nature humaine était autrefois double, et qu'en punition de ses fautes elle fut divisée en mâle et femelle.
>
> Il avait prouvé qu'il ne peut y avoir que cinq mondes parfaits, parce qu'il n'y a que cinq corps réguliers en mathématiques. Sa *République* fut un de ses grands rêves.   (p.15)

Thus we are told that the global theories propounded ever since Plato are dreams like his. 'Songer' and 'prouver' are equivalent. Plato's theories encompass the original order of human nature, the order of the universe (the perfection of mathematics and internal analogy) and the ideal civil order. The first is the myth of the androgyne. Primally, two were one. The third paragraph begins 'Voici un de ses songes'. This, another creation myth, becomes the principal narrative. It conforms to our folk-tale paradigm. 'Démiourgos, l'éternel géomètre' requires the subaltern angel Démogorgon to 'arranger ... le morceau de boue qu'on appelle la terre'. Mandator, hero and quest are manifest. His quest undertaken, the hero 'prétendait avoir fait un chef-d'œuvre': that is his dream/theory about

reality. 'Il fut bien surpris d'être reçu ... avec des huées' (p.15): that is
the mocking reception given to the dreamer by reality.

Another version of the original order appears in the unhelpfully titled
Petite digression. This is the story of the blind in the '[Hôpital des]
Quinze-vingts' who quarrel over colours. This clash of dreams ('prouver'
and 'songer' are the same) is however preceded by a dream of harmonious
origins. The incipit of this text runs 'Dans les commencements de la
fondation des Quinze-vingts, on sait qu'ils étaient tous égaux, ...'.
Everything proceeded 'parfaitement', '... et ils vécurent paisibles et
fortunés' (p.279). There is in this incipit a distinct element of irony, so
that the narrator takes a certain distance from his original harmony. But
the dream is proferred.

The couple sundered we can find at the start of other tales too. *Le
Blanc et le noir* is articulated upon the dualist ontology of Manicheanism.
The Good and Evil geniuses of the tale are a sundering of the One which
is Rustan the hero (or, ontologically, the sundering of Providential order).
However even this dualist theory of order has to go the way of the others
when it turns out that it was only a dream (p.278). At the start Rustan is
betrothed. 'On devait marier le jeune Rustan ... . Il devait ... rendre sa
femme heureuse et l'être avec elle'. However - sundering and journey
occur together - at Kabul he saw the Princess of Kashmir. 'Ils s'aimèrent
avec toute la bonne foi de leur âge'. They must separate - a second ideal
order sundered - but promise to meet in Kashmir. Rustan tells his two
geniuses of 'le projet de son voyage', and sets off (pp.255-57). *Les Lettres
d'Amabed* is an epistolary narrative. There are three correspondents: the
young Indian couple Amabed and Adaté, and their mandator the old
Bramin Shastasid. The text's incipit is a letter headed 'D'Amabed à
Shastasid' in which the young man argues that Eastern religions are the
most ancient. Our paradigm invites us to identify this as the primal
harmony. The two lovers and their correspondence with Shastasid are its
synecdoche. To this gentle Indian order the world's carnivalising violence
is brought by the Catholic priest Fa tutto. He sunders the lovers. He then
assaults Adaté. At the same time Shastasid's letters cease to appear in the
text (pp.492-94).

With these two works can be associated, respectively, *Le Taureau
blanc* and *La Princesse de Babylone*. Both the latter feature the divided
couple, the first associated with Manicheanism, the second with a
vegetarian Ganges. Thematisation is however less strong, especially at the

start. In *Le Taureau blanc* the couple are reunited thanks to the magus Mambrès and his fellow proponent of knowledge the Devil. The preliminary section offers diffused but clear traces of our paradigm. The incipit gives us the titular protagonist with a verb of movement: 'La jeune princesse Amaside, ... se promenait ...' (i, p.527). The imperfect tense however leads not to punctual action but to a general account (the pattern we noted in *L'Ingénu*). Several paragraphs present to us first Mambrès and then the fact of the mysterious absence of her lover whose name her father forbids her to pronounce. At the start we have the hint of a mandator and a project of knowledge: 'Mambrès ... lui enseigna tout ce qu'il est permis à une belle princesse de savoir des sciences de l'Egypte' (p.527). (Her quest for her lover, the narrative thread, will be expressed later as 'savoir ce que c'est que ce taureau blanc': iii, p.534.) The next paragraph, picking up the incipit, can now give us the classic launch. 'Comme elle avançait en silence vers les bords du Nil, elle aperçut de loin, sous un bocage ...' (p.528).

    La Princesse de Babylone begins:

> Le vieux Bélus, roi de Babylone, se croyait le premier homme de la terre; car tous ses courtisans le lui disaient et ses historiographes le lui prouvaient. (i, p.349)

The ironised absolutes show, and the echo of *Candide* confirms, that we are in the realm of pure theory. In place of a splendid philosophical construction however we have the splendour of heroic romance. Paragraphs celebrating the wonders of Babylon (Thunder-ten-tronckh less ironised) are followed by an equally ritual account of three great kings competing in magnificence for the hand of the Princess. 'Tout le monde avouait ... que l'essence de la nature humaine est de se réjouir', reports the narrator, adding drily 'cette excellente morale n'a jamais été démentie que par les faits' (p.352). (Theory, as in *Candide* or in the dreams of Plato or the 'Crocheteur', can be joyous because it is the domain where wishes are fulfilled.) The word 'faits' is immediately followed, in a new paragraph, by the launch. 'Comme on allait commencer ces essais ..., un jeune inconnu ... se présente à la barrière' (p.352). (Cp 'la porte', 'la fenêtre'.) The young man is our vegetarian hero. He and the Princess fall in love, but are promptly separated. His role as substitute protagonist is heralded too in his first utterance by a brief invocation of the journey and the quest for knowledge: 'l'étranger répondit ... qu'il était venu de fort loin par curiosité ...' (p.352).

'Je tâchai de m'instruire', announces the Turk at the start of his *Lettre*. This simplest form of the idealist project also appears in *Scarmentado*. Journey, first stop and project are announced together. 'Mon père m'envoya à l'âge de quinze ans étudier à Rome. J'arrivai dans l'espérance d'apprendre toutes les vérités.' The startling optimism is however accompanied by the rider 'car jusque-là on m'avait enseigné tout le contraire, selon l'usage de ce bas monde depuis la Chine jusqu'aux Alpes' (p.135). The world's voices debase his project ('reçu ... avec des huées'). This advance negation of the dream of perfection is almost as flat as in *Memnon* ('le projet insensé d'être parfaitement sage'). Its referential illogic - how could the innocent protagonist know the world's abuse already? - shows theme overanticipating narrative.

Aventure indienne is a variant in which the protagonist is not given his theory at the start but constructs it (rather like Zadig) from experiences. The other elements of our initial paradigm appear as normal. Protagonist, reality to be interrogated and gift of communication are all announced in the first sentence. 'Pythagore, dans son séjour aux Indes, apprit ... le langage des bêtes et celui des plantes' (p.281). The second sentence gives us once more the launch into reality. 'Se promenant un jour dans une prairie assez près du rivage de la mer, il entendit ...'. We recognise the shift to movement and punctual event, marked by 'un jour' and the present participle introducing the preterite. From a complaint by a blade of grass, then another by an oyster, Pythagoras establishes his theory. It is declared (a little impatiently again?) by the narrator as 'cette admirable loi par laquelle il est défendu de manger les animaux nos semblables' (p.281). Reality of course continually breaks the law ('cette excellente morale ... démentie ... par les faits').

Two other short *contes* feature philosophers as protagonists. These are *Les Deux consolés* and *Histoire d'un bon bramin*. Both protagonists begin in possession of their theory. Their wisdom however differs. The first is a parody of the Western philosopher, sententious and falsely stoic. In his aspiration to stoicism he resembles Memnon. The second has a more genuine wisdom, which the title declares to be modest and benevolent ('bon') and attributes to the East ('bramin'). Humane, it recalls that learned by Pythagoras. Both tales however operate on the usual dualism, opposing philosophy (theory) to reality. The dualism is implied in the title of *Les Deux consolés*. This work begins :

Le grand philosophe Citophile disait un jour à une femme désolée, et
qui avait juste sujet de l'être: 'Madame, la reine d'Angleterre, fille du
grand Henri IV, a été aussi malheureuse que vous'. (p.143)

(In the parenthetical clause 'et qui avait juste sujet de l'être' we might
perceive authorial impatience again. The narrator intervenes to state flatly
at the start where the truth is.) The *Bon bramin* begins: 'Je rencontrai
dans mes voyages un vieux bramin, homme fort sage ...'(p.235).
Protagonist(s), journey and first encounter are announced. But then the
paragraph continues with a descriptive presentation of the bramin, ending
'il s'occupait à philosopher'. In the second paragraph we are presented
more briefly with 'une vieille Indienne bigote, imbécile et assez pauvre'
who lives nearby.

Dualism, in both these tales, opposes a male theorist and a female
reality. This was also the scheme for Memnon and his seductrix. The
elevated philosopher in all these cases is assigned a little extra elevation:
'le *grand* philosophe Citophile'; 'un vieux bramin ... *riche*'; 'Memnon ...à
la *fenêtre* ...vit deux femmes que se promenaient *sous* ...'(p.126). This is
of course an extra irony, stressing the height from which they will fall. In
their oppositional role they are almost as interchangeable as the women.
They are however differentiated, named, and at the centre of narratives
often named for them, whereas the women are anonymous and peripheral.
In *Memnon* the female and the reality she stands for deserve only
contempt. In *Les Deux consolés* female realism is vindicated (as the equal
billing in the title partially recognises). The *Bon bramin* inclines to a
reflexive version of the male position, a theory that includes the awareness
of its own inadequacy.

This reflexivity in the *Bon bramin* is paralleled by the use of
successive protagonists. Initially as we saw the narrative is focalised
through 'je'. This narrator-protagonist is journeying, encountering and
implicitly interrogating reality. The bramin is an informant, part of that
reality. The third paragraph begins 'Le bramin me dit un jour ...', marking
the launch of the narrator's project (shift to preterite, 'un jour'). But the
bramin is then given a whole page in direct speech. 'J'étudie depuis
quarante ans' is the start of his long statement: clearly this is a new
narrator-protagonist with a new and more explicit project, its object being
that wisdom heralded in the first sentence. The bramin continues 'ce sont
quarante ans de perdues': again the narrator (here internal, as in
Scarmentado) anticipates the meaning of the narrative.

There are four or five *contes* in which the general meaning of the narrative is declared at the start. A narrator states the message. The narrative proper is then presented as an illustration of this general truth. *Le Crocheteur borgne* begins 'Nos deux yeux ne rendent pas notre condition meilleure'. The paragraph ends 'Mesrour en est un exemple', ushering in the story (p.3). *Cosi-Sancta* (already subtitled 'Un petit mal pour un grand bien') begins 'C'est une maxime faussement établie, qu'il n'est pas permis de faire un petit mal dont un plus grand bien pourrait résulter. ... il est aisé de le voir [=cet avis] dans le récit de cette petite aventure ...' (p.9). In its first section *Aventure de la mémoire* invokes the long-held belief 'que nous n'avions d'idées que par nos sens ...', qualifying this a little later as 'une vérité' (p.563). But here the pattern is not quite so clear, and the story is not presented as an example. *Les Oreilles du comte de Chesterfield et le chapelain Goudman* is tidier. The incipit: 'Ah! la fatalité gouverne irrémissiblement toutes les choses de ce monde. J'en juge, comme de raison, par mon aventure' (p.577). Since the narrator here is also protagonist he does not have the same conventional authority as in the previous cases. As protagonist he begins as a *naïf* and a victim. It is by no means clear however that we are to regard his view as mistaken.

This brings us to a peculiarly challenging group of later *contes*. *Chesterfield* does not keep to its declared programme. Thematic focus is displaced to include other topics, and narrative focus moved to other characters. This work has affinities with the more radically dislocated *L'Homme aux quarante écus*, and with the strange assemblage called *Pot-pourri*. The second and third texts consist of a series of short sections containing quasi-independent protagonists, episodes and issues. Both begin *in medias res*; *Pot-pourri* continues apparently without any logic.

Our paradigm can however help us to identify an initial structure. Section 1 of *Pot-pourri*, the paragraph beginning 'Brioché fut le père de Polichinelle', is a burlesque transposition. The genealogy of Christ is rewritten as the lineage of the 'Foire' - an almost literal carnivalisation. Section 2 begins:

> Comme je finissais ce premier paragraphe des cahiers de Merry Hissing dans mon cabinet, dont la fenêtre donne sur la rue Saint-Antoine, j'ai vu passer les syndics des apothicaires ... (p.239)

We recognise the classic elements of the launch. The protagonist looks out of his window; the start of the action is marked by the shift to a punctual tense (here the perfect instead of the usual preterite) by way of a participle clause ('comme je finissais' recalls most specifically Jeannot and Colin 'sur le point de finir'). Where then is the protagonist's theory or project? It should be what precedes the launch - here the burlesque genealogy of Christ. This is exactly what we are told by the reference to the first paragraph now identified as 'les cahiers de Merry Hissing'. But can a transposition of Christian history into the history of vulgar entertainment be called a theory? The *official* version of Christian history would be a good example of those received theories, myths or dreams through which the Voltairean *naïf* interrogates the world. Its burlesque version anticipates the burlesque breakdown brought about by the world. One might say that here it reflects a new ambiguity in the world, and in the protagonist. The world has partially exposed the Christian imposture - the syndics are confiscating drugs used by the Jesuits, who are losing their credit throughout Europe - yet charlatanism remains universal. The protagonist is a *naïf* yet also, from the start, something of a sceptic.

The beginning of *L'Homme aux quarante écus* both conforms to and modifies the paradigm a little more clearly. The latter in effect confirms our account of the start of *Pot-pourri*. The first paragraph begins 'Un vieillard ... me disait: Mon ami, la France n'est pas aussi riche qu'elle l'a été sous Henri IV' (p.415). The speaker continues to hold forth on the French economic situation for a page-and-a-half. Completing Section 1 of the text, a last paragraph begins 'Le raisonnement de ce vieillard, bon ou mauvais, fit sur moi une impression profonde; ... et je commence à réfléchir ...' (p.416). This can fairly readily be seen as mandate. We note the indices of mandator ('vieillard'), theory ('raisonnement'; a comprehensive statement introduced by a verb in a continuous tense; the initial invocation of Henri IV connoting a past Golden Age), project of understanding ('je commence à réfléchir') and even launch ('disait'>'fit'>'commence').

In Section 2 the narrator presents himself. The pattern is much as in *Pot-pourri*: a second section establishes a narrator-protagonist, following a quasi-independent Section 1. Here however the presentation is formal unto parody: 'Je suis bien aise d'apprendre à l'univers que j'ai une terre qui me vaudrait net quarante écus de rente, n'était la taxe à laquelle elle est imposée' (p.417). This establishes him as the titular protagonist. The size of his income, we learn a little later, is precisely the figure obtained by dividing the gross national product by the number of persons in France (pp.421-22): economically he is Mr Average. The principle of definition links him to Section 1 on the economics of France, establishing a thematic coherence. The paradigm perceptible within Section 1 is however repeated, more formally and more concretely, in Section 2.

The new protagonist identified, we are given the new theory. 'Plusieurs édits de quelques personnes qui, se trouvant de loisir, gouvernent l'État au coin de leur feu' require him to pay half the income of his smallholding in tax (p.417). The marks of theory are lofty and general discourse ('édits') proferred in a protected interior space ('au coin de leur feu') and couched in continuous tenses ('gouvernent'). After two more paragraphs we have a kind of launch: 'Un de leurs huissiers vint chez moi ...' (p.417). The theorists, as references in the text make clear, are the Physiocrats, who are caricatured as maintaining that since all wealth comes from agricultural production, all taxation should be levied upon that economic sector. But soon the attack is widened to encompass 'nouveaux systèmes' in general and theoreticians 'qui se sont mis sans façon à la place de Dieu, et qui ont créé l'univers avec leur plume' (p.439).

The paradigm, thus, can still be identified in *Pot-pourri*, *Quarante écus* and *Chesterfield*. It enables us to find an initial structure which seemed absent from the first two. It also enables us to perceive how they differ from earlier *contes* in terms of their meaning. This can be shown in the last text examined. 'Je commence à réfléchir' is not the old idealist project (like 'apprendre toutes les vérités', 'être parfaitement sage', '[comprendre] la destinée', '[croire que] tout est au mieux'). It is modest and critical. The protagonist of *Quarante écus* belongs to the disadvantaged classes in contemporary France and is thus partially (dis)abused from the start. His 'failure to understand' is less innocent and more explicitly argumentative. Not only is he less of an eiron and more the mouthpiece for direct judgement. In the paradigmatic confrontation between theory and reality he is closer to the other side, not so much struggling to englobe reality with his theory as to break down theory by his reality. This is part of the ideological shift towards bourgeois realism that we shall consider in Part III.

2.ii QUEST   b. JOURNEY and REVIEW

'Il est certain qu'il faut voyager', reflects Candide (*Candide*, xviii, p.188). The journey, made by the protagonist, is both literal and metaphorical. We take first the literal or normal sense of the term. This we might define as substantial physical displacement. The protagonist may be travelling because he chooses to. For example: 'il se mit à voyager' (*Micromégas*, p.20); 'Le désir de voyager me pressait toujours' (*Scarmentado*, p.138). He or she may be externally mandated. For example: 'L'oracle ... m'a ordonné de vous faire courir le monde. Il faut que vous voyagiez' (*La Princesse de Babylone*, iv, p.367); 'Va dans cette ville' (*Le Monde comme il va*, p.39). He or she may be fleeing from a peril, or pursuing the beloved (Zadig, Candide, the Princess of Babylon); at random, or towards a specific destination (Rustan in *Le Blanc et le noir* to Kashmir by choice, Amabed to Rome as a prisoner). Of course combinations are possible (*Zadig, Candide, L'Ingénu, Jenni*). Rarely if ever is the journey made for a strictly utilitarian or everyday purpose. (Even Cosi-Sancta's short trips are hardly routine.) Flight or pursuit, love, education or understanding are the usual motivations.

By genre convention (myth, tale, romance), often ironically emphasised, or by the socio-economic privilege assigned to them, these characters move rapidly and without practical impediment. This is particularly true of the earlier *Contes*. 'Babouc monta sur son chameau et partit avec ses serviteurs. Au bout de quelques journées, il rencontra vers les plaines de Sennaar l'armée persane ...' (*Le Monde comme il va*, p.39). Simple. Even in later *Contes*, when settings and motivations become more realist, the characters are eminently 'disponibles'. This is because - in a word - their motivation is far less important than their function. Their function, philosophically and figurally, is to encounter and review reality. But we stay first with the literal itinerary.

A journey by the protagonist occurs in most of the narratives, but not in all. In six or seven of the twenty-six *Contes* there is no journey in the normal sense of the term. These are *Memnon*, *Songe de Platon*, *Les Deux consolés*, *Petite digression*, *Aventure de la mémoire* and *Quarante écus* - to which might be added (ignoring the protagonist's nominal journey in the last chapter) *Le Taureau blanc*. The first five listed here are all short (four pages or less) and no doubt this is a factor. But it does not apply to the last two.

In another six *contes* a journey by the protagonist is a preliminary. It occurs or has occured at the beginning of the story, and is mentioned at the start of the narration. The case of Babouc in *Le Monde comme il va* - the only one at all elaborated - we have just cited. It appears in the incipit of the *Bon bramin* ('Je rencontrai dans mes voyages un vieux bramin ...'), that of *Aventure indienne* ('Pythagore, dans son séjour aux Indes ...'), and that of the *Lettre d'un Turc* ('Lorsque j'étais dans la ville de Bénarès sur le rivage du Gange ...') when juxtaposed with the titular reference to origins. In *Chesterfield* ('Je cours du fond de ma province à Londres': p.577) the clause evoking the journey does not occur until the third sentence of the second paragraph. It is not foregrounded as in the previous cases. In *Jeannot et Colin*, the former's journey from Issoudun ('pour le mettre à Paris dans le beau monde': pp.269-70) is mentioned only elliptically in the third paragraph. Clearly these last two instances are similar. The journeys are set in the here and now. They take the protagonist from province to capital city in pursuit of worldly advantage (Goudman in *Chesterfield* is solliciting a preferment). The journey in the first four texts is very different. Not only is the reference far more prominent. The Turk, Pythagoras and Babouc, if not also the Bramin's interlocutor, travel to quite alien cultures. Their motivation is to seek moral truth and philosophical understanding. In all six however the journey itself is given no substance, except that of transporting the protagonist from what is implicitly 'home' to the reality he does not know.

In another seven or eight *contes* journeys, constituting a part of the tale, are given some narrative development. Events and encounters occur on the way. Zadig goes from Babylon to Egypt to Balzora (Basra), off into Arabia again, then back to Babylon (chs ix-xvi). Micromégas goes from Sirius to Saturn, then via Jupiter and Mars to Earth (chs i-iii). The second half of *La Princesse de Babylone* takes the separated protagonists from her home via his to a dozen countries between China and Spain, and finally back (§§iv-xi). The hero of *L'Ingénu* lands at St Malo soon after the start of the narrative, having come we are told from Huron Ontario via England. Later he makes a more modest and purposive journey to Versailles, given some substance in time and place by his encounter with the Huguenots at Saumur (ch.viii). Amabed and Adaté are taken from their native Bénarès to Goa, then via the Cape of Good Hope and Lisbon to Rome. Events occur at each stage. The journey is involuntary but purposive, for they are being taken to Rome by the Portuguese Inquisition.

With *Amabed* and *L'Ingénu* we are - again - moving away from tale and romance towards realism.

Then there are *contes* which feature a single journey. Tidy contrast is more difficult. Cosi-Sancta is set in North Africa and antiquity. But its claim to the status of 'nouvelle' is supported by the concrete nature of the heroine's journey (Hippo to Aquila and back, to fetch a doctor). At the other extreme is the oriental *Crocheteur borgne* where the journey - if such it can be called - is unlocated and gratuitous. Mesrour runs beside Mélinade's coach; they walk; they discover a palace. In *Le Blanc et le noir*, another oriental tale, Rustan's incident-filled journey takes him from Kabul to the capital of Kashmir. In the last two cases the journey occupies all but the start and end of the tale, edging us into our next category.

Of two or three *contes* it can be said that the journey is the narrative. Candide is kicked out of the German castle in the last paragraph of chapter i, and takes possession of his 'métairie' in the final chapter. Between, his wanderings take him successively to Holland, Portugal, Paraguay, Eldorado, Surinam, France, Venice and Constantinople. At none of these places does he remain for more than a few chapters. In *Scarmentado* the protagonist leaves his native Crete for Rome at the start of the second paragraph. He visits ten cities or countries in fewer pages, returning home in the last sentence of the tale. Along with these human travel narratives we must list the allegory called *Éloge historique de la raison*. The *Éloge* has Reason and her daughter Truth emerging from their well to receive a few Greek refugees from sacked Constantinople. Two-and-a-half centuries on, they tour Europe noting how the seeds planted then are now bearing fruit.

In the last two categories the journey constitutes an important narrative element. As in folk-tale and romance, the protagonist's journey tends to be the narrative armature, events being linked less by causality than by temporal sequence and by analogy. As in those other genres too the journey approximates to the quest. The object sought in the *Contes* is more abstract, some form of understanding. But we have just seen how often it is sought through travelling. A major quality of the protagonists, or of the narrative, is sheer energy. Linked to this - and noted earlier - is curiosity. To establish the relation between theory and reality requires a global review. However, this need not entail massive physical displacement. Classical wisdom and scientific hypothesis both suggest that reality is everywhere the same. Satiric or propagandist message will claim to show this. Figural power is achieved by offering an emblematic totality. The review is carried out not just by the protagonist but beyond him by the story and the narration.

We move now to a more general account of the characteristic features of the narrative in the *Contes*. This will work outwards from the examination of two very short tales, *Lettre d'un Turc* and *Aventure indienne*. On a small textual scale effects are more condensed and schematisation is more evident.

Aventure indienne begins by announcing its protagonist, Pythagoras. We have the launch or first encounter. 'Se promenant un jour ... il entendit ces paroles'. The words of his informant are then given, as a single continuous utterance presented to us in direct speech. They are, explicitly and exclusively, a complaint against violence. The next paragraph begins 'Pythagore avança quelques pas'. He encounters his second informant; he and we are given a second unitary utterance - containing with different reference the same message - in direct speech; again this ends the paragraph. 'En retournant à la ville' he observes many further examples of biological violence. These instances are presented by the narrator, using plurals and a continuous tense, in serial summary: 'il vit des araignées qui mangeaient des mouches, des hirondelles qui mangeaient des araignées'. 'En entrant' he comes upon a new instance, which becomes the major encounter in the tale (pp.281-82).

The *Lettre d'un Turc* uses first-person narration. Physical displacement again combines with visual survey. The serial character of the instances is still more strongly marked. 'Un jour nous allâmes ...' launches the protagonists. 'Nous y vîmes plusieurs bandes de fakirs' promptly declares the reality to be examined. 'Dont les uns ..., et les autres ...' generalises already. The next paragraph begins 'Je passai devant un fakir qui ...'. Then 'A quelques pas de là ...je fis réveill[er] un fakir ...'. A new paragraph introduces serial summary by the narrator, much of it in the imperfect tense. 'Je passai aux autres ...: il y en eut plusieurs .... D'autres dansaient ...; d'autres voltigeaient ...; d'autres allaient ...'. 'Il y en avait ..., d'autres ...; quelques-uns ...'. Again the major encounter comes last, when he and Omri meet the fakir Bababek (pp.131-32).

In *Aventure indienne* - unusually - a theory or mandate is not declared at the start. A vegan philosophy is perhaps implicit in the choice of title and protagonist. But Pythagoras does not initially seek to examine reality. His first encounter is random, and he is given no reaction to the complaint against violence which he hears. It is the narrator who glosses the event by invoking 'cette admirable loi par laquelle il est défendu de manger les animaux nos semblables' The second complaint is introduced by the narrator as 'ces mots attendrissants'. After this second encounter, we are told, 'Pythagore tressaillit, il sentit l'énormité du crime ...'. To the protagonist is attributed a primary affective response; the ethical judgement still seems to belong more to the narrator. But Pythagoras too is beginning to seek general meaning: 'Comme il rêvait profondément à cette aventure ...'; 'Tous ces gens-là, dit-il, ...'. He interprets reality globally. Where he is wrong, the narrator implies the error by the choice of verb ('Pythagore crut ...') then flatly declares it ('point du tout': the combination of spontaneity and omniscience however seems to go beyond either voice). When he is right, the verb of presentation is more positive ('Pythagore jugea').

In the *Lettre d'un Turc* the protagonist possesses an initial mandate both explicit ('je tâchai de m'instruire') and implicit (social harmony overrides religious difference). When confronted with instances of reality, however, neither his emotions nor his judgement seem directly engaged. The narrator seems equally indifferent. This is in contrast to their responses in the other tale. Reality in this case is more ridiculous than shocking. But that is not the whole explanation. In the parallel episode of the *Lettre*, disjunction will be established through irony. Disjunction here is achieved through a mock-naïvety relayed less through the protagonist than through the discourse. The incoherence of reality is signalled through laconic oxymoron. The fakir's 'lumière céleste' appears '[au] bout de mon nez' (incompatibility within his own utterance). His 'extase' is compensated by 'une roupie' (incompatibility between fakir's utterance and protagonist's reaction). The instrument of divine observance is a bed of nails, evoked by the narrator as 'de petits clous fort jolis' (incompatibility within narrator's utterance).

Thematisation, thus, can occur explicitly through the utterance of a protagonist, an informant or the narrator. Indirectly it occurs through utterances which 'fail to understand': situation or narratorial presentation invite us to rectify them. An apparently neutral narration incorporates oxymoron or is itself affectively and ethically incompatible with the impact of the story. Throughout each *conte* the topos is the same, and the thematic focus insistent. The message is multiply reinforced. All these techniques occur widely in the *Contes*. We can also generalise about narrative structure. In the two *Contes* above it is almost identical. The protagonist has two successive encounters; further instances, nominally seen through his eyes, are summarised by the narrator; there is an extended final encounter. This points to the fact that any instance can be more or less expanded. It can be presented in a phrase, a sentence, or one or several paragraphs, as in our two examples; or it can be developed to the amplitude of a section (as in *Le Monde comme il va*), a chapter (*Candide*) or dozens of pages (*L'Ingénu*).

The three segments into which both our Indian tales fall shows the pattern two/many/one. In *Zadig* the first instance of unpredictable destiny is Sémire's infidelity, followed by that of Azora in chapter ii. Two examples of female inconstancy are provided. The protagonist opts for the observation of nature. Chapter iii gives us two parallel cases of the dangers of observation, 'le chien' and 'le cheval', then a third - the prisoner - because Zadig learned the wrong lesson. A dyad is followed by a triad incorporating reversal. Most of the *Contes* of the early and middle periods, right up to *L'Ingénu*, can be reduced to geometrical schemes of this kind.

The overall division of the Indian tales into three parts is particularly interesting.   The successors of Propp identify three 'tests' in the paradigmatic folk-tale.[5] This could readily be applied to our examples. It can also be applied to many of the major *Contes*. By setting, three parts can be identified in *Micromégas* (Sirius, Saturn, Earth), and *Jenni* (Spain, England, America). *Candide* proceeds through Old World, New World and Eldorado. *Zadig* divides into Babylon/travels/Babylon, and *L'Ingénu* into Breton comedy/prison debate/Parisian tragedy.[6] But the most striking case is *Memnon*, which is pervasively structured on threes.

The final episode in the body of each of our two exemplary *contes* is also the longest. It will be useful to examine these parallel episodes in detail. They provide further rhetorical devices in the service of theme and figure. As reference and as narrative they are more expansive. Taken in

---

[5] Adam, *op.cit.*, p.69.

[6] The case for the triple division of the last two works is argued in persuasive detail in the relevant chapters of Sherman, *op.cit.*, pp.98ff, 208ff.

themselves and in relation to what has preceded them, they enable us to point to many more paradigmatic elements and variations in the *Contes* in general.

The principal episode in *Aventure indienne* has Pythagoras borne along by a crowd who are gleefully heading for a public execution. Two men are about to be burned alive. Pythagoras assumes that they are 'deux grands philosophes' who are seeking a new incarnation. 'A la place publique,' we are then told,

> il vit un grand bûcher allumé, et vis-à-vis de ce bûcher un banc qu'on appelait un *tribunal*, et sur ce banc des juges, et ces juges tenaient tous une queue de vache à la main, et ...

An 'honnête homme' among the judges explains to Pythagoras the real nature of 'la fête qu'on allait donner au peuple indou'. The two men are being burned, by popular demand, for purely speculative heresies. Pythagoras is distressed to discover suffering 'depuis l'herbe jusqu'à l'homme'. 'Il fit pourtant entendre raison aux juges, et même aux dévotes', though - adds the narrator - this has never happened since (pp.282-83). The parallel episode in *Lettre d'un Turc* is a dialogue. 'Mon ami Omri me mena dans la cellule d'un des plus fameux [fakirs]; il s'appelait Bababec.' The 'long entretien' between Omri and Bababec, reported in alternating direct speech without narratorial commentary, opposes socially-useful religion and obscurantist ceremonial religion.

> Je tâche, dit Omri, d'être bon citoyen, bon mari, bon père, bon ami; je prête de l'argent sans intérêt aux riches dans l'occasion, j'en donne aux pauvres; j'entretiens la paix parmi mes voisins. - Vous mettez-vous quelquefois des clous dans le cul? demanda le bramin.

The debate continues. Finally, we are told, Omri 'le persuada ... à venir chez lui mener une vie honnête'. 'Il vécut quinze jours d'une manière fort sage' (pp.132-33).

These principal episodes emphasise the narrative and thematic oppositions established already. Protagonist, humane feelings and civilised values are confronted by pervasive violence in the first tale, pervasive folly in the second. Folly is institutional and popular, violence ontological as well. Victories over these forces may occur, but they are - we are told - rare and temporary. Overall, a mandated ideal (non-violence, social harmony) is exposed to a world of barbarity and absurdity.

Dualist opposition is marked formally and figurally. In the final episode, as in the earlier serial accumulation of instances, each side is represented as a totality. Reality in *Aventure indienne* is said to reveal suffering 'depuis l'herbe jusqu'à l'homme': the alliterative form emphasises the totalising sense. In the other narrative the totalising statement is that made by Omri on behalf of order. It is pointedly opposed, so to speak, by Bababec's 'clous dans le cul' - balanced unto alliteration again, but apparently random and ridiculous in sense. Omri's long enumeration of order ('bon citoyen, ...') has its parallel in the narrator's enumeration in *Aventure indienne* of the circumstances of the tribunal. Omri's utterance however proposes the harmonious ideal. This is signified not only by its ethical reference but by its geometrical form: four parallel phrases; two parallel clauses; one clause. The narrator's enumeration in the other text is equally insistent on the disorder of reality. This too is signified both by the sense (random and sometimes ridiculous details) and by the form: phrases and clauses of irregular length; the parataxis of dislocation.

The two final episodes are exemplary in other respects. In *Aventure indienne* we have a ceremonial public event: the crowd, the tribunal, victims and a 'fête' in the 'place publique'. In the *Lettre d'un Turc* we have a private event: a debate involving two or three people happens indoors. (Note how the two titles imply respectively the public and the private, by genre and by reference.) These two modes occur in all the *Contes*. A few deal almost exclusively in public ceremony (*Scarmentado*, *La Princesse de Babylone*), and a few principally in private and verbal transactions (*Chesterfield, Quarante écus*). More frequently the protagonist moves between the formal rituals of the outdoors (processions, battles, punishments) and the informal rituals principally of the indoors (suppers, conversations, amours). The former are usually the more corporeal and figurally grotesque; the latter are the more solidly anchored in time, place, concrete speech and interlocution. All are collective cultural practices presented as ritualised interactions.

A further difference is that the protagonist Pythagoras begins and continues as a *naïf*. Innocent and feeling, the *naïf* arouses our sympathy, and thus our hostility towards that which harms him. He functions as an *eiron*, his idealistic misunderstanding of reality serving to point up the scandal of the world. He may acquire through repeated exposure to reality a degree of practical wisdom. But his own last word is usually rueful.

Versions of the *naïf* as protagonist are of course almost ubiquitous in the
Contes. (Even Micromegas is not entirely an exception.) Omri on the
other hand is an authoritative voice. He is a 'sage'. However he is not the
primary protagonist. In a sense he is an episodic figure. This is generally
the case for the wise men in the *Contes*. Episodic are the Hermit in *Zadig*,
the 'vieux lettré' in *Le Monde comme il va* (ch.ix), Démiourgos in *Platon*,
in *Candide* the 'vieillard' and the King of Eldorado along with the old
Turk in the final chapter, in *Quarante écus* the Géomètre (pp.419-32,
442-48) and the Chirurgien (pp.460-64), in *Jenni* Parouba. (More doubtful
'sages' would include certain informants in the latter part of *La Princesse
de Babylone*, and Dr Grou in *Chesterfield*.) The exceptions are Mambrès
in *Le Taureau blanc* and Freind in *Jenni*, both present throughout.

Omri is also a surrogate protagonist. This too can be applied to the
last three 'sages' named. Another surrogate protagonist is Amazan in *La
Princesse de Babylone*. In the first half of this tale narration is focalised
through the Princess of the title, while the second half follows the
experiences of her lover Amazan. An analogous shift of focalisation
occurs formally in the epistolary *Amabed*. The story is told through the
letters of the titular hero, except for a sequence of seven by his wife Adaté.
The reason for these two shifts seems obvious. To the women are assigned
the 'romanesque' elements - Babylonian glamour or secret rape - while the
men are given the 'philosophique' matter. (In fairness however, we should
note that the Princess is presented as bored by Babylon and fascinated by
the Phoenix; Princess Amaside, not Mambrès, debates with the Serpent in
Le Taureau blanc.) Shifts in focalisation occur only in later *contes*. But
even these three remain linear. Only *L'Ingénu* follows two protagonists
successively through the same period of time.

The final episode in *Aventure indienne* tells a story. In *Lettre d'un
Turc* however the final episode consists principally of people talking. One,
that is, presents a sequence of events occuring in real time and space, the
other the verbal event of a conversation about reality. The *Contes* in
general review the world in these two ways. Almost every *conte* uses
both, in varying combinations. Later tales however tend to move away
from the former and towards the latter.

Aventure indienne is narrated in the third person, like most of
Voltaire's *Contes* (and most tales generally). *Lettre d'un Turc* is in the
first person. Half-a-dozen other *contes* use the latter form: *Scarmentado*,
Pot-pourri, *Quarante écus*, *Amabed* (epistolary), *Chesterfield* and *Jenni*.

In a few more a narratorial 'je' appears occasionally (*Micromégas*), notably at the beginning (*Candide*). But this 'je' of the storyteller, rare anyway, is very different from that of the diegetic narrators in the six or seven *Contes* just listed. Use of the diegetic narrator however is in itself straightforward only in *Scarmentado*. Later *Contes* combine it with other other modes of presentation, in increasingly complex ways. Conversations may be presented in the form of theatrical dialogue. This occurs in *Quarante écus*, *Chesterfield* and *Jenni*. (It also occurs in one narrative using the third person, *Le Taureau blanc*.) Or a narrative may begin in the first person, then switch without explanation to the third person. This occurs after chapter ii of *Chesterfield*, and about half-way through *Quarante écus*. Then there is the most disruptive device. *Pot-pourri* and *Quarante écus* each consists of a number of semi-discrete sections, treating different topics in the voices of different fictional authors. These switches may be regarded as forms of ironic wit. It is possible to see some as carelessness.[7] More generally, one might surmise that Voltaire is less than happy using first person narration, which tends to deny him the aesthetic distance needed for his art.

Both our exemplary *contes* are satirical. In order to mock the reality they depict, they objectivise it. We have already noted some of the devices for disjunction in the *Lettre d'un Turc*. The effect is to deprecate the spiritual claims of the fakirs. They are debased by juxtaposing them with the corporeal ('la lumière céleste ... [au] bout de mon nez'; 'mon âme passera dans le corps d'un lièvre'). Quality is reduced to quantity ('les voyelles que je comptais'; 'je lui donnai une roupie'). An analogous effect is sought by ironic antiphrasis ('petits clous fort jolis'). On the narrative level we have the rapid listing of varieties of practice, or events. Such joyous accumulation serves to make the referents themselves seem mechanical and incoherent. These techniques are fundamental in all the *Contes*. Cultural connectives are suppressed, and concrete phenomena in isolation are foregrounded.[8] Through this narratorial 'failure to

---

[7] The sceptical view is taken by Vivienne Mylne, 'Literary techniques and methods in Voltaire's *contes philosophiques*', *SVEC* 57 (1967), pp.1055-80.

[8] These effects have been excellently identified on the level of style. 'Voltaire réduit au minimum ... les conjonctions, relatifs, et tous autres termes de coordination et subordination': G. Lanson, *L'Art de la prose* (Paris, 1930), p.155. 'L'écriture de

understand' (shared with the protagonist), reality appears as random and disordered.

Incomprehension is of course selective. Alongside the narrative carnivalisation of reality we also have authoritative judgement on it. Context and form clearly authorise Omri's statement that asceticism is merely 'l'effet d'une excessive ambition'. Brama favours those who will 'rend[re] ... service à la patrie'. In *Aventure indienne* the impersonal narrator intervenes to judge. Vegetarianism is 'cette admirable loi'. Pythagoras 'fit entendre raison'. The universals of the classical 'moraliste' or the Enlightenment philosopher appear intermittently in all the *Contes*. So does epigram and, more rarely, exhortation.

It is evident that in the main the cultural norms proposed here are those of French high civilisation. Most obviously, the very concept of 'la patrie' or '[la] raison', as well as the value assigned to them, have everything to do with the Enlightenment and nothing to do with ancient Hinduism. The earlier account of fakir asceticism however is sufficiently strange and detailed to give it a limited authenticity.[9] Such 'historical' elements appear in all the *Contes*. They serve to give specificity and referential or discursive depth, but in their new comic contexts they also appear as parodic of these conventional effects. Where the pattern assigned to an alien culture resembles one that is more familiar, we readily perceive allusion. It is impossible to say whether *Lettre d'un Turc* is 'really' about Hindu ascetic practices or those of Catholicism. In the last part of *Aventure indienne* however the specificity clearly fits Christianity. All the details of the tribunal, the crime and the punishment invite us to read this account as a transposition of Catholic Inquisitional practice.[10] Later

---

Voltaire procède par coupures, ellipses, litotes - par toutes les formes de la *soustraction*' [author's emphasis]: J. Starobinski, 'Sur le style philosophique de *Candide*', *Le Remède dans le mal* (Paris, 1989), pp.123-44 (p.124).

[9] Direct borrowing from the account of such practices in Bernier's *Voyages* has been established: The note in René Pomeau's edition of the *Romans et contes* (Garnier Flammarion), p.117, is clearer - and more accurate - than the Pléiade, p.805.

[10] 'Avoir dit que la substance de Xaca n'est pas la substance de Brama' surely transposes the Arian heresy of distinguishing the Son from the Father. The formula contrives both to sympathise with this deistic view and to mock Father and Son alike. ('Xaca' sounds interchangeable with 'Brama', thus also contaminating the latter with

Contes present contemporary European cultural reality directly, thus partially losing the distance which fable requires to mark off its exemplarity. It is however maintained by the continued reliance on the naive protagonist and simplified issues. Disjunction and antithetical irony still serve to satirise both reality and idealist theory.

The main episode in *Aventure indienne*, and the whole of *Lettre d'un Turc*, take place in cities. For the classically-minded Voltaire, the emblem of totality is not so much the universe or the Earth as the city. Figuratively of course they are the same. As Micromégas tours the universe, and Scarmentado the Earth, so the Turk tours Benares. As the main episode of *Micromégas* occurs on the Earth, so that of the Indian adventure occurs in the city. Babouc encounters and tries to judge reality constituted as Persepolis; Memnon encounters and is assaulted by reality constituted as Nineveh. Certain other cities are used in not just one *conte* but several. This is most strikingly the case for Babylon. *Le Taureau blanc* ends there; *Zadig* begins and ends there, as does *La Princesse de Babylone*. Benares is not only the setting for the *Lettre d'un Turc* but also where Amabed begins. *Amabed* ends in Rome. Rome too is the first school for Scarmentado, a stopover for Amazan (*La Princesse de Babylone*) and La Raison (the *Éloge*), and the starting place for La Vieille in the interpolated 'Histoire' in *Candide*. Candide is delayed in Paris, where Jeannot is taken to learn what is important. *Candide* ends near Constantinople, where Scarmentado also widens his education. Venice is a halt on the journeys of Candide, Amazan and La Raison.

The city is almost as significant as the journey in the *Contes*. Both of course are great emblems in our inherited culture. They communicate to the *Contes* their own archetypal power. The choice of cities in the *Contes* includes a referential and historical function. But this is usually far less important than the mythical function. All represent - and mockingly celebrate - the worldly City. Babylon is *the* luxurious pagan city, in the Christian tradition the antithesis of Jerusalem. Nineveh was the great and wicked city which angered God and Jonah. Persepolis was the great city - the 'polis' - of the Persian empire. Rome is the capital equally of the ancient pagan and the modern Christian empires. Constantinople has the same double status (in temporal reverse) and also joins East and West.

---

its infantile repetition and scatological associations.)

Venice, joining land and sea, had been a great power. (Not only Vanity Fair, but *sic transit gloria*, are further and major ironic meanings conveyed by Voltaire's choices.) Benares (Varanasi) is the holiest city of Hinduism. This seems to make it the odd one out. But of course it thus doubles the Christian holy city. It is both Rome (more so in *Lettre d'un Turc*) and anti-Rome (pointedly so in *Amabed*). Persepolis, Nineveh and Babylon especially are all - by satirical allusion - Paris. Paris is 'itself' in the later and more realist tales. But it too is also strongly emblematic. For the protagonists, and for Voltaire's readers, it is the capital of worldliness. All these cities are 'le monde (comme il va)'.

Central to our two tales, and to the *Contes* in general, is the encounter and conversation. Often, as we have noted, it involves not just a couple but a group. Often the group is also sharing a meal. The whole event (group, meal, conversation) constitutes social observance and exchange. Such gatherings can be found in most of the *Contes*, including all the major ones. Here is a partial list of these events: *Le Monde comme il va*, xii; *Memnon*, p.113; *Zadig*, iv, xii ('Le Souper'); *Candide*, xviii, xxvi; *L'Ingénu*, i; *Quarante écus* ([§] 'D'Un Bon Souper ...'); *La Princesse de Babylone*, viii; *Amabed*, xii; *Le Taureau blanc*, vi ('... Un Bon Dîner'); *Chesterfield*, v-vii; *Jenni*, vii. Table talk is another archetype within our inherited culture, pagan and Christian alike. Again it gives the *Contes* an emblematic dimension. This is the more so in that it functions in the *Contes* as a privileged figure of meaning. Journey and city signify travel and place: travel to a place, and a place within which (as in our Indian *contes*) one travels. They signify line and circle, or accumulation and totality. Table talk too is accumulation and totality. It offers the accumulation of participants, views, topics or references to reality. It offers totality as the collectivity united and divided. The circle contains the lines of exchange which the world sends in and which refer back out.

Here is a pleasing example from *Zadig* of the superposition and dynamics of these figures of meaning. The protagonist visits

> la grande foire de Balzora, où devaient se rendre les plus grands négociants de la terre habitable. Ce fut pour Zadig une consolation sensible de voir tant d'hommes de diverses contrées réunis dans la même place. Il lui paraissait que l'univers était une grande famille qui se rassemblait à Balzora. Il se trouva à table, dès le second jour, avec un Egyptien, un Indien gangaride, un habitant du Cathay, un Grec, un Celte, et plusieurs autres étrangers qui, dans leurs fréquents voyages vers le golfe arabique,

avaient appris assez d'arabe pour se faire entendre.
(xii, p.87)

The market is within the city which in turn is within the (human) world. It draws diversity together in one place. The universe, the family, the meal repeat the initial equivalence of collectivities at three more levels. (We may note too a third occurrence of 'grand', and the continuous 'se rassemblaient' balancing the stasis of 'réunis'.) Diversity is itemised in the first part of the last sentence, an accumulation of national representatives. This enumeration remains open-ended ('et plusieurs autres étrangers'), but we are then returned once more to the focus of gathering. The linguistic means for universal intercommunication is summarily provided by the narrator. The protagonist - too? - finds the great gathering to be a 'consolation sensible'. Clearly then the human family is not often in harmonious conjunction. Nor is it here, as the totality united by trade becomes the totality divided by religious differences. Each diner (like each fakir in the *Lettre d'un Turc*) speaks up for the view of reality held by his group. The review of the world by encounter on the journey has become the review of the world by conversation in the city.

Almost all of the *Contes*, as we have observed, partake of this bipolarity. From the earlier to the later *Contes*, journeys tend to contract and conversations to expand. At the extreme, the world journey may serve as an almost nominal preliminary to the world review within the conversation. The paradigm is no less marked. 'M. Husson me parlait hier de ses voyages ...' *(Pot-pourri, x, p.249)*. 'Le docteur Grou vient dîner chez moi: ... il a fait le tour du monde ...' *(Chesterfield, iv, p.586)*. 'J'ai remarqué, me disait-il, ... cette contradiction de l'espèce humaine ...' (p.249); 'Je remarque, dit le docteur Grou, que malgré la variété infinie répandue sur ce globe, cependant tous les hommes que j'ai vus ...' (p.587).

The governing principle of the narrative or main part of the *Contes* we have called journey and review. More broadly one might say that it is the totalising accumulation of representative instances of reality, their significance thematised in relation to an initial theory or mandate.

The protagonist - and the reader - are often offered some form of revelation. This marks the end of the serial accumulation of instances which has constituted the body of the *conte*. It prepares the end or closure of the whole narrative. The revelation is the thematic climax of the tale because it concerns the object of the protagonist's quest. Sometimes it corresponds with the narrative climax. The protagonist has been raised to a state of bliss, like Mesrour in *Le Crocheteur borgne*. Alternatively and more frequently he has been reduced to total abjection (Memnon) or near-death (Rustan in *Le Blanc et le noir*). Bliss and abjection are combined for Zadig, and for Candide. For the Ingenu they are successive. In all these last four cases the narrative climax is the rediscovery of the beloved. The last three also involve a broader integration, with home (Zadig), the group and a new home (Candide), or the group and civilisation (the Ingenu).

Scarmentado also comes home, though for him this marks the end of an explicit programme of investigation. 'Il me restait de voir l'Afrique' (p.167), announces the last segment of a review that is both systematic and almost literally global. Others too might be said to have carried out systematic reviews. They include Babouc near the end of *Le Monde comme il va*, Memnon, Micromégas, the Turk of the *Lettre*, the Bramin of the *Bon Bramin*, Goudman in *Chesterfield*. All these were explicitly mandated at the start. We may add those mandated *de facto* (Zadig, Candide), or who have at least carried out a review *de facto* (Pythagoras in the *Aventure indienne*, M. André in *Quarante écus*, Amazan in *La Princesse de Babylone*, Amabed, Cosi-Sancta). Tales in the latter category also include several where the protagonist is scarcely more than a cipher: *Platon*, *Jeannot et Colin*, the allegorical *Petite digression* and *Éloge de la Raison*.

It can be argued, nevertheless, that the moment of revelation is arbitrary. The preceding narrative and review alike usually consist of a series of semi-discrete segments. Narrative events are linked as sequence, but rather less as cause and effect. Realist plotting is usually mimimal when the armature is a journey. It is scarcely required when the armature is conversation. The re-encounter with the beloved undeniably constitutes a narrative climax. But rarely does it arise necessarily from the accumulation of previous events, which could be readily augmented or diminished without affecting it. *L'Ingénu* is an exception (but the preceding conversations, chs xi, xii and xiv, are only broadly germane). *Candide* is an exception to some extent (though the penultimate chapter is in fact the second re-encounter for the lovers). Zadig re-encounters Astarté by chance. Rustan finds his Princess by intelligent design, but the eight incidents which beset him on the way could be any other number. Citophile reviews five examples of sorrowing noblewomen, but the number is random.

Can any review be said to be complete? Scarmentado makes the claim. The narrator implies it for Babouc in *Le Monde comme il va* (§xi). Another case might be *Platon*, which examines all the six heliocentric planets known to eighteenth-century science. However it is cursory on five, omits to refer to the Sun, and forgets the rest of the 'globes innombrables' first mentioned (pp.15-17). Completeness is possible only if the initial mandate is strictly circumscribed. Memnon's programme of abstinence contains three categories, and all are tested. The same applies to the programme of triple infidelity laid down for Cosi-Sancta. But essentially the universalising claims are made by the discourse itself. Instances are accumulated. Their signification is pointed and doubled by internal reviews. Each is offered as representative and therefore already total in itself. As sense, as emblem and as figure, the review is insistently global. There is not a shortfall but a massive redundancy of instances, and of thematised meaning. Revelation and closure are amply prepared.

The revelation is invariably to some degree ironic. The ironic effect results in part simply from its location near the end of a comic narrative. It is ironic secondly because it is rueful, or occasionally euphoric - diverging in content or tone from sober wisdom. In the best-known tales the rueful instances are more frequent, and we tend to think of them as more typical generally. They are also in literary terms the most elaborate. These are ironic, thirdly, because they question, reject or reverse the initial proposition. Finally we shall look at the revelation ironised through reflexive repetition.

Probably the simplest cases are those in which the narrator declares a moral at the start, illustrates it, then confirms it at the end. In §2.ii.a we listed several *contes* of this type. *Cosi-Sancta* and the *Crocheteur* are the most obvious. The formulae 'Nos deux yeux ne rendent pas notre condition meilleure' and 'Un petit mal pour un grand bien' are ironic from the start because they collapse, if not - by their dualism - reverse our conventional expectations. But their truth is shown by the tale, and finally formally restated. The first formula is both subtitle and capitalised exurgit in *Cosi-Sancta*. The *Crocheteur borgne* opens with the second, and closes with 'Mais Mesrour n'avait point l'oeil qui voit le mauvais côté des choses' (p.8). Analogous is *Aventure de la mémoire*, where the initial proposition, having been illustrated, is finally repeated in similar terms by the authoritative voice of Memory. *Les Deux Consolés* ends with the capitalised formula 'A CELUI QUI CONSOLE' (p.144), addressed to Time by the two protagonists. This moral recalls the title, while its referent is ironic in relation to the stoicism attempted by those in the tale. It seems clearly authorised.

The pattern appears in two substantial late *contes*. *Chesterfield* opens and closes with the assertion 'la fatalité ... gouverne ... toutes les choses de ce monde' (pp.577, 595). *Jenni*'s subtitle, *le sage et l'athée*, is partially picked up in the exurgit 'Vous conviendrez qu'un sage peut guérir des fous' (p.655). In both these tales the utterances are assigned to diegetic narrators, less evidently authorised than an impersonal narrator outside the fiction would be. But the second especially is almost devoid of irony (only 'des fous' as hyperbole is mildly comic), like the latter part of the tale it closes and confirms. Entirely sober is the closing moral proferred by the narrator of *Jeannot et Colin*. But the repetition and improper declension preceding it retain the gently comic tone: 'Et Jeannot le père, et Jeannotte la mère, et Jeannot le fils, virent que le bonheur n'est pas dans la vanité' (p.277).

What we think of as the classic revelation, however, is not offered directly by the narrator. It is offered within the fiction, by an apparently authoritative speaker. It fails to satisfy the protagonist. Sometimes it is just incomprehensible. The Hermit offers Zadig the book of destiny. '[Il] ne put déchiffrer un seul caractère du livre' (*Zadig*, xviii, p.109). Micromégas offers the earthmen a revelation still greater, a book containing 'le bout des choses'. It turns out to be 'tout blanc' (*Micromégas*, vii, p.37). Rustan tries to understand the revelation offered to him by his two genii. But 'il y a quelque chose ... que je ne comprends pas' (*Le Blanc et le noir*, p.265). In other cases the protagonist discovers the revelation to be merely a delusion. Rustan is about to learn the truth for himself. But then 'il se réveille en sursaut, tout en sueur, tout égaré' (p.265). The same device is used in *Le Crocheteur borgne*. Mesrour is rudely awakened, to find that his ideal world was only a dream (p.7). In both these cases the reader too has been tricked. *Songe de Platon* on the other hand tells us in advance that we are hearing about a dream. But while reading we forget this warning, until the brutal exurgit. 'Voilà ce que Platon enseignait à ses disciples. Quand il eut cessé de parler, l'un d'eux lui dit: *Et puis vous vous réveillâtes*' (p.17).

Then there are the cases where the protagonist resists, declining to accept the revelation. Again *Zadig* provides the most familiar example. The angel explains, at last, the moral logic of the universe. Zadig seems to accept the answer, but his reiterated 'Mais ...' mark a dissatisfaction (xviii, pp.113-14). The revelation is ironised and the question left open. A supernatural representative also appears towards the end of *Memnon*. This time the revelation is treated by the protagonist with some impatience (*Memnon*, p.128). Another 'génie' appears in *Le Monde comme il va*. Babouc's review, like those by the other protagonists, leads him to deny any self-consistent order. But Babouc's contestation is at once more general and more tactful. His heterogeneous statue, emblem of the heterogeneity of the world, is fully understood by the 'génie'. 'Il résolut ... de laisser aller *le monde comme il va*. Car, dit-il, *si tout n'est pas bon, tout est passable*' (p.54). Here human and divine agree. But, contrasting with the initial demand for an absolute judgement, this might be called a counter-revelation. Insofar as they are understood, the messages offered by all the subaltern divinities are resisted.[11]

On the human plane, the equivalent message is proposed by Pangloss. Throughout *Candide* he affirms metaphysical order. At the end we have the protagonist's counter-revelation: 'Il faut cultiver notre jardin'. In *L'Ingénu* the last word of the protagonist balances pessimism and a degree of hope: '*malheur est bon à quelque chose*'. But the narrator adds a more negative observation. 'Combien d'honnêtes gens dans le monde ont pu dire: *malheur n'est bon à rien!*' (xx, p.347). This double conclusion appears in some tales as a narrative sequence. Moral order is achieved, but only temporarily. The *Éloge de la Raison* reviews the new order of Europe, but in the exurgit Reason suddenly turns sceptical. 'Jouissons de ces beau jours; restons ici, s'ils durent; et, si les orages surviennent,

---

[11] On the subaltern divinities, see W.H. Barber, 'Voltaire's astronauts', *French Studies* 30 (1976), pp.28-42.

retournons dans notre puits' (p.575). Elsewhere the narrator tells us of the reversal. This we find in the two Indian tales we examined in §2.ii.b. Bababec's metaphysics are opposed by the more modest counter-revelation of citizen Omri, and the metaphysician is persuaded. But - we are told in the exurgit - after a fortnight he returns to spiritual mystification 'pour avoir de la considération' (*Lettre d'un Turc*, p.133). The revelation of a 'loi admirable' which forbids violence is successfully conveyed by Pythagoras to the judges and the people, in *Aventure indienne*. The tale ends: 'Ensuite il alla prêcher la tolérance à Crotone; mais un intolérant mit le feu à sa maison: il fut brûlé, lui qui avait tiré deux Indous des flammes. *Sauve qui peut!*' (p.283). The narrative reversal reoccurs in *Petite digression*. There the blind eventually cease to argue over colours. But there is a coda:

> Un sourd, en lisant cette petite histoire, avoua que les aveugles avaient eu tort de juger des couleurs; mais il resta ferme dans l'opinion qu'il n'appartient qu'aux sourds de juger de la musique. (p.280)

We have looked at revelation and closure in their simpler form, then in the more interesting and characteristic form incorporating resistance or counter-revelation and reversal. Lastly we note cases of reflexive repetition. The short *Histoire d'un bon bramin* moves dialectically between the models of the unhappy philosopher and the happy imbecile. The philosopher prefers his own state. Yet to prefer unhappiness is itself senseless. The tale concludes:

> Après y avoir réfléchi, il paraît que de préférer la raison à la félicité, c'est être très insensé. Comment donc cette contradiction peut-elle s'expliquer? Comme toutes les autres. Il y a là de quoi parler beaucoup. (p.237)

At the end of *Le Blanc et le noir* Rustan again complains that he cannot understand. Again he is promised revelation: 'j'ai un perroquet qui vous le fera aisément comprendre ...'. But again he and we are disappointed, for 'l'histoire du perroquet' is unfortunately lost (pp.266-67). *La Princesse de Babylone* also spirals off into reflexivity. The narrator ends the story with a reference to poets, then successively to the muses, other tales he has written, his publisher and his literary enemies (pp.413-14). Within the realist conventions of the epistolary form, *Amabed* increasingly presents social rituals - including a play - which function as the *abyme* of the tale. *Le Monde comme il va* does not actually end with the italicised formula

('*...tout est passable*') that we cited. The narrator then contrasts Babouc's judgement with the Biblical judgement of Jonah on Nineveh. However, he observes finally, the interior of a whale is less pleasant than the theatre and good society (p.54). Reflexivity encompasses both the literary system and the society to whom the tale is offerred.

It is clear that in general narrative closure in the *Contes* is both arbitrary and strongly marked. It is determined and defined less by plot than by theme. It offers some form of revelation. This is foregrounded in several ways: attribution (angel, hero, book, narrator); reprise (of an initial proposition) or gloss (upon the whole narrative or its climactic event); epigrammatic quality and often typographical emphasis. It constitutes a final flourish, sometimes prolonged but more often punctual. Disabled in one way or another in the more substantial *contes*, it fails to deliver the promised truth.

3. PASTICHE and PARODY; PLAY and PLEASURE

Any general account of the *Contes* must recognise their insistently literary character. By this I mean not just their conventionality or even their literary ironies, but their ironic literarity. They are conventionally literary in their strong generic patterning. At the same time, through various forms of play, they both mock and celebrate the order that is literature. This is the source of much of the pleasure that they give. It is also the source of much of their meaning, because literature itself represents - in both senses of the term - an ideal order.

Our identification of paradigms in the twenty-six narratives has established a structural homogeneity and a collective internal consistency which are by definition literary. So are the terms we used. 'Hero' is a literary as much as an ethical category. 'Mandate' and 'quest' are literary metaphors. These formalist or structuralist concepts were originally extrapolated from folk-tale, and are most obviously applicable to other archaic genres. But they are likely to be no less germane to the analysis of their apparent opposite, the highly self-conscious narrative. Voltaire's tales partake of both the archaic and the highly self-conscious.

The *Contes* have much of the narratalogical and moral simplicity, the patterning by repetition and contrast, of folk-tale. They have the thematic and didactic focus of fable. A number of the best-known *contes* employ the topoi of romance: the handsome young lovers, the separation, the journey, the adventures, ... A few use the machinery of epic. Some use the animist world of fairy-tale, many the exoticism and some the supernatural of the oriental talc. A few function as allegory; a few others use the new apparatus of 'sensiblerie'; a few are principally discussions or debates. With the possible exception of the last two categories, all not only follow established generic conventions but ironically draw attention to them.

Can certain *contes* be said to rewrite specific works? *Le Monde comme il va* uses the narrative outline and the theme of the *Book of Jonah*, to which it explicitly alludes at the end. *Le Taureau blanc* - composed twenty-five years later - draws much of its cast and its nominal plot from the Old Testament. Here too allusion and re-writing are explicit. The name, characteristics and situation of the protagonist of *Le Crocheteur borgne* are to be found in the *Mille et une nuits*. *Zadig* at the start explicitly evokes the same work. But it is presented there as part of a subgenre ('... des *Mille et Une Nuits*, des *Mille et Un Jours*, etc') - 'les *Mille et Un*' (p.56). And of course *Zadig* draws upon a vast range of literary antecedents. Any one of them may be itself derivative, rewritten, directing us more widely. For example, the chapter 'L'Hermite' uses Parnell's verse narrative. But that poem is itself a retreatment of an ancient topos. The chapter 'Les Combats' is clearly inspired by Ariosto. But the topos of the Games was more recently renewed by Fénelon's *Télémaque*. It goes back to Homer. Voltaire himself will use it again at the start of *La Princesse de Babylone*.[12]

From this brief discussion we can establish not one but two distinctions. Firstly, there are a great variety of possible relations between a text and its antecedent. For present purposes we should at least distinguish between borrowing (use of 'sources'), pastiche ('serious imitation', especially of style) and parody ('satirical imitation', of a work, a genre or a style).[13] The chapter 'L'Hermite' is an example of borrowing. *Le Crocheteur borgne* is closest to pastiche. *Le Taureau blanc*

---

[12] For the fullest documentation on antecedents, see the edition of *Zadig* by G. Ascoli and J. Fabre cited above, i, §5 'Les Sources du roman'.

[13] Undoubtedly the most systematic attempt to analyse and classify such relations is Gérard Genette, *Palimpsestes: la littérature au second degré* (Paris, 1982).

is in broad terms a parody. Here we are concerned with the latter, more
literary, procedures. Secondly, the playful literarity of the *Contes* may
include specific allusion. But antecedents are usually multiple. More
characteristically we are dealing with the reworking of generic topoi.

The models of the Old Testament, the epic and the tale are
complemented by that of the romance. Indeed the romance - which can
partake of all three, and much else - is certainly the most important model.
Numerous parallels have been established between *Candide* and Prévost's
Cleveland. However, in any specific instance the parallel may well be
found elsewhere as well. For example, the 'three utopias' in the central
chapters of *Candide* are said to recall the three in *Cleveland*. But
Télémaque, familiar to Prévost and to Voltaire, also has three utopias. In
fact those critics who perceive Prévost's fictions in *Candide* seem to accept
nevertheless that we should talk not about specific allusion but about
generic patterns. Voltaire's tale is 'the parody of a certain variety of novel
which *Cleveland* can be held to represent', namely 'the long, heroic novel
(or romance)'.[14]

Most modern readers of Voltaire's *Contes*, unlike his contemporaries,
do not know *Cleveland*. Modern readers can nevertheless recognise in the
tales the topoi of romance, because these are still familiar to us from a
thousand narratives antecedent or subsequent to *Candide*. The effect of
parody in the *Contes* can also be recognised independently of our
knowledge of any specific text. Generic conventions are exaggerated, thus
foregrounding them. They are shown forth, placed within quotation marks,
double-voiced. Thus the hero is thoroughly sympathetic; his enemies are
duly the opposite. He, or the couple, suffer numerous vicissitudes. Events

---

[14] Philip Stewart, 'Holding the mirror up to fiction: generic parody in *Candide*',
French Studies 33 (1979), pp.411-19 (pp.418, 411); see too R.A. Francis, 'Prévost's
Cleveland and Voltaire's *Candide*', *SVEC* 208 (1982), pp.295-303. Similarly, the
resemblance of certain episodes in *Candide* or in *Zadig* to some in *Manon Lescaut*
reflects the function of Prévost's most famous novel as 'a model of heroic romance'.
See C.J. Betts, 'Echoes of *Manon Lescaut* in *Candide*', *French Studies Bulletin* 28
(Autumn 1988), pp.14-16, and Haydn Mason, '*Zadig* and *Manon Lescaut*', *ibid.* 29
(Winter 1988), pp.21-22 (p.21). The parallel between *Cleveland* and *Télémaque* is
made by James Gilroy, 'Peace and the pursuit of happiness in the French utopian
novel', *SVEC* 176 (1979), pp.169-87. My '*Télémaque* et *Zadig*: apports et rapports',
SVEC 215 (1982), pp.63-75, examines a range of possible relations between these two
texts.

multiply, as do reversals. They arrive in such rapid succession that the sequence seems to be speeded up. Not only the human but the literary is made to seem mechanical. The comic effect may also be achieved by the opposite means. Instead of moving us on rapidly, the narration may linger. The convention or cliché is underlined. Passion is overwritten. Coincidence is emphasised. Through speeding up or slowing down, the paradigms are displayed for our amused contemplation.[15]

The stories featuring young love, as we noted, are generally those we know best. When Zadig falls in love with Astarté, his symptoms and their presentation are emphatic:

> Ses yeux se couvraient d'un nuage; ses discours étaient contraints et sans suite; il baissait la vue ... . Zadig sortait d'auprès d'elle égaré, éperdu, ...
> (viii, p.76)

Many adventures later, Zadig chances upon a majestic, veiled woman who sighs as she traces a word in the sand:

> Il vit la lettre Z; puis un A: il fut étonné, puis parut un D; il tressaillit. Jamais surprise ne fut égale à la sienne ... . [Il s'écria] d'une voix entrecoupée: O généreuse dame! ... (xvi, p.100)

Here we have a pastoral setting, a mysterious beauty, the sweet sorrows of love, engraving the name; surprise, suspense, recognition; elevated (and courtly) apostrophe ... . By wondrous fate it is the beloved - long-lost and believed to be dead. These are all commonplaces. By affective exaggeration and stylistic emphasis they are double-voiced and ironised.

The clichés of first love, chance encounter, and recognition after many adventures, are presented in a similar manner in *Candide* (chs i, vii). The ritual competition of suitors for the royal hand is used in *Zadig* (ch.xvii), and writ larger in *La Princesse de Babylone* (ch.i). Animals speak in *Aventure indienne*. Animals are fabulous in *La Princesse de Babylone* (the phoenix, the unicorns). They are ubiquitous in *Le Taureau blanc*. Marvels of other kinds too accumulate in *Le Blanc et le noir*. Through overemphasis, pastiche which imitates becomes parody which mocks.

By taking an affectionate distance - pastiche, parody, deprecation - the

---

[15] See Jean Sareil, 'Le Rythme comique, accélération et ralentissement dans les *Contes* de Voltaire', *Colloque '76: Voltaire*, ed. Robert L. Walters (London Ontario, 1983), pp.141-54.

Contes can delight in the literary. We have seen how the stuff of traditional tale, fable and romance is offered and enjoyed as ironic quotation. The clichés of contemporary literature are also held up for inspection. Zadig protests against the phrase '"*l'esprit et le coeur*! car ... on ne voit que des livres où il est question du coeur et de l'esprit"' (*Zadig*, 'Appendice', p.120). The mockery is compounded by its impossible attribution to a Babylonian. The theme of moral education through travel is distanced almost literally - by scale - in *Micromégas*. 'Il se mit à voyager de planète en planète, pour achever de se former *l'esprit et le coeur*, comme on dit' (i, p.20). Yet the ethos of the journey as education, ironically rewritten, is indeed that of the *Contes*. Alternatively they deal in the conversation as education. This too is marked ironically: 'C'est ainsi que l'homme aux quarante écus se formait, comme on dit, *l'esprit et le coeur*' (*Quarante écus*, p.464).

The education of the reader is a serious purpose. And of course satire in the *Contes* is often not smiling but ferocious. Yet satire itself is a form of indirection. It too displays the wit of the writer and addresses that of the reader. The lessons pass much more easily thanks to brevity, lightness of touch and a degree of self-mockery. Even the harshest tales take pleasure in their wit and celebrate their own fabulation. In more sober moments tales themselves are perceived as merely a means. Didactic fictions are to be approved, says the Ingenu, while the others are to be condemned as imposture or scorned as infantile. '*J'aime les fables des philosophes, je ris de celles des enfants, et je hais celles des imposteurs*' (*L'Ingénu*, xi, p.318). Yet sober Amazan is seduced in the capital of frivolity, Paris. (And worthy Amabed is seduced in the capital of imposture, Rome.) Amazan the philosopher quits the French

> en leur recommandant d'être toujours légers et frivoles, puisqu'ils n'en étaient que plus aimables et plus heureux. 'Les Germains, disait-il, sont les vieillards de l'Europe; les peuples d'Albion sont les hommes faits; les habitants de la Gaule sont les enfants, et j'aime à jouer avec eux.'
> (*La Princesse de Babylone*, x, p.404).

The *Contes* themselves are playful diminutions. As our Introduction noted, this is true of the very genre (fairy-tale, oriental tale) in the period. Epic and romance are cut down to size. It is true within the literary production of the age's most famous epic and tragic poet, Voltaire. The great dreams are rewritten small. Baroque becomes rococo, in literary scale, tone and ethos. *Petite digression* and *Micromégas* thematise littleness in their titles. The latter sends its hero on a 'petit voyage philosophique' which will eventually land him on 'notre petite fourmilière' (chs i, ii, pp.19, 24). Memnon begins with his 'petit plan de sagesse', and ends wondering whether 'notre petit globe terraqué ne soit précisément les petites-maisons de l'univers' (pp.126, 129). Amazan arrives in Babylon equipped with 'une petite boîte' and 'une petite lame d'ivoire' with which he writes 'petits vers' in the form of a 'petit madrigal' (*La Princesse de Babylone*, ch.i). Mélinade has a 'petit chien', 'de fort petits pieds et des souliers encore plus petits' which equip her for the society of 'petits-maîtres' (*Le Crocheteur borgne*, p.5). Solid Colin on the other hand rides in an unfashionable vehicle '[qui] n'allait pas comme le char d'un petit-maître'; but he is a 'petit homme', accompanied by 'ma petite femme' (*Jeannot et Colin*, p.276). The emblem of human society, or the summary of Babouc's experience, is 'une petite statue' (*Le Monde comme il va*, p.54).

We see how the meiosis of the rococo and that represented by bourgeois good sense, apparently antithetical, are linked. Overall in the *Contes* there is nevertheless a development from fantasy towards realism. We can trace the development through the changing use of another topos. Truth is shared knowledge. Juxtaposing it with the stuff of romance serves to mock both. Improbable coincidence is hailed in this way. 'Tout le monde sait que Cacambo ... connaissait ... cette langue [d'Eldorado]' (*Candide*, xvii, p.185). Fabulous events likewise: 'Chacun sait comment le roi d'Ethiopie devint amoureux de la belle Formosante ...' (*La Princesse de Babylone*, xi, p.412). The allegation of shared knowledge within the fiction seems to serve the same function. *Le Blanc et le noir* begins: 'Tout le monde, dans la province de Candahar, connaît l'aventure du jeune Rustan' (p.269). But what then of the incipit of *Jeannot et Colin*? 'Plusieurs personnes dignes de foi ont vu Jeannot et Colin à l'école dans la ville d'Issoire en Auvergne, ...' (p.269). Here no ironic distancing is evident. To realist time and place are joined more intimate knowledge and writer-reader relations. *Jenni* begins 'Vous me demandez, Monsieur, quelques détails sur ...' (p.597). This is now a version of the new authenticated narrative.

The old opening rituals however are more frequent. They promise the old pleasure of the tale. 'Du temps du roi Moabdar il y avait à Babylone un jeune homme nommé ...' is the incipit of *Zadig* (p.57). 'Il y avait ...'

also begins *Micromégas*, *Cosi-Sancta* and *Candide*. Along with 'Once there was ...', the simplest formulaic incipit for storytelling is 'One day ...'. *Cosi-Sancta* (p.9), *Le Monde comme il va* (p.39), *Memnon* (p.125), *Les Deux Consolés* (p.143), *Candide* (p.146), the *Bon Bramin* (p.235), *Aventure indienne* (p.281) and *L'Ingénu* (p.285) all begin their narratives with 'Un jour ...'.

Chapter 2   DISABLED POWERS

Physical disablement - damage to the human body - is a recurring feature in the *Contes*. The theodicy problem - that of reconciling belief in a benevolent Deity or Providential order with the moral incoherence of the world - is a constant theme. Clearly these are linked at the level of narrative. Progressive assaults on the protagonists lead them, and us, to a questioning of initial naive optimism and a perception of the disorder of the universe. There is also here a parallel with Newtonian scientific method, and with Lockean epistemology. General theory is submitted to particular facts; the *a priori* gives way to sense-experience. In terms of rhetoric, the received order is disrupted by the repeated introduction of low elements - the particular, concrete or down-to-earth - into the normative high register.[1] All this occurs within the *conte* which is in its most characteristic form an ironic rewriting of the order of heroic fiction.

We shall look systematically at three kinds of disabling. The first category is persons in the *Contes* who are deprived, physically, of a cognitive dimension. Secondly we have beings whose power in the world is much less than it seems. The final and principal section shows how all narrative forms are declared to be unauthorised, mediated, unreliable. It is evident that these powers are analogues, respectively, for classical human dignity (disabled through the body), for God and for discourse. We are dealing with burlesque forms of irony and self-irony. We shall see that, having declared invalid the claims of other literary genres, the *Contes* quite properly go about disabling themselves. Emphasis in this chapter falls less on the figures than on the *thematics* of disablement, and less on the celebration than on the criticism of disorder.

---

[1]   On the philosophical significance of style, see my 'The Burlesque as a philosophical principle in Voltaire's *Contes*', *Voltaire and his World*, ed. R.J. Howells, A. Mason, H.T. Mason and D. Williams (Oxford, 1985), pp.67-84. The parallelism of style, event and theme is indicated by Jean Starobinski apropos of *Candide*. 'Dans son style même (style de la soustraction avons-nous dit), *Candide* mime la diminution physique que le mal inflige à l'intégrité des êtres, - partant, il mime la réplique du monde à ce que l'optimisme croit pouvoir en dire': 'Sur le style philosophique de *Candide*', *Le Remède dans le mal* (Paris, 1989), pp.123-44 (pp.129-30).

Pangloss, and Memnon, each lose an eye in the course of the story
(*Candide*, iv, p.154; *Memnon*, p.127). But for the eponymous protagonist
of *Le Crocheteur borgne* this is a pre-existent condition (p.3). A more
radical deprivation of sight defines the 'Quinze-vingts' of *Petite digression*
(pp.279-80). There the three hundred blind men are finally judged by one
who is deaf. *Les Oreilles du comte de Chesterfield* presents a patron
disabled by defective hearing. *Aventure de la mémoire* also alludes in its
title to an essential cognitive capacity, which everyone in the story will
lose. The titular protagonist of *Le Taureau blanc* is unable to speak; the
real and interesting protagonist, wise old Mambrès, is a eunuch.

The allegorical significance of these states is sometimes made explicit.
The one-eyed can only see the good side of things (the 'Crocheteur'), or
the bad side (Memnon). The blind attempt precisely those judgements
which require sight. Memory is hypostatised as a concept and a goddess.
The condition of Mambrès, however, is not assigned a specific value. It
is clearly ironic in that his role in the story is to assist young love. But it
does not deny him a desired sexual plenitude (unlike the eunuch in
Candide, chs xi and xii). What it does is to literalise a more general
impotence. 'Madame, lui répondit Mambrès, je vous ai avoué déjà que ma
science baisse à mesure que mon âge avance' (iii, p.534). 'Le grand
Mambrès y présidait, mais il n'avait plus le même crédit qu'autrefois' (iv,
p.540). Here it is presented diachronically, as a loss of power. But it is
also a permanent state. 'Tout prophète que je suis, je sais bien peu de
choses' (v, p.543). The power of the Count of Chesterfield to benefit his
protegés, on the other hand, is not in doubt. Yet he fails to do so, because
he is incapacitated first by deafness, then by death. Both these high
personages, 'mage' and 'comte', are good-willed. Both have, or had,
power. Yet both are disabled.

In *Le Taureau blanc* Mambrès has a problematical double. The Snake
- alias Satan - claims that in encouraging Eve to eat of the Tree of
Knowledge he acted with the best of intentions. His interlocutor
apparently accepts this, observing that others too, '[des] ministres ..., de
vrais savants et de grands génies', have been persecuted for spreading
useful knowledge. The Snake however denies that he has lost credit or
power. Indeed, 'J'oserais presque dire que toute la terre m'appartient' (iii,
p.536). One could accept this last statement were it made - as by Martin
in *Candide*, ch.xx - of Satan as the enemy of the proper and Divine order.

But this Satan claims to serve the Divine order. Can he unite in himself knowledge, and power, and benevolence? He cannot, as contradictions appear in his own account of himself. He recognises that knowledge may involve 'quelque danger' (p.537). The narrator, in turn, conceding Satan's good intentions but not his knowledge, observes that he always did harm 'en croyant bien faire' (ix, p.556). He himself admits to being less than he used to be: 'j'ai perdu depuis quelque temps l'imagination et la mémoire' (p.554). It seems that the Serpent does not after all have full capacity. In any case, in its contradictions his account disables itself.

Numerous other authority figures in the tales face the same problem. Their power is not as great as it seems.

> Le ministre lui avoua qu'il était un homme très malheureux; qu'il passait pour riche, et qu'il était pauvre; qu'on le croyait tout-puissant, et qu'il était toujours contredit; qu'il n'avait guère obligé que des ingrats, et que, dans un travail continuel de quarante années, il avait eu à peine un moment de consolation. Babouc en fut touché, ... (*Le Monde comme il va*, xi, pp.52-53)

Some sympathy is required for the human potentate, but also for the subaltern divinities. 'Démogorgon ... ayant arrangé [la terre] ... prétendait avoir fait un chef d'oeuvre. Il ... attendait des éloges, même de ses confrères; il fut bien surpris d'être reçu d'eux avec des huées.' It is revealed moreover that none of his colleagues have organised their respective planets any better. Their master, 'le grand Démiourgos, l'éternel géomètre', explains that they, are all limited; only he can produce 'des choses parfaites et immortelles' (*Songe de Platon*, pp.15-17). It appears that God - solely - is free of disablement. But a later tale denies this too. Chaplain Goudman is drawn to the other conclusion: 'Dieu est donc esclave tout comme moi?'. His interlocutor replies 'Il est esclave de sa volonté, de sa sagesse, des propres lois qu'il a faites, de sa nature nécessaire' (*Chesterfield*, iv, p.585-86).

The subaltern divinity is the most obviously ironic case. From our human point of view the 'ange' or 'génie' is superior. He must have both dominion over human affairs and an understanding of the universal order. Alas, this presumption is increasingly denied. Memnon's 'bon génie' is confident of possessing the understanding: he reassures Memnon that 'tout est bien ... en considérant l'arrangement de l'univers entier'. But he has no reply when Memnon reproaches him with lack of power. He claims

only to 'veiller' and to 'consoler' (pp.128-30). Topaze, the 'bon génie' of
Rustan, describes his role in the same way: 'ma charge était de veiller
auprès de toi jusqu'au dernier moment de ta vie; je m'en suis fidèlement
acquitté'. Rustan too is less than satisfied. Adducing like Memnon his
own unhappy condition, he too demands 'A quoi un génie est-il bon?'.
This time the subdivinity ruefully admits to incomprehension. He knows
no more in this world than the protagonist; he is far from confident of full
revelation in the next. Rustan, dying:

> Il y a quelque chose là-dessous que je ne comprends pas. - Ni moi non
> plus, dit le pauvre bon génie. - J'en serai instruit dans un moment, dit
> Rustan. - C'est ce que nous verrons, dit Topaze.
>   (*Le Blanc et le noir*, pp.264-65)

The limitations of Topaze (and Démogorgon) are confirmed by a
superior being in an early tale. 'J'arriverai peut-être un jour au pays où il
ne manque rien; mais jusqu'à présent personne ne m'a donné des nouvelles
positives de ce pays-là' (*Micromégas*, ii, p.22). The capacities of the
subaltern divinity may seem complete in *Zadig*. The chapter 'L'Hermite'
shows that Jesrad has the power to intervene, not simply to advise or warn
as will be the case in *Le Blanc et le noir*. As he dispenses destinies, so at
the end he prestigiously dispenses explanations of the universal scheme.
This includes the assertion that there is an 'ordre ... parfait ... dans la
demeure éternelle de l'Etre suprême' (*Zadig*, ch.xviii). Yet his
explanations seem marginally put into question in three ways. There is the
repeated interruption of *Zadig*'s famous 'Mais ...'. The angel's withdrawal
from earth might be read not as a triumph but as a retreat, a physical
curtailment occasioned by the inability to explain. (An avatar, therefore,
of the more pointed punctuation by the dervish who slams the door on the
questions of Candide.) Thirdly, the several explanations proffered are so
diverse as to be scarcely compatible with each other.

All the last three tales we have cited also include an episode involving
a written account of the order of things. Great hopes are raised. (The
promise of revelation, offered by various agencies, we noted in Chapter 1,
2.ii.c.). In each case, again, the hopes are disappointed. Jesrad begins by
showing *Zadig* 'le livre des destinées'. But Zadig cannot decipher a single
letter (xviii, p.109). Micromégas ends by giving to the earthmen 'un beau
livre de philosophie ... [où] ils verraient le bout des choses'. The book is
blank (vii, p.37). The tale of Rustan ends with Topaze offering him an

explanation of the logic of all events in the history of the world. But an editorial note tells us that this manuscript has unfortunately been lost (*Le Blanc et le noir*, pp.266-67). The parallel is surely clear. The discourses of the subaltern divinity and of the written text, each carrying great prestige, raise expectations of attaining the truth. Both - sadly and comically - are revealed to fall short.

By implication, the book which repeatedly deals in these defective forms of authority is itself disabled. Reflexivity is our concern in the third part of our analysis. We look at how the *Contes* undermine the status of all forms of utterance as accounts of reality.

At one time or another in the text of the tales a score of genres or subgenres are invoked. These include the following: 'roman', 'récit', 'mémoires', 'chronique', 'histoire [publique]', 'histoire [privée], 'histoire [inventée]', 'tragédie', 'comédie', 'poème épique', 'livre sacré', 'fable', 'conte', 'prophétie', 'almanach', 'éloge', 'dialogue', 'lettre' and 'extrait'. Most occur a number of times, in different tales. Alongside these appear various quasi-narrative categories. We encounter 'oracle', 'prière', 'testament', 'titre', 'généalogie'. Then there are quasi-generic categories: 'songe', 'rêve', 'aventure', and the problematical 'traduction'. All are more or less disabled not only by the general context of irony in which they appear, but by particular juxtapositions or overt judgements. All constitute both a *mise en abyme* and a generic metatext for the *conte* itself. The *conte* also declares more directly its own invalidity.

Most history is mere fiction. 'Je soupçonne, depuis que je me suis mis à lire, que le même génie qui a écrit *Gargantua* écrivait autrefois toutes les histoires' (*Quarante écus*, p.471). Ancient history in particular deserves such a label. 'Je ne vois avant Thucydide que des romans semblables aux *Amadis*', says the Ingenu. Here the sceptical implications are spelled out in a list that is almost a set of literary subgenres in itself: 'Ce sont partout des apparitions, des oracles, des prodiges, des sortilèges, des métamorphoses, des songes expliqués, et qui font la destinée des plus grands empires et des plus petits états: ...' (*L'Ingénu*, xi, pp.317-18). But this foolishness is more widespread: 'Je suis las de toutes les fadaises dont tant d'historiens prétendus ont farci leurs chroniques' (*Chesterfield*, vii, p.594). Objections to the history of the Jews, the Old Testament, are multiple and more violent in tone:

[Le peuple juif] se forgea une histoire pendant sa captivité, et c'est dans cette seule histoire qu'il ait jamais été question de Noé. Quand ce petit peuple obtint depuis des privilèges dans Alexandrie, il y traduisit ses annales en grec. Elles furent ensuite traduites en arabe ... . Mais cette histoire est aussi méprisée [aujourd'hui] que la misérable horde que l'a écrite. (*Amabed*, p.483)

In this latter judgement the verb 'forger' clearly carries a secondary sense of 'fake'. Something similar is going on, in the modern period, with historical texts which are given a false pedigree.

Il cite le testament du grand ministre Colbert, et il ne sait pas que c'est une rapsodie ridicule faite par un Gatien de Courtilz; ... ; il cite le testament du cardinal de Richelieu, et il ne sait pas qu'il est de l'abbé de Bourzeïs. (*Quarante écus*, p.437)

Overall, then, most histories are no better than 'fables', risibly childish or deliberately falsified: '*je ris de celles des enfants, et je hais celles des imposteurs*' (*L'Ingénu*, xi, p.318).

History may be disabled by alleging various types of contradiction. The lack of corroboration elsewhere for one history's claims about Noah is used to suggest falsehood. So, alternatively, is the failure of a supposedly comprehensive account to mention certain major facts. 'C'est une histoire universelle du monde entier, dans laquelle il n'est pas dit un mot de notre antique empire, rien des immenses contrées au-delà du Gange, rien de la Chine, ...' (*Amabed*, pp.480-81). A history may be damaged by internal contradiction, as with the apparently differing dates for the Creation in three versions of the Bible (*loc.cit.*). Or two histories may negate each other - the implication drawn by sarcasm: 'si ces deux historiens se contredisent, c'est une preuve de la vérité du fait ...' (*Pot-pourri*, i, p.239). Or an obviously false history may be bracketed with one supposedly true, leaving them to sink rather than swim together: 'ces histoires [Hercule, saint Pierre], tout authentiques qu'elles sont, ...' (*Jenni*, iii, p.605).

Why, apart from foolishness or deliberate imposture, should the scribes of history produce defective accounts? The neutrality of truth is very difficult to achieve. 'Je vais raconter ingénument comme la chose se passa, sans y rien mettre du mien, ce qui n'est pas un petit effort pour un historien' (*Micromégas*, iv, p.29). What is difficult for one historian is impossible for several. 'Elles racontèrent toutes à leurs amants cette aventure étrange, et chacune avec des circonstances différentes, qui en augmentaient la singularité, et qui contribuent toujours à la variété de toutes les histoires' (*Le Taureau blanc*, iv, p.540). Sheer ignorance may be a cause, to be added to that of unreliable transmission. 'J'ai lu comme vous, dans Florus, cette incroyable anecdote [sur la table d'hôte d'Atticus]; mais apparemment que Florus n'avait jamais soupé chez Atticus, ou que son texte a été corrompu, comme tant d'autres, par les copistes' (*Quarante écus*, p.472). The problem may be contemporary ignorance, or that of later historians who misinterpret the documents (*Chesterfield*, vii, p.594). The conclusion from all this is clear, and perhaps also self-disabling in its reflexivity. Juxtaposed with each of the last two examples is a line of verse, unattributed, which is actually from a play by Voltaire himself: 'Et voilà justement comme on écrit l'histoire'.

Particular authorities may be evoked in ironic contexts. *Le Taureau blanc* supports a minor narrative detail with the assertion 'comme il est dit dans Manéthon' (vii, p.552). Shortly before, a Latin proverb is attributed to 'mon maître Zoroastre' (v, p.547). In *La Princesse de Babylone* the heroine is pompously presented with various sacred animals, two mummies and 'les livres du grand Hermès' (which are presumably hermetic). Another suitor offers her more beasts and 'le *Veidam*, écrit de la main de Xaca lui-même' (i, p.351). Here the disablement is both diegetic, in the fatuous misuse of books, and narratorial, through ironic overemphasis and comic juxtapositions. In *Zadig* the narrator likes to invoke the authority of 'le grand livre du *Zend*' (iii, p.62; xvi, p.104). The last two sacred texts appear together in the *Lettre d'un Turc*, where the Veidam is announced hyperbolically as 'assurément le plus ancien livre de toute l'Asie, sans en excepter le *Zend-Vesta*' (p.131). Here the status of the book is also disabled by its misuse. 'Je passai devant un fakir qui lisait un livre. "Ah! malheureux infidèle! s'écria-t-il, tu m'as fait perdre le nombre des voyelles que je comptais"' (*loc.cit.*).

We return finally to the revered text that leaves one no wiser even when it is approached properly. But now the text is spoken. 'Ezéchiel et Jérémie parlèrent aussi très longtemps dans un fort beau style, qu'on ne pouvait comprendre' (*Le Taureau blanc*, vi, p.550). The unintelligible style of the prophets is attributed elsewhere to a mock pope, who may be using it more knowingly: 'on n'entendait pas un mot de ce qu'il disait; mais il avait un galimatias fort convenable' (*Pot-pourri*, vii, p.246). But perhaps the incomprehension is on all sides. An almoner receives money 'pour dire des prières dans une langue ... que personne de l'équipage n'entend; peut-être ne l'entend-il pas lui-même' (*Amabed*, p.500). Emitter and/or message and/or receiver are disabled.[2]

The tales, ironically invoking by genre and by name the authoritative texts, or overtly deprecating their truth, nevertheless imitate those texts. *Le Taureau blanc* draws its material from the Old Testament, foregrounding and juxtaposing various episodes concerning unlikely animals so as to create a more evidently fantastic story. The Biblical episodes are repeatedly compared to similar pagan legends. *Les Lettres d'Amabed* use both main text and editorial footnotes to confront Biblical with Indian sacred narratives. The oriental story is the reference point for several *contes* including *Zadig*, *Le Blanc et le noir* and *La Princesse de Babylone*. This genre shades off in turn into the broader outlines of the romance which stand behind most of the major tales. In all cases the received order is held up for inspection, ironically undermined, cheerfully or harshly disabled. More directly to the present point, the problematical relationship is often announced in the titles of the tales. These, as we noted in Chapter 1, are insistently generic. Examples included *Cosi-Sancta ... nouvelle africaine* and *Histoire des voyages de Scarmentado*. Other received generic categories invoked in titles include: *Histoire* (d'un bon bramin; de Jenni); *Lettre* (d'un Turc) and *Lettres* (d'Amabed); *Aventure* (indienne; de la mémoire); *Éloge* (historique de la raison); *Songe* (de Platon). Alongside we have too the new composite *Histoire philosophique* (= *Micromégas*), the apparently pleonastic *Histoire véritable* (= *L'Ingénu*), the rather suspect *Vision* (de Babouc), the mocking *Pot-pourri* and the self-deprecating *Petite digression*.

This ironic conspectus is repeated within the longer tales. Most of the tales are broken down into brief semi-discrete narrative episodes. In the longer tales these units have their own headings. In several, these pastiche

---

[2] An important exception here is the oracular power attributed to Freind in the *Histoire de Jenni*. Freind himself asserts in turn that the Divine Script(ure) is translatable and readable, fully available to us: 'nous lisons le testament de notre grand-père dans notre propre langue' (iii, p.604). We shall observe how this very late work (as to a lesser extent *Jeannot et Colin* and *L'Ingénu*) retreats from the principle of disablement. My account accords here with the remarkable reading offered by Jack Undank, 'The Status of fiction in Voltaire's *Contes*', *Degré Second* 6 (July 1982), pp.65-88.

the chapter-headings of the popular romances. Thus: 'Comment une vieille prit soin de Candide, et comment il retrouva ce qu'il aimait' (*Candide*, ch. vii); 'Le Roi Tanis arrive. Sa fille et le taureau vont être sacrifiés' (*Le Taureau blanc*, ch.vii). Some employ generic naming in their chapter-titles. The *Histoire de Jenni* includes 'Aventure' (ch.i), 'Suite des aventures' (ii), 'Précis' (iii) and 'Dialogue' (viii). In *Quarante écus* successive segments are labelled 'Entretien', 'Aventure', 'Audience' and 'Lettre'. Thus we can say that the tales as a collection, and many of the individual works, offer a fragmented review of literary genre. This offers a parallel to those dislocated reviews of public or private history which constitute the narratives themselves.

But we have yet to note the disabling elements that many of the tales carry in their own titles. These works are sometimes attributed to very unlikely sources. Thus we have *L'Ingénu. Histoire véritable tirée des manuscrits du P. Quesnel.* Alternatively, or in addition, they may be 'translated'. Thus *Les Lettres d'Amabed. Traduites par l'abbé Tamponet*; or *Le Taureau blanc. Traduit du syriaque par M. Mamaki* .... For allegedly foreign tales this latter presentation is, on the surface, not a disabling but an authenticating device. But not only does the burlesque tradition, since the *Quixote*, suggest an ironic reading. Everything in the *Contes* implies that this is a form of damage to the original message. The Jewish historical record was deprecated through reference to its being in translation. The *Contes* contain a number of remarks about the mutual impenetrability of different languages. (Only in Eldorado do the royal witticisms successfully translate.) *La Princesse de Babylone* in particular makes of the question a running joke. There it involves not only Chaldean and French poetic styles (i, p.353), and the language of animals (iii, p.363). One passage delightfully juxtaposes English and French idiom, literal meaning and final meaninglessness.

> Il regarda un moment Amazan, et lui dit: *'How dye do?'*, à la lettre: *Comment faites-vous faire?* et dans la langue du traducteur: *Comment vous portez-vous?* ce qui ne veut rien dire du tout en aucune langue. (viii, p.389)

Within the subtitles themselves the reader's suspicions may also be aroused by mildly comic names: Tamponet, Mamaki; *Traduit par M. de la Caille* for *Jenni*. Or by curious details: *Traduit de l'allemand de M. le docteur Ralph, avec les additions qu'on a trouvées dans la poche du docteur* ....

Or by direct deprecation: *Aventure indienne. Traduite par l'ignorant.*[3]
Not only do the tales frequently begin by implicitly disabling
themselves, they sometimes end by explicitly doing so. Several disqualify
all that has come before by declaring it to have been an illusion. 'Alors
tout disparut. Rustan se retrouva dans la maison de son père, dont il
n'était pas sorti, et dans son lit, où il avait dormi une heure' (*Le Blanc et
le noir*, p.265). The protagonist in *Le Crocheteur borgne* has the same
experience, except that he wakes up in the street (p.7). In both these cases
the reader too has been fooled by the illusion. *Songe de Platon*, a third
'dream' tale, warns us in advance. There a *narrataire* within the fiction
abruptly deflates Plato's dream of wisdom: '"*Et puis vous vous
réveillâtes*"' (p.17). It follows from this device that the genres 'Songe' and
'Vision' are always suspect, at least in prose.[4]
     A connection can also be made between the mock-authentication in the
titles and the excessive claims made at the end of certain tales. The
epistolary *Amabed* concludes with an editorial note. 'Ici finit le manuscrit
des *lettres d'Amabed*. On a cherché dans toutes les bibliothèques de
Maduré et de Bénarès la suite de ces *lettres*. Il est sûr qu'elle n'existe
pas.' So beware of false imitations (*Amabed*, p.525). *La Princesse de
Babylone* denounces 'continuateurs téméraires'. Let them not dare to
corrupt 'les vérités que j'ai enseignées aux mortels dans ce fidèle récit' (xi,
p.413). Moral truth, mission to all mankind, literal truth: no book could
claim much more. No claim could throw much more mockingly into
question the claims of all narratives.
     None of the tales actually calls itself a *conte*. But of course this term
appears within some tales. In various contexts it has varied senses. One
sense is that of falsehood ('Ce sont apparemment mes ennemis, madame,
qui vous ont fait ces contes': *Le Taureau blanc*, iii, p.537). Another sense
is that of frivolous, infantile or absurd literary genre (oriental tales are
described as 'des contes qui sont sans raison, et qui ne signifient rien':

---

[3] *Aventure indienne*, and *Petite digression*, both appeared originally as part of *Le
Philosophe ignorant* (see the Pléiade edition, pp.962-65). This explains their respective
references to ignorance and to digression; the ironic force of the references however
remains.

[4] They remain a non-ironic species when protected by the genre marker of heroic
verse, as in *La Henriade*, vii.

Zadig, 'Epître', p.56). These meanings are perhaps joined in the suggestion that theological propositions are best classed with 'contes de ma mère l'oie' (*Quarante écus*, p.466). But the term is also formally examined in its literary sense. Two of the tales offer not only discussion but firm definition of what the *conte* should be. 'Je veux qu'un conte soit fondé sur la vraisemblance, et qu'il ne ressemble pas toujours à un rêve' says Princess Amaside (*Le Taureau blanc*, ix, p.553). A similar demand is attributed to another intelligent young woman. 'La princesse fit acheter ... tous les contes que l'on avait écrits ...; elle espérait qu'elle trouverait dans ces histoires quelque aventure qui ressemblerait à la sienne' (*La Princesse de Babylone*, vii, p.388). But both demands are internally collapsed by the impossible titles on the royal reading-lists. We are told told that the Princess of Babylon has been perusing *La Paysanne parvenue* and *Le Sopha*; the other princess has read 'l'*Entendement humain* du philosophe égyptien nommé Locke'. Both demands moreover are undermined by their narrative contexts. The appeal for verisimilitude and relevance appears in the middle of tales which are wildly fantastic. The incoherence is doubly pointed. With this most direct form of ironic reflexivity the principle of self-disablement is manifested once more.

PART II

INTRODUCTION

So far we have focused mainly on narratological and reflexive aspects of the *Contes*, only sketching in the carnivalesque implications. Part II offers two specifically carnivalesque readings. First we look at *Le Monde comme il va*. This tale belongs to the first group of major *contes*. *Memnon*, *Zadig*, *Le Monde comme il va* and *Micromégas* all appeared between 1747 and 1752. Our second text will be *Candide*, published in 1759. *Candide* stands out from all Voltaire's work, including the other *contes*, as his masterpiece. It is however also in effect the turning point between the earlier tales and those, beginning with *Jeannot et Colin*, which we shall consider in Chapter 5.

The tales published around 1750 are set almost out of time and place. Nominally located in the ancient world, or other worlds, their lack of specificity enables them to function as both exotic tales and as satirical doubles of eighteenth-century civilisation. Narrative integration is not strong. Marked off in quasi-independent units - chapters, sections, even paragraphs - episodes and moments succeed each other. External time and place, and an internal continuum which would 'make sense', are undeveloped. When we reach *Candide* however we have specific time and place, and a more developed human consciousness. Consciousness indeed is multiple, that of a whole group of beings. They are inserted into contemporary history. Place is a more concrete referentiality, and time is process. Change however is still limited at the level of human consciousness. We are more aware of bodies and desires than of experience integrated, more aware of indomitable entities than of developing individualities. Events, similarly, are still radically stylised to bring out shape rather than specificity. Engagement in the physical world is nevertheless much stronger. In *Le Monde comme il va* the body is scarcely filled out. Figure is brilliant, but almost abstract. It tends to be stripped to a kind of geometric purity: duplication, hierarchy, line and circle. In *Candide* it will be more corporeal and heterogeneous, joyously embracing a referential as well as emblematic totality.

Chapter 3   FIGURE IN *LE MONDE COMME IL VA*

The tale begins thus:

> Parmi les génies qui président aux empires du monde, Ituriel tient un des premiers rangs, et il a le département de la haute Asie. Il descendit un matin dans la demeure du Scythe Babouc, sur le rivage de l'Oxus, et lui dit: ...

The first sentence establishes strongly a register that is elevated. 'Génies', 'président', 'empires du monde', 'premiers rangs'; even perhaps, reinforced by what precedes it, 'haute'. The one exception is 'département', a term more administrative than angelic. This comic dissonance signals the pattern to come. Referentially, nevertheless, so far all is in perfect stasis. At the start of the second sentence we have a radical shift. 'Il descendit' takes us from static verbs ('président', 'tient', 'a') to a verb of movement, and from an atemporal present to a temporal and punctual past. And of course it takes us down. Ituriel descends from the realm of ideal order to enter the world. This is his launch. Thus he is - or will be - not only the mandator of Babouc. He is his avatar. The first few lines of this *conte* can be read as a frame narrative about Ituriel, and they constitute a preliminary *mise en abyme* of the figure of induction into the world. The final paragraph of the *conte* will return us, in reverse, to this metanarrative.

Babouc at the start is identified with the ideal, in several ways. His quest is mandated by the angel Ituriel. It requires him to make an absolute and global judgement ('corriger la ville ou l'exterminer'). He is a Scythian, a race proverbial for its savagery.[1] This last identification - also made in *Zadig*, ch.xii, and in *La Princesse de Babylone* - might seem unrelated to the first. But the text will later place the angelic and the savage in parallel. 'Babouc, tout Scythe et tout envoyé qu'il était d'un génie, s'aperçut que, s'il restait à Persépolis, il oublierait Ituriel pour Téone' (§xii). On the one hand is the moral absolute: barbaric (Babouc)

---

[1] See n.1 to p.39 of the Pléiade edition. I have not included page-references for quotations from the text, because this is a short work (15 pages). It is divided into twelve sections (§), and I have given these instead, for reference to any edition.

or angelic (Ituriel). On the other is human civilisation (Persépolis), its synecdoches the woman (Téone) and particular affection. For 'Persépolis' we can read any other civilised capital city - likewise *polis*, polite, policed. Specifically we are to read *the* capital city, Paris, for which Persépolis is not only one more witty displacement. Persépolis is Paris's alliterative echo and perhaps - since Montesquieu's *Lettres persanes* - its metaliterary mirror. The injunction 'Babouc ... va dans cette ville' repeats formally but also as figure 'Ituriel ... descendit [sur la terre]'. Babouc is instructed to 'examine[r] tout' (see Chapter 1, 2.ii.a and b, above). He is to review a human totality.

'Babouc monta sur son chameau et partit avec ses serviteurs'. The incipit of the second paragraph gives us the protagonist's launch. It is marked, again, by the first instance of movement. 'Babouc monta' both reverses and repeats 'Ituriel ... descendit'. One might say indeed that the barbarian rises, as the angel comes down, to the level of the human. 'Babouc ... partit' establishes horizontal movement. From a point of origin, a line extends towards the large circle of the collectivity. The spatial and temporal gap is traversed so rapidly that the figure of movement is almost pure abstraction. 'Au bout de quelques journées, il rencontra vers les plaines de Senaar l'armée persane ...'.

This first encounter, with the Persian army, is promptly segmented and structured within itself. 'Il s'adressa d'abord à un soldat qu'il trouva écarté. 'Il lui parla, et lui demanda quel était le sujet de la guerre ...'. In the next paragraph, 'Babouc ... entra dans le camp. Il fit bientôt connaissance avec le capitaine, et lui demanda ...'. The fourth paragraph begins 'Babouc, étonné, s'introduisit chez les généraux; il entra dans leur familiarité. L'un d'eux lui dit enfin ...'. Figuration here is complex and precise. We have three kinds of social space: on the margins with the soldier ('écarté'), inside the collective area of the camp with the captain ('entra'), then within the quasi-private space of the generals ('dans leur familiarité'). Soldier, captain, general thus offer succession inwards. As an independent series they also offer hierarchy upwards. They constitute an emblematically complete enumeration. (Note too the grammatico-logical totalising of the article: '*un* soldat', '*le* capitaine', '*les* généraux'.) The three modes of encounter are also differentiated so as to represent totality. We have an hierarchy of respect: 'il s'adressa ... à un soldat'; 'il fit ... connaissance avec le capitaine'; 'il s'introduisit [sans poser sa question] chez les généraux'. Clearly the soldier is socially below Babouc, the captain his equal and the generals above him. Their utterances constitute a figure in triples. First is the soldier who simply speaks his piece. Then we move to the captain whose two utterances flank one by Babouc: three in all. Thirdly the general again simply speaks his piece. But, marking climax and closure, he has the answer. Gradation is also marked by the degree of narratorial intervention. The first utterance is simply presented, without affective reaction by Babouc or commentary from the narrator; Babouc however is 'étonné' following the second; a narratorial 'enfin' precedes the third and last.

But the totality of the Persian army is just half of an englobing and more dynamic figure - that of the war. This doubling and its dynamism are signalled from the start. Babouc encountered 'l'armée persane *qui allait combattre l'armée indienne*'. As doubling it is echoed by the alternative offered in the captain's speech, '[chercher] la fortune *ou* la mort', and by the ironic equivalence offered in that of the soldier, 'mon métier est de tuer *et* d'être tué'. As dynamism it appears in the soldier's summary 'on se bat' and the captain's summary 'on s'égorge'. Following the exposition of the Persian (demi)totality, battle is joined with the Indian double. Inter-army battle however is also intra-army. The latter occurs vertically ('satrapes qui firent ... battre leur chef') and horizontally ('soldats qui ... égorg[èrent] leurs camarades'). In the next paragraph specularity is established through Babouc's own movement into the other totality. 'Il passa dans le camp des Indiens.' Identity is made explicit: 'Il y fut aussi bien reçu que dans celui des Perses ...'. 'Il y vit tous les mêmes excès [que chez les Perses]' declares negative ethical identity. 'Dans l'une et l'autre armée, il apprit des actions de générosité ...' reverses and repeats this as positive ethical identity. 'Cependant la paix fut déclarée', the incipit of the next paragraph, offers a conceptual reversal and - in a sense - a synchronic identity. Peace doubles what has been till now the totalising figure of war.

Before leaving the war episode, we can pick up further emblematic patterns. We saw how the utterances of the Persian soldier and then the captain reinforced the figure of war. The general and - 'enfin' - his utterance completed the series. But his climactic account of the war between Persia and India takes us spiralling rapidly back down to its trivial past origins.: 'il s'agissait d'... à peu près la trentième partie d'une darique, ...'. Then we expand, in the present, far beyond the confines of the war: 'l'univers souffre'. The next sentence evokes '[le] genre humain'. Quitting the human plane, we then have a vertical expansion both ways to take in the subhuman and the angelic. The long account of the Persian army is concluded by the protagonist's reaction. 'Sont-ce là des hommes, s'écria Babouc, ou des bêtes féroces? Ah! je vois bien que Persépolis sera détruite.' The agent of destruction is the angel. The visit to the Indian army however also causes him to double the superhuman agency. 'Si l'ange Ituriel veut exterminer les Persans, il faut donc que l'ange des Indes détruise aussi les Indiens'. The declaration of peace completes the armies episode. We have had a second and more substantial preliminary *mise en abyme* of Persépolis. Babouc and we are ready to enter the city proper.

For the capital, a new chapter. The incipit of §ii is 'Il arriva dans cette ville immense par l'ancienne entrée'. The second paragraph begins 'Babouc se mêla dans la foule', and the next sentence 'Cette foule se précipitait ... dans un enclos'. Here we have three successive figures of entry. Babouc is taken into the city, then into the crowd, then with the crowd into an enclosure. 'Se mêla' also suggests exchange, which continues in the church with '[le] mouvement qu'il y remarqua, ... l'argent que quelques personnes donnaient à d'autres, ... plusieurs femmes ... regardant les hommes de côté'. Uncouth voices in song 'faisaient retentir la voûte'. Babouc 'se bouchait les oreilles; mais il fut prêt à se boucher encore les yeux et le nez, quand ... des ouvriers ... remuèrent une large pierre, ... on vint poser un mort dans cette ouverture, et on remit la pierre par-dessus'. As referentiality and as figure this is carnivalesque: the public venue; collective, improper exchange; money and sexuality debasing the sacred, the audience as performers, accord and discord; the vault above and the grave beneath; turning over; life and death. But Babouc in the middle tries to block off his senses. The popular is not for him. We move on to its double.

'Cependant le soleil approchait du haut de sa carrière. Babouc devait aller dîner à l'autre bout de la ville ... .' Thus the incipit of §iii. As the sun crosses its zenith, Babouc crosses the city. Movement is linear from one quarter to the other. But we might equally read in the sun and its career the figure of the circle. This is prepared just before by a reference to 'le globe terrestre'. We would then superimpose it on Babouc's movement in the city in the third sentence of §iii. As the sun circles the globe, Babouc 'fit d'abord plusieurs tours dans Persépolis'. He encounters the respectable double of what he found before. 'Il vit d'autres temples mieux bâtis et mieux ornés, remplis d'un peuple poli, et retentissants d'une musique harmonieuse.' The public squares offer both the orderly and disorderly versions: 'des places où semblaient respirer en bronze les meilleurs rois qui avaient gouverné la Perse; d'autres places où il entendait le peuple s'écrier "Quand verrons-nous ici le maître que nous chérissons?"' The official king from the past, safely frozen in bronze, is clearly preferable in this presentation to the popular and carnivalesque king of the future.[2] Previously we had '[les] morts, et ... [les] vivants rassemblés et pressés dans le même lieu'; now we have an intermediate state, amply accommodated, 'une maison [de retraite] immense'. Previously we had bilateral chthonic activity: 'ils ... jetèrent à droite et à gauche une terre ...'. Now we have bilateral grand stasis: 'les palais bâtis à droite et à gauche'. Nevertheless, Babouc is still in the street. Its civilised double will be a new indoors. 'Il entra enfin chez la dame qui l'attendait à dîner avec une compagnie d'honnêtes gens.'

Thus Babouc has been taken successively from the open countryside ('les plaines de Senaar') to urban public space and then to semi-private space. We have moved from the extreme physical violence of warfare to the uncouth jostlings of the crowd to the 'dîner avec ... [les] honnêtes gens'. The hierarchic review of the military totality, upwards from soldier to general, can now also be seen as the avatar of the review of the urban totality upwards from 'foule' to 'honnêtes gens'. A brilliantly simple horizontal linkage has Babouc conveying a letter to his hostess from her officer husband. (The line is taken into the inner circle, in more than one sense.) It moves us from the masculine to the feminine. We are however still dealing with '*une compagnie*' - not only a plurality but a collectivity.

---

[2] 'Semblait respirer' apparently offers a hint of life in the bronze kings. It really signifies the opposite, for it is a nervously literalist rectification of the epic conceit of the 'speaking shield' (see the *Iliad*, Book xviii). The 'Moderne' Charles Perrault had criticised the conceit in Homer, 'Que jamais d'un burin ... / Le langage muet ne sçauroit dire', rectifying it in his celebration of the sculptures at Versailles which include 'Ces Chevaux du Soleil qui marchent, qui bondissent, / Et qu'*au rapport des yeux on croiroit qu'*ils hanissent' [my emphasis]: 'Le Siècle de Louis le Grand', in *Parallèle des Anciens et des Modernes* (4 vols, Paris, 1688-97), ed. H.R. Jauss and M. Imdahl (Munich, 1964) (pp.165, 168). Fénelon - much more likely to have influenced Voltaire - makes the same rectification in *Télémaque*, Book xiii. The popular catch-cry by contrast is not imitation of received high art but part of contemporary street life. It alludes to the Jansenist 'convulsionnaires' and hopes of a Second Coming.

The 'dîner' still constitutes ritual group activity. From now the narrative will stay indoors and with the privileged classes. But, likewise, it will continue to deal in collective practices. §§iv and v present the company and its luncheon. §vi takes Babouc to a better class of church, the theatre and a fashionable boutique. In §vii he visits a religious order; in §viii he has the fraternity of scribblers to lunch. In §ix he is in conversation. §x takes him to a courtroom and §xi to the antechamber of a minister. In §xii - the last - he sups and dines with small groups. All is refined. Inside the social circumference, the line and the circle are less evident. But the narrative representation is as before of interpersonal and especially collective practices - including conversations which both are and are about social practice. The figures are still of doubling and exchange.

The first indeed becomes deliciously bodily. §iv begins thus:

> Cependant il s'aperçut que la dame, qui avait commencé par lui demander tendrement des nouvelles de son mari, parlait plus tendrement encore, sur la fin du repas, à un jeune mage. Il vit un magistrat qui, en présence de sa femme, pressait avec vivacité une veuve, et cette veuve indulgente avait une main passée autour du cou du magistrat, tandis qu'elle tendait l'autre à un jeune citoyen très beau et très modeste.

In the initial sentence the lady doubles her husband with her 'jeune mage'. Emphasis is laid on the parallel ('tendrement'), the gradation ('plus ... encore') and the opposition ('commencé', 'sur la fin'). We have a triad of persons. This is repeated in the next sentence: the magistrate doubles his wife with the widow. But by gender the latter triad is also an inversion. This time the third element reciprocates. But she too divides herself, between magistrate and citizen. We have a series of four persons linked. The total is seven. They offer a conspectus of their social world: 'dame', army officer husband, 'mage' (presumably abbé), 'magistrat', 'sa femme', 'veuve', 'citoyen'. The links become progressively more corporeal. The 'dame' is engaged with her two men only verbally (written/spoken). One is absent. The linkage of the foursome is not only more complex but it is physical: "présence' becomes 'main', 'cou', 'l'autre [main]', 'pressait', 'pass[ait] autour d[e]'. All this occurs around the luncheon table. The luncheon gives the event its focus, its classical shape, its physical and social structure. The effect of grotesque ritual is characteristic of Voltaire. At table among the group any further intensification of physical relations would be indecent. An 'écart' - so to speak - must occur. 'La femme du magistrat se leva de table la première, pour aller entretenir dans un cabinet voisin son directeur, qui ... lui parla dans ce cabinet avec tant de véhémence et d'onction que la dame avait, quand elle revint, les yeux humides, les joues enflammées, la démarche mal assurée, la parole tremblante.' Physical has become physiological. The figure of 'around' (the table) has become the figure of 'within' (the cabinet). Female dalliance is complemented by male aggression; social, sacred and sexual are in comic play. The woman returns to the group.

Immediately after the scene just recounted, Babouc is told its moral significance. 'La dame ... lui confia son goût pour le jeune mage, et l'assura que dans toutes les maisons de Persépolis il trouverait l'équivalent de ce qu'il avait vu dans la sienne.' Meaning is thematised and universalised by straight assertion. From now it should be more difficult for Babouc, and for the narrative which is partially focalised through him, to 'fail to understand'. External forms will tend to lose their importance. A pleasing example of their expressive power however can still be found in §vi. With Babouc we visit a theatre. This is preceded by his attendance at 'un des plus superbes temples de la ville'. The church presentation offers a positive antithesis to the uncouth worship presented earlier. It functions, more immediately, to contrast negatively with the theatrical experience following, as a far less effective vehicle for moral teaching. However the theatre - unlike the church - is not explicitly identified as such. It is defamiliarised, requiring us to look again, by evoking only its external forms. These are presented as ambiguous, and then as reversible.

'On le mena voir une fête publique qu'on donnait tous les jours de l'année; c'était dans une espèce de basilique, au fond de laquelle on voyait un palais.' This is a public event. It is everyday yet ritual and festive. It resembles a religious observance by its container; it seems to be royal by its contents. Then comes a still more suggestive misunderstanding. 'Les plus belles citoyennes de Persépolis, les plus considérables satrapes, rangés avec ordre, formaient un spectacle si beau que Babouc crut d'abord que c'était là toute la fête'. By a horizontal reversal (here naturalised by explicitly adopting Babouc's innocent eye), the audience is the show. Royalty however appears and performs at the palace end. Babouc, deeply moved by 'la principale reine, qui avait débité dans ce beau palais une morale si noble et si pure', wishes to meet her afterwards. 'On le mena par un petit escalier, au second étage, dans un appartement mal meublé, où il trouva une femme mal vêtue ...'. Narrow stairs and vertical axis provide a mildly expressive figure (though going upwards sets social referentiality against our symbolic system). But the indices lack specificity and are almost directly moralised ('beau'/'mal').

Sections vii and viii place Babouc in further groups. He *goes out* and *into* a seminary ('il se transporta dans un collège de mages'); he *comes in* and *invites to his table* scholars and writers ('retiré chez lui, ... il pria quelques lettrés à dîner'). But the collective figures are secondary to the wholesale moral judgements made against the social groups represented. In §ix Babouc, deeply alienated, encounters 'un vieux lettré qui ... fuyait toujours la foule'. This notation confirms that we are at the point of maximum hostility to collectivities large or small. But it is established here by setting up a twosome. Better, 'un autre lettré les joignit'. Now we are three. 'Leurs discours furent si agréables et si instructifs, si élevés au-dessus des préjugés, et si conformes à la vertu ...'. Is this figure plural or monologic? The wise men speak as one, but their lesson - 'le bien résulte quelquefois de[s] ... abus mêmes' - is pluralist. Likewise Babouc learns both pluralism ('les grand corps ... se choquant ..., chaque société des mages était un frein à ses rivales') and monologism ('ils enseignaient tous la même morale'). The two-sided wisdom is then derived complementarily at the courts of justice, not from the agéd and learnéd but their antithesis 'les jeunes', 'les hommes nouveaux' (§x). It is clear at least that Babouc's crisis of alienation is over. His return to the world is thematised. In the next section it is figured.

'Comme il voulait pénétrer dans toutes les conditions humaines, il se fit mener chez un ministre' (§xi). Implicit here is the notion that Babouc's review is complete. Completeness is declared as the ambition. Completion is suggested by his accession to a minister, at the apogee of society (as were the generals to whom he finally acceded in the army). Babouc once more penetrates. But now the line enters the innermost circle. What do we find within it? 'L'antichambre [du ministre] était remplie de dames de tout étage, de mages de toutes couleurs, de juges, de marchands, d'officiers, de pédants.' This world is a filled space, multi-layered and parti-coloured. Its contents are not only a microcosm of the larger world. They represent in particular most of the cast of the narrative. Already reviewed sequentially, they are now reassembled within a single time and place.

Babouc's audience with the minister himself is interrupted by another return. This begins the last segment of the narrative, §xii. (Twelve can itself be seen as an emblem of totality: twelve months in the year, twelve gates to the city [Revelations, xxi, 12], ...) 'La belle dame chez qui Babouc avait dîné' enters to sollicit a place for her husband the army officer. The synchronic review of Babouc's sequential review is completed, now - ending with the army where we started - in reverse order. Totality is offered not only as *abyme* but almost as palindrome. Then the lady tells Babouc that her husband and his mistress are later to join her and her ecclesiastical admirer. Here the totality is a chiasmus. It becomes civilised carnival with the invitation to Babouc. 'Nous soupons ensemble ce soir avec mon mari et mon petit mage, venez partager notre joie'.

The next day Babouc participates in the final collective meal. It is a luncheon - like the first. He dines *chez* Téone, a lady in whom a doubtful reputation and many excellent qualities are combined. She is of course a synecdoche of Persépolis, and in turn of the world. Ituriel's absolutes are inadequate to the complexity of reality. How then is Babouc to present to the angel 'le compte qu'il allait rendre'? The final paragraph of the narrative tells us. It is a figure in more than one sense. '[Babouc] fit faire par le meilleur fondeur de la ville une petite statue composée de tous les métaux, des terres et des pierres les plus précieuses et les plus viles'. The city produces from within itself the *abyme* of its heterogeneity. 'Ituriel entendit à demi-mot' - a nice expression for the response to ambivalence. It also marks the prolongation of the palindrome. We return to the angel, with whom we began. At the same time the relation is reversed. Then the angel instructed the man, here the man instructs the angel. The final figure is a joyous superposition. Babouc's affection for Persépolis is contrasted with 'Jonas qui se fâcha de ce qu'on ne détruisait pas Ninive'. The narrative explicitly invokes its own metatext - both the Bible as the authoritative Book and the particular archetype of Jonah. 'Mais quand on a été trois jours dans le corps d'une baleine, on n'est pas de si bonne humeur que quand on a été à l'opéra, à la comédie, et qu'on a soupé en bonne compagnie.' The narrator signs off by celebrating the most social of the narrative arts, the meal as observance, and the civilised collectivity which produces, consumes and is mirrored in this tale.

Babouc indeed has not been in the *belly* of the world-whale. The narrative eschews the concrete and vulgar term 'ventre', just as it tends throughout to eschew concrete detail and the vulgar populace. 'Honnêteté' circumscribes the register entirely and the reference mainly. The crowd and the street were soon left behind. Within the civilised world however

Babouc's itinerary is both everyday and festive. The latter as public observance we have noted: church, theatre, boutique, college, lawcourt, ministerial waiting-room. We have also noted the frequent occurrence of collective meals. The collective meal, undifferentiated, points towards conversation, the principle of verbal communication and exchange so important in the *Contes*. In the other direction, differentiated, it points to time of day. Babouc's circuit of civilised rituals is in fact clearly marked off into segments which are determined by the diurnal as much as the social order. He enters Persépolis in the morning. As the sun signals midday he set off to dine with the lady and her other guests. 'Après dîner' occurs his attendance at church, then the theatre. 'Sa soirée' is passed at the fashionable boutiques. 'Le lendemain matin' (=Day 2) he visits the seminary, then has the authors to lunch, then goes out again 'pour aller le soir à la promenade'. He encounters the wise scholar, '[qui] le mena le lendemain au grand tribunal'. At this point (= Day 3) temporal duration becomes imprecise. We might read here an allusion to the archetype (Jonah spent *three days* in the whale). Certainly we have an accurate representation of the morning, afternoon and evening activities of the privileged classes in Paris. This realism underlies the order and the fantasy of fiction, of quest, of Biblical archetype.

In this *conte* satire - variously upon Paris, Eastern tales and the Old Testament - is also celebration. The joyous mockery of the everyday and of the mythical brings the two levels together in ambivalent play. We noted earlier the reference to popular hopes of the Second Coming (§iii). The tale returns to the great dream. At the seminary a lay brother tells Babouc 'Je vois bien que l'œuvre va s'accomplir: car Zerdust est revenu sur la terre; les petites filles prophétisent, en se faisant donner des coups de pincettes par-devant et le fouet par-derrière.' Violence fore and aft, the world upside-down (female children showing the way), prepare for the popular Coming. Its enemy is the ruler in place, 'ce pontife-roi' (§vii). Other versions of subversive kingship are more cursory and less disturbing. They occur nevertheless in most sections of the narrative. 'Quarante rois plébéiens' - an allusion to the company of tax-farmers in France - control Persia (§v). 'Sa Majesté ... mal vêtue' is the unfortunate actress (§vi). The great work opposed by the Papal monarch is in §vii. The minister in place turns out to be powerless: 'on le croyait tout-puissant, et ... il était toujours contredit' (§xi). We began with the Divine and masculine rule of the 'génies qui président aux empires du monde' (§i). We end with human and feminine rule, as Babouc dines at 'une maison où régnait tous les plaisirs. Téone régnait sur eux' (§xii). He realises he is in danger of forgetting Ituriel for Téone, the transcendant mission for the civilised collectivity, the line of enquiry for the circle of humanity.[3]

---

[3] It has been argued that this should be seen as an error on the protagonist's part: Roy S. Wolper, 'The Final foolishness of Babouc', *Modern Language Review* 75 (1980), pp.766-73. This seems to me a rather willful reading. I would see Babouc's new affective involvement with another person - as distinct from all his previous seeing and hearing - as a positive event. Insofar as Babouc at the end is an object of satire, so is not only the society to which he is attracted but the society which produces this tale. My reflexive reading would concur with that offered by D.I. Dalnekoff, '*Le Monde comme il va*: a satire on satire', *SVEC* 106 (1973), pp.85-102.

Chapter 4 *CANDIDE* AS CARNIVAL[1]

Candide is the most widely known and the most highly regarded of the *Contes*. Its text has been subjected to a vast amount of analysis.[2] Among the most suggestive approaches, serving to explain at least in part the nature and power of *Candide*'s hold on our imagination, are what one might call 'archetypal' readings. The power that they identify is mythical and comical.[3] From these approaches to that of the carnivalesque is not too far.[4] The carnivalesque however lays less emphasis on narrative sequence and thematic structure, and more on dynamic figure. It is uniquely able to account for the joy aroused in us by *Candide*, in appearance a harsh and negative satire. I shall treat first the opening chapter of the work. Then I shall offer a 'grotesque' reading of the whole. This will identify successively a number of carnivalesque figures which are universalising and ludic: the body, interpenetration, the meal, verbal accumulation, naming, utopia and ceremonies.

Thunder-ten-tronckh, from its name onwards, is a realm of excess and of dislocation. Candide himself appears to derive from a disorderly desire.

---

[1] This chapter is a modified version of the article '"Cette Boucherie héroïque": *Candide* as carnival', which appeared in the *Modern Language Review* 80 (1985), pp.293-303. I am grateful to the Modern Humanities Research Association for permission to use this material.

[2] The most complete survey, up to the mid-1980s, is probably that contained in Part One of *Approaches to Teaching Voltaire's 'Candide'*, ed. Renée Waldinger (New York, 1987).

[3] See especially Patrick Henry, 'Sacred and profane gardens in *Candide*', *SVEC* 176 (1979), pp.133-52; J.-M. Apostolidès, 'Le Système des échanges dans *Candide*', *Poétique* 48 (1981), pp.449-58; Michel Gilot, 'Le Cycle des semaines dans *Candide*', *Lettres et réalités: mélanges de littérature générale et de critique romanesque offerts au professeur Henri Coulet par ses amis* (Aix-en-Provence, 1988), pp.117-29. On the comic vision itself as an archetype, see James Andreas, '*Candide* as comic *conte*', *Approaches to Teaching Voltaire's 'Candide'*, pp.124-33.

[4] The titles themselves furnish a sufficient indication: 'sacred and profane', 'échanges' and 'cycle', all within 'comic'.

His origins are doubly against cultural order: sexual congress outside the approved structures of class and marriage produces in turn a by-product surely not intended. He is marginal and accidental. The comic victory of nature over cultural structures is further marked by the fact that the father's genealogy is incomplete, due to 'l'injure du temps'. Here indeed, metaphorically, is the first assault. The number of 'soixante et onze quartiers' appears to be random, yet emphatically so by its apparent generosity, its mathematical unevenness complementing its verbal clumsiness. Dislocation is also suggested by the hesitation over the narrator's authority - 'je crois' - which might be linked with the diegetic uncertainty regarding Candide's origins. The origins of the text are also placed in question. Contingency and excess are suggested by the full title of the whole, 'Traduit de l'allemand de M. le docteur Ralph, avec les additions qu'on a trouvées dans la poche du docteur, lorsqu'il mourut à Minden, l'an de grâce 1759'. These details constitute parody slipping into the freer play of imagination. Even taken at face value, they present the text as heterogeneous, inflated by insertions. The latter are born of death, determined by chance.

The fatuity of Thunder-ten-tronckh is joyous. The doubling of the various domestic functions results in a lively ambiguity. This ludic bivalence is comically reinforced by the accumulation of instances: 'chien/meute', 'palefreniers/piqueurs', 'vicaire/grand aumônier'. The Baron is addressed as 'monseigneur' by all, 'et ils riaient quand il faisait des contes'. Is the laughter merely deferential? It seems likely that in such a lyrical domain it is genuine too. There are also implications here about the present *conte*, its telling and the laughter it may arouse in its audience. Thunder-ten-tronckh is a domain of physical generosity: 'Madame la baronne, qui pesait environ trois cent cinquante livres, ...'; 'Cunégonde, âgée de dix-sept ans, était haute en couleur, fraîche, grasse, appétissante, ...'. A domain indeed of sexual desire. The 'unofficial' circuit probably began with the Baron's sister. It eventually returns to her putative offspring, by way of the pleasures taken by Pangloss and Paquette, which Cunégonde offers to imitate in a third transgression. For Candide however the kiss is promptly doubled by a kick. This alternation, which will characterise his adventure in the world, launches it here. Each of the young persons is assaulted - for him 'grands coups de pied dans le derrière', while she is 'souffletée'. Here the doubling is repeated: face and 'fesses', front and back, higher and lower. And of course each assault is rhythmic, ushering in the pattern of violence at once ritual and lyrical.

The violence done to the protagonists in the course of the tale is that done to the doctrine of Optimism. That doctrine is presented initially as part of a pristine state - well-being, ignorance, egocentrism, theory - shared by all at Thunder-ten-tronckh. The assault begins with the dislocation of rhetoric. The conjunction is used to signal disjunction: 'un des plus puissants seigneurs de la Westphalie, *car* son château avait une porte et des fenêtres'. The adverbial phrase is referentially ambiguous: 'La baronne, qui pesait trois cent cinquante livres, s'attirait *par là* une très grande considération'. Pangloss teaches 'la métaphysico-théologo-cosmolonigologie'. The name is concatenated, and at the same time literally broken up by the insertion of 'nigo'. Such ludic excess will continue, in the narrator's account ('il prouvait *admirablement*') and that of the philosopher ('tout est *au mieux*').

The doctrine is lyrically collapsed through two forms of expression. The argument from Final Causes appears in the series beginning 'les nez ont été faits pour porter des lunettes, aussi avons-nous des lunettes'. One or two examples would do, but we are joyously given four. The corroboration of the latter clause is weakened by the choice and variety of conjunction: 'aussi avons-nous' becomes in the three subsequent propositions 'et', 'aussi monseigneur a' and a comma. The examples are chosen to mock high philosophy: cultural contingencies such as 'les lunettes' are declared to be the final causes of natural phenomena. But the phenomena themselves - 'nez', 'jambes', 'pierres', 'cochons' - have their own value. We have human extremities with a hint of the sexual in the first and of movement in the articulated second; solidity in the third and the promise of appetite ever-renewed in the fourth ('nous mangeons du porc toute l'année'). The abstract terminology of Optimism is also juxtaposed with human energy when Pangloss's sexual congress with Paquette is described in terms of 'la raison suffisante', 'les effets et les causes'. 'Les expériences réitérées' signals the enthusiasm both of the participants and of the narrator who has ranged beyond Leibnizianism to the vocabulary of experimental science. The passion of Cunégonde and Candide will soon express itself not only through classical eyes but through active hands, mouths, knees; its opposition through slaps and kicks.

'Tout est au mieux' is the discourse of Optimism invoked throughout *Candide*. This universal superlative is voiced by Pangloss. 'L'oracle de la maison', Pangloss is the divine scaled down to the domestic. He is a parodic version of the sage. His avatars in this traditional comic role include Panurge in the *Pantagruel*, Sancho Panza and Sorel's Hortensius. All irrepressibly spout versions of received wisdom. The name Pangloss surely signifies not 'toute-langue' (he is much more), but '[celui qui sait] tout gloser'. (We may recall that the philosopher who glosses all sorrow in *Les Deux Consolés* is called Citophile - surely 'celui qui aime citer'.) In Pangloss the pedant's encyclopaedic discourse is modernised. The universal wisdom whose fragments he purveys is that of his own age. Optimism can gloss everything.

The narrative in *Candide* is equally comprehensive. Epic, romance and the fabulous voyage are parodied. The journey takes in the Old World, the New World, and utopian Eldorado. Its protagonists experience or encounter a vast range of institutions, moral, social, and economic conditions. Thematically almost every form of human order and belief is questioned: providence, morality, religions, societies, classes, nature, high culture, true love. This has been observed many times and in detail.[5] But insufficient attention has been given to the creative and figural aspects of the writing. On all levels, paradox and satire become carnival. The debasing process, and the debasing world itself, are characterised by lyrical energy. The enunciation of the doctrine proceeds into logical folly: 'Les malheurs particuliers font le bien général, de sorte que plus il y a de malheurs particuliers, et plus tout est bien' (iv, p.154). The tale unfolds its compendium of particular sufferings drawn from contemporary reality, constantly confronting them with truncated forms of the doctrine to produce a multiple insanity.

A single 'malheur' may provide a universalising figure. Pangloss offers an account of the venereal disease he caught from Paquette:

> J'ai goûté dans ses bras les délices du paradis, qui ont produit ces tourments d'enfer dont vous me voyez dévoré; elle en était infectée, elle en est peut-être morte. Paquette tenait ce présent d'un cordelier très savant qui avait remonté à la source; car il l'avait eue [sic] d'une vieille comtesse, qui l'avait reçue d'un capitaine de cavalerie, qui la devait à une marquise, qui la tenait d'un page, qui l'avait reçue d'un jésuite, qui, étant novice, l'avait eue en droite ligne d'un des compagnons de Christophe Colomb. (iv, p.153)

---

[5] Perhaps the most systematic account is that of William F. Bottiglia, *Voltaire's 'Candide': Analysis of a Classic*, SVEC 7 (1959).

The imaginative flight of the final sentence offers a range of ages, social functions, sexes and sexual preferences, while linking past and present, one country and another, New World and Old. The first sentence - on Pangloss's own condition - joins heaven with hell, and tasting with being consumed. The great paradox of 'l'amour', source of life yet source of death, is figured in this chain of grotesque couplings.

The speaker, Pangloss, has himself been physically carnivalised. He is described as 'tout couvert de pustules, les yeux morts, le bout du nez rongé, la bouche de travers, les dents noires, et parlant de la gorge, tourmenté d'une toux violente et crachant une dent à chaque effort' (iii, p.151). Here we have the individual human form of the 'grotesque body'. The description deals in bumps and hollows, a protuberance eaten away, fragments repeatedly precipitated into the world. This continual exchange figures the whole universe as matter in motion. We may recall that Pangloss caught his disease while giving 'une leçon de physique expérimentale'. He was embraced ('dans les bras') while penetrating.

Here are some further instances involving bodily exchange.

> Le matelot court incontinent au milieu des débris [de Lisbonne], affronte la mort pour trouver de l'argent, en trouve, s'en empare, s'enivre, et, ayant cuvé son vin, achète les faveurs de la première fille de bonne volonté qu'il rencontre sur les ruines ... . (v, p.156)

In this account we have purposeful yet random movement, material exchange amid the fragments, appropriating and being appropriated, entering and being entered, appetite and satisfaction, life pursued amid death. The historic present, short clauses, and frequent verbs, further convey the insouciant energy of the event. Another instance is furnished by the contrasting couple Don Issacar and Le Grand Inquisiteur. Wealthy Jew and chief Catholic, they seem united only by their mutual hate. But they are mutually dependent because of their material power over each other (money-lender, heretic-burner), to which is added their desire for Cunégonde, resulting in their shared arrangement with her. In death on the two sides of midnight, their two sabbaths, they are united by Candide's sword. This being Catholic Portugal, 'on enterre monseigneur dans une belle église, et on jette Issacar à la voirie' (chs viii, ix) - where presumably the first body will return to undifferentiated matter almost as quickly as the second.

No doubt the most extreme form of human exchange is cannibalism.

The ingestion of part of one human body by another is proposed in the Oreillons episode in the New World, but achieved in the civilisation of the Old World. It is killing monkeys who were pinching the bottoms of their human lovers which puts Candide and his servant in the cooking pot, as it is having killed the brother of his own beloved which saves them (ch.xvi). La Vieille loses half her bottom to feed the soldiers who are guarding her to satisfy the desire of a chief janissary, just before all the men are slaughtered (ch.xii). Pangloss and the young Baron are united by their origins and their obstinacy, by their pattern of death and resurrection, and by their sexual desires, which are also opposed. They find themselves side by side in the galley, poking an ineffectual oar in the great sea, as a result of similar interchanges. The Baron and a male companion, naked, had bathed together. Pangloss had attempted to place a bouquet between the breasts of a young woman (ch.xxviii). Here once more is the grotesque body: the intrusions upon the extrusions, the figures of immersion in the world and penetration of the other.

The punishments exercised upon Pangloss and the Baron are identical. One hundred strokes on the feet, condemnation to the galleys where 'le levanti patron appliquait de temps en temps quelques coups de nerf de boeuf sur leurs épaules nues' (xxvii, p.224). Rhythm and ritual are important in all the assaults. So, in relation to the grotesque body, is the literal opening up of the body to the world. Candide deserts from the Bulgar army.

> Il n'eut pas fait deux lieues que voilà quatre autres héros de six pieds qui l'atteignent, qui le lient, qui le mènent dans un cachot. On lui demanda juridiquement ce qu'il aimait le mieux d'être fustigé trente-six fois par tout le régiment, ou de recevoir à la fois douze balles de plomb dans la cervelle. ... il se détermina ... à passer trente-six fois par les baguettes; il essuya deux promenades. Le régiment était composé de deux mille hommes. Cela lui composa quatre mille coups de baguette, qui, depuis la nuque du cou jusqu'au cul, lui découvrirent les muscles et les nerfs. (ii, pp.148-49)

There is an overall sequence of linear movement and enclosure (walk, binding, walk, beating). The remarkable sequence of numbers - two, four, six (one), thirty-six, twelve, two thousand, four thousand - is ludic, while evoking both the military ambience and the climax of material assault. The blows open up the the trunk of the body, from end to end, extremes marked by the phonetically minimal pair 'cou' to 'cul'. Pangloss will experience little less: 'Il me fit d'abord une incision cruciale depuis le nombril jusqu'à la clavicule' (xxviii, p.226). Many of the assaults and deaths involve penetration. Cunégonde has been 'éventrée par des soldats bulgares, après avoir été violée autant qu'on peut l'être', according to the first report (iv, p.152). (Three versions of the sack of the chateau are given. The details vary somewhat: the text is not concerned with naturalistic self-consistency.) The female inhabitants of the Abare village were treated likewise, while the males were 'criblés de coups' (iii, p.150). Shooting and piercing are frequent, as is mere whipping.

In these cases the world enters the human body. But equally the body may be swallowed up by the world. At Lisbon the earth itself fissures. Jacques the Anabaptist is 'englouti' by the sea. Candide, Pangloss and the sailor are also immersed when 'le vaisseau s'entrouvre' (v, p.155). The term designating Jacques's fate occurs again to conclude the account of the loss of Vanderdendur's ship with all on board: 'le vaisseau ... s'enfonçait', 'coula à fond', 'en un moment tout fut englouti' (xx, p.197-98). As the primal elements of earth and water are involved, so is that of fire. Burning and cooking - approaches favoured by the cultural extremes of Catholic and savage - also reconvert the body to the world. Inorganic confrontation joins all the elements at Lisbon, in the places of public exchange. 'La mer s'élève en bouillonnant dans le port, et brise les vaisseaux qui sont à l'ancre. Des tourbillons de flammes et de cendres couvrent les rues et les places publiques; les maisons s'écroulent, les toits sont renversés sur les fondements, et les fondements se dispersent' (v, p.156). This apocalypse is a larger version of the total breakdown of Thunder-ten-tronckh: 'quant au château, il n'est pas resté pierre sur pierre' (iv, p.152). This in turn is paralleled by the dismantling of the human body. Candide walks 'sur des membres palpitants ou à travers des ruines' (iii, p.150). The chatelaine is treated like the chateau: 'madame la baronne a été coupée en morceaux' (iv, p.152). The same happens to the mother and companions of La Vieille, 'déchirées, coupées, ...' (xi, p.169). She loses a buttock, the slave in Surinam an arm and a leg, the eunuch his 'c ...' (chs xii, xix, xi). Others will have their heads removed, or their hearts (chs xxx, xxvi).

Bodies separate, but they also join together. They are ingested by the world, but they also ingest. Eating and drinking are very frequent in *Candide*. Almost invariably, meals are collective. At Thunder-ten-tronckh Cunégonde and Candide exchange their kiss 'après le dîner, comme on sortait de table' (i, p.147). Over a score more occurrences of shared eating and drinking will follow. The settings vary from inn to jungle to palace, the participants with Candide from recruiting-sergeant to king, the dishes from ham to humming-bird. Sometimes 'faim' is the spur (ii, p.148; viii, p.163; xvi, p.180); at others, social ritual and conviviality (xiv, p.177; xviii, p.189; xxv, p.215). Communion may mask disunion: 'les hommes ne sont faits que pour se secourir les uns les autres' is the protestation of the army-recruiters; the Jesuit-Colonel-Baron and Candide enjoy 'un excellent déjeuner ... tandis que les Paraguains mangèrent du maïs' (ii, p.148; xiv, p.177). It may realise genuine Christian charity, under the two species: 'Jacques ... l'amena chez lui, ... lui donna du pain et de la bière' (iii, p.151 - we may recall that Candide had just been 'baptised' with excreta from a chamber-pot). 'Quelques citoyens secourus par eux leur donnèrent un aussi bon dîner qu'on le pouvait dans un tel désastre' (v, p.156). It may be inspired less by *agape* that by *eros*, as with Cunégonde's feeding of Candide (ch.vii). In Paris it is the nearest thing to harmony, within disharmony: 'Je trouve que tout va de travers chez nous ... excepté le souper, qui est assez gai et où il paraît assez d'union' (xxii, p.205).

The meal is an aspect of the grotesque body. This list already shows its multiple value. But contradictions may be held together in a single occurrence. The most striking is probably the one in Cunégonde's account: 'Enfin, pour détourner le fléau des tremblements de terre, et pour intimider don Issacar, il plut à monseigneur l'inquisiteur de célébrer un auto-da-fé. Il me fit l'honneur de m'y inviter. Je fus très bien placée; on servit aux dames des rafraîchissements entre la messe et l'exécution' (viii, p.162). Here consumption and consummation, desire and disaster, the interpersonal, geological and religious are celebrated together. A delicate example appears in the Parisian episode. Candide, about to visit a French actress he has just seen playing Elizabeth of England, asks 'comment on trait[e] en France les reines d'Angleterre. "Il faut distinguer, dit l'abbé; en province, on les mène au cabaret; à Paris, on les respecte quand elles sont belles, et on les jette à la voirie quand elles sont mortes"' (xxii, p.202). The abbé's distinctions emphasise the strange conglomerate of festivity, respect and garbage which is the life and death of an actress. Commoner is yoked with queen, Paris with province, and France with elsewhere. The sufferings of La Vieille begin when the celebrations for her marriage are suddenly transformed into death:

Les noces furent préparées. C'était une pompe, une magnificence inouïe; c'étaient des fêtes, des carrousels, des opera-buffa continuels; ... quand une vieille marquise qui avait été maîtresse de mon prince l'invita à prendre du chocolat chez elle. Il mourut en moins de deux heures ... (xi, p.167).

What one might call verbal accumulations are frequent in *Candide*. Rapid successions of clauses and phrases can readily be found in the quotations above. Strings of single words, nominal or adjectival, are a notable feature of the text. Rhetorically surprising in itself, this device stands out the more in a highly economical narration. As an abrupt succession, within itself each string imitates the sequential impact of the events in the narrative. But - like the events - it is also totalising and ludic. Taking four as the minimum number of terms required, we can find a score of such strings. The record is the proper names of thirty-one kings, from Hebrew to Henri IV, who met violent deaths (xxx, p.232). As time, so place: 'ce pirate ne nous a-t-il pas menés au cap de Matapan, à Milo, à Nicarie, à Samos, à Petra, aux Dardanelles, à Marmora, à Scutari?' (xxvii, p.223). Nineteen common nouns or adjectives list the undesirable qualities of humankind (xxi, p.200). The universal abilities of Cacambo are already implicit when we are told 'il avait été enfant de choeur, sacristain, matelot, moine, facteur, soldat, laquais' (xiv, p.175).

Feasts are sometimes detailed: 'il ... les invite à venir à son hôtellerie manger des macaronis, des perdrix de Lombardie, des oeufs d'esturgeon, et à boire du vin de Montepulciano, du lacrima-christi, du chypre et du samos' (xxiv, pp.211-12). Local colour hardly accounts for the generosity of this list, or for those elsewhere of food and drink collectively enjoyed (xvii, pp.185-86, nine items; xxx, p.232, eight items; xvi, p.180, five items). Thus in the tale the heaps of dead (Abares, Lisboans, Moroccans) are repeated and opposed on a more modest scale by heaps of food. Heaps of words may be mimetic and ludic. Candide performs military drill 'avec tant de grâce, de célérité, d'adresse, de fierté, d'agilité, ...' (x, p.166). They may have the generosity and the savour of desire: 'elle avait entre ses deux tétons un beau bouquet de tulipes, de roses, d'anémones, de renoncules, d'hyacinthes et d'oreilles-d'ours' (xxviii, p.227).

One minor protagonist has a name which constitutes a string: 'Don Fernando d'Ibaraa, y Figueora, y Mascarenes, y Lampourdos, y Souza'. The choice of proper names for the protagonists in *Candide* is another playful aspect of the text. The principles governing this choice are mixed; but the names are always more than particular. At the least they type by nationality or race, like 'Issacar', which is further pointed by the incongruous prefix 'Don'. By classical convention too they may incorporate an element of direct moral typing: the pitiless Dutch merchant 'Vanderden*dur*'. 'Cunégonde' incorporates national and historical reference to a virgin saint, with a comically opposed syllabic suggestion of orifice and articulation. 'Cacambo' to European ears sounds appropriate phonetically, by repetition, suffix, and syllabic simplicity, for a South American coloured. Again, however, there is a suggestion of internal contradiction here between the two parts of the name, the scatological and the 'beau'. All these incorporate in their form an element of the ludic. Various meanings have been canvassed for the perfectly simple names of 'Jacques', the Anabaptist, and 'Martin' the Manichean. Evidently then we expect these names to signify. It is perhaps part of their social and moral simplicity that most of the protagonists have only one name, but this again points beyond naturalism. 'Paquette', connoting a fresh but common flower, is a morally-typing name. But it is the ludic element in the writing which then engenders 'Giroflée' as her companion. 'Pococuranté' types wittily, combining the character's language and his moral quality of world-weariness. Both 'Candide' and 'Pangloss', the hero of the tale and the proponent of its doctrine, are universals by name and by function. The second is he who can gloss everything, the first he who who is open to all experience.

Eldorado is the antithesis and the complement of the rest of the world. It is reached when Old and New Worlds have been found wanting (xvii, pp.183, 186). It is as much above expectation as they were below it. It comes in the middle of the text. It is a world-upside-down, inverting or rectifying what surrounds it - amid the disasters a festive kingdom. This other world is reached - as from Odysseus to Alice - by a perilous journey of self-abandonment. Here it is both a total figure in itself and a part of the larger figure which is Candide's comprehensive journey. Its relationship to the 'real' world, and to the utopian genre, is both serious and comic. The Eldoradan order in commerce, religion, politics and science is presented with approval. But this world is mediated by the naive reactions of the protagonists, and the amiable ironies of the narrator. Passages like that beginning 'Ils entrèrent dans une maison fort simple, car la porte n'était que d'argent, ...' (xviii, p.187) make fun of the romance and the fabulous voyage. The assurance that 'partout l'utile était agréable' (xvii, p.184), like the information that the royal apothegms did not lose their savour in translation (xviii, p.190), also remind us of the element of metaliterary playfulness throughout. Details are accompanied by lyrically generous numbers: 'trois cents colibris', 'douze ... domestiques', 'la millième partie de la ville', 'vingt millions de livres sterling', 'cinquante moutons'.

Numerical play also begins the account of Candide and Cacambo's reception at the royal palace. 'Vingt belles filles de la garde ... les conduisirent aux bains, les vêtirent ...'. The two are then led to the King 'au milieu de deux files chacune de mille musiciens'. Cacambo enquires

> comment il fallait s'y prendre pour saluer Sa Majesté; si on se jetait à genoux ou ventre à terre; si on mettait les mains sur la tête ou sur le derrière; si on léchait la poussière de la salle; en un mot, quelle était la cérémonie. 'L'usage, dit le grand officier, est d'embrasser le roi et de le baiser des deux côtés'. Candide et Cacambo sautèrent au cou de Sa Majesté, qui les reçut avec toute la grâce imaginable et qui les pria poliment à souper. (xviii, p.189)

Here is the complement and antithesis to the 'baguettes' episode of chapter ii, when the guards led Candide to prison. There too he was conducted between two lines, who beat not hymned him, to end up on his knees before a king. In Eldorado, where one walks upright, the event itself is joyous. But the writing is joyous in both episodes. The Eldorado passage too shows us the grotesque body. It begins with a comic reversal of norms (female guards), and a cheerful indifference to realist self-consistency (if there are no law courts and no prisons, why guards?). It proceeds through a series of contortionist fantasies on base aspects of the body, its centre and protuberances (knees, belly, head, bottom, tongue). It leads to embracing and reception, or the joyful leap and the gracious gathering in, and the shared meal. The episode is ludic (the numbers, the inventive series of positions). It is both lyrical and formal, that is, ritual. Perhaps the key word in it is 'cérémonie'.

The *auto-da-fé* - which shares with the Eldorado episode the particulars of dressing-up and music - involved the execution of several men 'à petit feu, en grande cérémonie' (vi, p.157). The ceremonious term is used too for the repeated feeding and anointing of the wounded Candide by La Vieille on behalf of Cunégonde: 'Elle fit encore les mêmes cérémonies' (vii, p.159). Each of these figures is itself a grotesque ritual, and the two here are complementary as well as sequential. The same term again

qualifies the physical practice of the pirates in the story of La Vieille. All
those captured are stripped 'nus comme des singes, ... Mais ce qui me
surprit davantage, c'est qu'ils nous mirent à tous le doigt dans un endroit
où nous autres femmes nous ne nous laissons mettre d'ordinaire que des
canules. Cette cérémonie me paraissait bien étrange' (xi, p.168). Here is
a double displacement (finger for phallus, back for front) within what is
both a reduction (men and women stripped down to monkeys) and a
universal figure (anticipating the 'soldats, matelots, noirs, basanés, blancs,
mulâtres' who will kaleidoscopically battle it out later in this chapter).

The episode in France offers a collective figure on several successive
levels, the latter a *mise-en-abyme* of the former. Martin tells us first: 'j'ai
parcouru plusieurs provinces. Il y en a où la moitié des habitants est folle,
quelques-unes où l'on est trop rusé, d'autres où on est communément assez
doux et assez bête, d'autres où l'on fait le bel esprit; et dans toutes ...'.
Then, contained topographically, 'j'ai vu Paris; il tient de toutes ces
espèces-là; c'est un chaos ...' (ch.xxi). Within this again, they go to the
theatre. The implications of the theatrical figure are developed on all
levels by Candide's question 'quelle était l'étiquette' ['la cérémonie'] and
the reply linking not only Paris and provinces again but art and life
(ch.xxii). Here actors and audience intermingle. But playing also has
other senses. The first event at which Candide and Cacambo are present
in Eldorado involves 'quelques enfants du village, couverts de brocarts d'or
tout déchirés, [qui] jouaient au palet ...'. Their clothing is paradoxical. So
is their pastime, since the pieces they use are 'des émeraudes, des rubis'.
When the children leave them on the ground, Candide and Cacambo
intervene, assuming that these counters have the same value as in 'l'autre
monde' (xvii, p.185). The riches pursued by adults in the other world
become children's toys in Eldorado. The 'real' world is reversed and
resumed as a game.

Finally we have the carnival literally, as reference as well as figure.
The setting is Venice.[6] At an inn Candide finds himself eating with 'six
étrangers qui étaient venus passer le carnaval à Venise'. Successively,
each of the six is addressed by his servant as 'Votre Majesté'. General

---

[6] A broader account of the Venetian episode is offered by Christiane Mervaud,
'Du Carnaval au carnavalesque: l'épisode vénétien de *Candide*', *Le Siècle de Voltaire:
hommage à René Pomeau*, ed. Christiane Mervaud and Sylvain Menant (2 vols,
Oxford, 1987), ii, pp.651-62.

astonishment among 'les convives'; it is assumed that this must be 'une mascarade de carnaval'. But the first one replies:

> Je ne suis point plaisant, je m'appelle Achmet III. J'ai été grand sultan plusieurs années; je détrônai mon frère; mon neveu m'a détrôné; on a coupé le cou à mes vizirs; j'achève ma vie dans le vieux sérail; mon neveu le grand sultan Mahmoud me permet de voyager quelquefois pour ma santé, et je suis venu passer le carnaval à Venise.

Each of the others then offers in turn his parallel explanation, concluding with the same final clause. The sixth is in financial difficulties and the other 'kings' each make him a modest gift, to which Candide joins a very large one. Afterwards Candide wonders at the event, though Martin regards it as 'très commun' (xxvi-xxvii; pp.219-23).

Here is a universal figure indeed. All present are travellers, lodging and eating together at a common inn. Candide and Cacambo dine with six foreigners who have come to Venice for the carnival. Six complementary pairs, master-and-servant, reveal the former to be kings but ex-kings. All of the six speakers are part of a cycle of dethroning, which takes in time and space (six different countries brought together). The cycle also involves literal opening up ('le cou coupé') and breaking down (disconnected syntax conveys the abrupt succession of events). The last pair however collapse the structure of opposition into identity (the ex-king and the servant are one in debt) and invert it (the commoner Candide gives alms to the ex-king; he gives far more than do other ex-kings). This is initially called a 'plaisanterie', but those involved are not 'plaisant[s]' - yet clearly in the narrative they are. It is called a 'mascarade', but these are in fact contemporary historical cases - though the festive event in the narrative is imaginary. Its centre, 'six rois détronés [qui] soup[ent] ensemble au cabaret', is astonishing yet everyday. The truth looks just like the carnival. So the carnival looks like the truth.

Must we say that the carnival of *Candide* is principally one of destruction? There is almost throughout the text an effect of unremitting energy. This appears in the speed of events, the frequent use of the historic present, the violence of the assaults, the force of imagination in the writing. It is evident in the continual cycle of matter interpenetrating, the consuming and being consumed. We are swallowed up in death, (but) we swallow food and drink. Meals are frequent; so is sexual activity. Both involve joining together. The characters are unregenerate and unkillable.

Pangloss appears in the opening chapter, reappears as a 'fantôme' in chapter iv, is hanged in chapter vi, and turns up once again near the end. Cunégonde was killed at the sack of the chateau, and survives. Her brother the Baron met death at the same time. He reappears in Paraguay as Jesuit-Colonel, is assassinated once more, and surfaces with Pangloss on the Black Sea. Nothing can put them down. Their enthusiasm for life is marked equally by their intellectual obstinacy and their sexual energy.

To Candide himself these rebirths are important. 'Une chose me console, je vois qu'on retrouve souvent les gens qu'on ne croyait jamais retrouver' (xxiv, p.214). Here is a reply to the negativity of Martin. The latter had predicted that Candide, having naïvely entrusted his wealth to a half-breed valet, would never see him again. Not only is the 'Manichean' in this case wrong. The narrator comments that 'Martin n'était pas consolant' (xxiv, p.211). The same voice remarks earlier: 'Candide avait un grand avantage sur Martin, c'est qu'il espérait toujours revoir Mlle Cunégonde, et que Martin n'avait rien à espérer' (xx, p.196). Pangloss, on the other hand, offers not just metaphysical glosses but certain universal moral principles. He affirms human equality: 'Maître Pangloss m'a toujours dit que les hommes sont égaux' (xv, p.179). He affirms that the earth is for us all: 'le bon Pangloss m'avait souvent prouvé que les biens de la terre sont communs à tous les hommes' (x, p.165). It seems fair to say that Candide generally behaves along these lines. It is the voice of the narrator, again, which says that Candide was 'un fort bon homme' (xiv, p.175). Poor or rich, he is actively generous with those whom he knows (Pangloss, Paquette), and those he does not know (the citizens of Lisbon, the many rivals of Martin).

This brings us back to the question of energy. It is habitually asserted by critics that Candide is passive. This is plainly untrue. We see him walking resolutely out of the army, acquiring a captaincy by his skills, shooting the monkeys, purchasing Pangloss and the Baron. He flatly contradicts the last-named over his sister, and for good measure kills him. That is his third killing. Already at his second he remarks how suffering has changed him (ix, p.164). Cunégonde too is strengthened by adversity: 'Une personne d'honneur peut être violée une fois, mais sa vertu s'en affermit' (viii, p.161). La Vieille sums it up: 'Les malheurs donnent des droits' (xiii, p.174). It is La Vieille too who offers a startling metaphor for the penetrating and consuming of life, 'caresser le serpent qui nous dévore, jusqu'à ce qu'il nous ait mangé le coeur'. Even she, whose adventures leave all others in the shade, confesses: 'Je voulus cent fois me tuer, mais j'aimais encore la vie' (xii, p.172). At the end, she and most of the other unkillables are not only alive but together. They are the motley cultivators of the garden. From past cycles, we doubt how long this will last. Here is another totalising figure, a 'corps grotesque', an organic image of growth which will eventually return to earth and surely grow again.

PART III

Chapter 5   TOWARDS BOURGEOIS REALISM:
SIX LATER *CONTES*

INTRODUCTION

We shall now look more broadly at six of the later *Contes*. Compared to those of the earlier period, including *Candide* (1759), they show various changes. They engage more closely with corporality and process, and they develop new modes of narration. They offer new forms of the carnivalesque figure. But we shall also find a retreat from the carnivalesque consciousness, towards what Bakhtin calls 'the lie of pathos' on the one hand, and as a deep ambivalence towards the body on the other.

These six tales will be: *Jeannot et Colin* (published in 1764), *Pot-pourri* (1765), *L'Ingénu* (1767), *L'Homme aux quarante écus* (1768), *Histoire de Jenni* (1775) and *Les Oreilles du comte de Chesterfield* (1775). They are characterised by a new degree of realism. They deal in something like the here and now in its contingent detail. All six are set in France or in England. All are also located historically, at some time within the previous hundred years. Some use first-person narration, or theatrical dialogue. Rendering fictional experience more immediately, this also constitutes a kind of realism. All engage directly with contemporary social issues.

The rise of realism is associated, historically, with the rise of the bourgeoisie. It is in effect the literary programme and the literary consecration of that class. (The connection is most evident in the English novel and the French *drame* in the eighteenth century.) The six *contes* I have chosen illustrate the new bourgeois consciousness. To some extent they illustrate two apparently contradictory tendencies within it. These might be called 'le bon sens' and 'les bons sentiments'. The first is sceptical, burlesque and materialist. The second is didactic, sentimental and deist. Three of the tales fall broadly into the first category. These are *Pot-pourri*, *Quarante écus* and *Chesterfield*. The other three - *Jeannot*, *L'Ingénu* and *Jenni* - fall into the second.

Certain indices of difference or contrast between the groups can be perceived. The three 'commonsensical' tales all feature bourgeois autodidacts, male and - one feels - middle-aged. They deal less in narrative than in domestic conversation. The three sentimental tales are closer to the romance formula. The protagonists are attractive youths. There is a journey. There is a love interest. In *Jeannot et Colin* and *Jenni* there are happy endings. All three - *L'Ingénu* as well - end on a note of general reconciliation and shared feeling. In the commonsensical group, on the other hand, we are invited to be sceptical about ethical claims.

This contrast is mirrored in the tone and the modes of narration of the two groups. The commonsensical trio tend to be aggressive in tone. Narration, as we observed in Chapter 1, is fragmented. Its radical dislocation figures that of the worldly reality represented. The other trio however are affectionately comic at the start, then sentimental and didactically monologic at the end. The narrator of *L'Ingénu* demands our emotional engagement in the pathos of the deathbed scenes. *Jeannot et Colin* invokes witnesses at the start, using the interpersonal perfect tense rather than the distancing preterite: 'Plusieurs personnes dignes de foi ont vu Jeannot et Colin...' (p.269). Jenni is presented to a diegetic reader by the tender Sherloc, who has participated in the events and seeks a response identical to his own: 'vous partagerez tous mes sentiments' (p.597).

The three sentimental tales deal not just in good feeling but in family feeling. Romantic love is increasingly eclipsed by family love. They invite an oedipal reading. Within the new bourgeois ethos of the family, the role of the father assumes greater importance.[1] The pattern appears progressively in our three late *contes*. *Jeannot et Colin* ends with the reintegration of the family. *L'Ingénu* starts thus. At the end Gordon, surrogate father to the Ingenu, replaces the fiancée Saint-Yves. Freind's loving domination of his son Jenni is evident throughout. The father

---

[1] It can be argued that the Oedipus complex is an historical phenomenon, which emerges with the bourgeois family, or with the transfer of religious respect from the Divine to the human father. See Paul Pelckmans, *Le Sacre du père: fictions des Lumières et historicité d'Œdipe 1699-1775* (Amsterdam, 1983). Independent evidence of its presence in the most influential contemporary literature is furnished by Roland Barthes, *Sur Racine* (Paris, 1963) - starting the trail a little earlier - and by the chapter on Rousseau's *La Nouvelle Héloïse* in Tony Tanner, *Adultery in the Novel* (Baltimore, 1979).

successfully suppresses a principle of sexual desire and disorder which is linked to the feminine.

Though the youths Jenni and the Ingenu are both associated with Hercules, they are also feminised. The Ingenu, naked in the water, is described as 'une grande figure assez blanche' (iii, p.297). In this state he is watched and desired by women. This image is reinforced by the parallel scene in which Jenni is seen emerging from his bath, clad only in 'ses cheveux blonds, qui descendirent en grosses boucles sur la plus belle chute de reins' (i, p.599). Their women have masculine names: Saint-Yves, Clive-Hart. Jeannot's faithless widow is unnamed. But she is replaced by Colin. Colin carries off in his arms the weeping Jeannot, and bestows on him his sister. Likewise Freind consoles the weeping Jenni (twice: vii, p.625; xii, p.654), and bestows on him his choice of female. Indeed, the last paragraph tells us that 'Freind leur a servi de père à tous' (p.655). The male companions of our three heroes have names which are at once solidly masculine and curiously similar: Colin, Gordon, Birton. The same applies still more, but in gender reverse, to the protagonists themselves. Jeannot and Jenni are both names with a distinctly feminine ring. They are also strikingly similar, a phonetic resemblance the more remarkable in that it is picked up in the third name: *zano, zɛni, [ĩ]zɛny.*

The commonsensical trio of *contes* deal almost exclusively in male and verbal exchange. In *Quarante écus* and *Chesterfield* the conversations attend increasingly to what Bakhtin calls 'the base material stratum'. They reveal a fascination with biology and sexuality. Seeds, spontaneous generation, transformism, venereal disease, are all matters of concern in both. In part this represents Voltaire's engagement with new thinking in the sciences, which has replaced the mechanical model of reality with a physiological model. Bourgeois realism allows the scientific discourses of biology and sexuality to be admitted to the literary tale. They are treated with comic violence. But the carnival here is distinctly uneasy.

Finally in this contrastive survey we may look again at the titles. They can be read as supporting our analysis. The sentimental tales place themselves under a human and - I have argued - a feminine sign: *Jeannot, L'Ingénu(e?), Jenni.* The titular protagonists are taken back into families and order. The commonsensical tales have titles in which the emphasis falls on the masculine, but no less on materiality. *L'Homme aux quarante écus* defines the male ('homme') in relation to quantity ('quarante') and money ('écus'), with a hint too of orifice and obscenity (*ky*). *Les Oreilles*

du comte de Chesterfield does very much the same: the male ('comte')
qualified by the corporeal and the orifice ('oreilles'), and a secondary
sexual meaning as subtext. *Pot-pourri* can now be seen as remarkably
similar again. Broken down into its two components, this title suggests in
its first a material container (body) and in its second an organic process
that is distasteful but fundamental to life.

The contrasts indicated here reflect a new dissociation of sensibility.
The brilliant equilibrium of the earlier eighteenth century, holding
heterogeneous elements in ironic interplay, breaks down. The early 1760s
are clearly the turning point. 1761 sees the publication of Rousseau's *La
Nouvelle Héloïse*. An enormous success, its perfervid tone, pre-Romantic
idealism and sublimation of the erotic in the familial voiced a new
sensibility. At the same time we have the rise of the rationalist atheism
associated most closely with d'Holbach. Voltaire was hostile to both
camps. The latter part of *L'Ingénu* is often seen as an attempted corrective
to Rousseau's sentimentalism; the latter part of *Jenni* is likewise seen as
a reply to d'Holbach's materialism. But of course Voltaire belongs to the
age; he too is changing. We have identified a pattern of diachronic shifts
in his tales. They point towards a sentimental moralism on the one hand,
a materialist scepticism on the other. We have found them to begin,
precisely, around 1760.

Historically, however, the new bourgeois ethos covers both. Our
analysis of the six *contes* may identify two groups, but it must show what
they have in common. We have observed that they share a tendency
towards literary realism, as story if not also as narration. All six bring us
closer to the time and place of narration. *Jeannot et Colin* uses the perfect
tense at the start. The others end the story in the here and now. 'C'est à
présent ...' (final sentence of *Pot-pourri*); 'L'Ingénu ... a paru...'
(penultimate paragraph); 'ni M.André ni moi ne soupons ...' (final sentence
of *Quarante écus*); 'nous ... . Jenni et lui sont aujourd'hui ...' (final
paragraph); 'il est devenu ...' (final sentence of *Chesterfield*). Dislocation
of story and narration alike characterises the three commonsensical tales.
But we also have a certain dislocation in the narration of *L'Ingénu* and
Jenni. Each switches part way through from a tone of affectionate
mockery to one of fervent peroration. Nor is peroration confined to the
three sentimental tales. *Quarante écus* includes a passionate denunciation
of torture, presented as 'ces fragments [de texte] que l'éloquence avait
dictés à l'humanité' (pp.458-59). Its provincial rather than Parisian

provenance is emphasised (p.459). The antithesis between country and city, thus, is no longer used ironically and dialogically as in the earlier eighteenth century. It is as in *Jeannot* exclusive.

Jeannot becomes a bourgeois, as does the protagonist of *Quarante écus* and that of *Pot-pourri*. Each of these three heroes begins as socially disadvantaged. Reformism is a value present in all six *contes*. It takes the liberal guise of toleration in several (*Pot-pourri, L'Ingénu, Jenni*). It is also institutional (attacks on the venality of offices in *Pot-pourri*; on inefficiency and corruption at the centre of government in *L'Ingénu*). In the two commonsensical tales set in France reformism is economic (attacks on regressive taxation, and on unproductive feast-days). It is distinctly anti-festive. In all of course it is strongly critical of the Catholic Church.

Seeing the paths to the Revolution of 1789 is not too difficult. Nor is it hard to perceive here the rise of wider bourgeois secular values. These might be summarised as individualism, materialism, sentiment and the family. Yet a priesthood can also be identified. In *Chesterfield* the protagonist is a poverty-stricken ordinand, in *L'Ingénu* Gordon is a persecuted Jansenist ecclesiastic. Both in their very different ways represent the lower orders within the Christian institution, resenting the Anglican episcopacy or resisting the Catholic establishment. The French protagonists of *Pot-pourri* and *Quarante écus* are violently hostile to Rome and the regular clergy, especially the Society of Jesus. But their reasons are economic and political. They are gallicans, proponents of a national Church. Freind in *Jenni* is a minister of such a Church. He is both an oracular secular voice and the privileged representative of a civilly-constituted clergy.

Freind is also in these *contes* the principal father. In all of the sentimental trio of tales, the 'feminine' titular protagonist is mastered. Males end by dominating, as they dominate throughout the sceptical trio of tales. In almost all the six *contes* (the earliest, *Jeannot et Colin*, is the exception) sexuality is a subject for concern. It is associated with matter, corporality, cycle and violence. In the sentimental tales the body is controlled. In *L'Ingénu* and in *Jenni* it is progressively sublimated as a semantic presence in the text and as a threat to order in the story. The three sceptical tales are, successively, more openly obsessed with corporality. Ambivalence towards the corporeal is increasingly marked.

This *conte* can be said to break new ground as story, as narration and as meaning. The story concerns the titular couple, provincial youths. Their close friendship is shattered when one, Jeannot, adopts the airs of his parvenu father who has summoned him to Paris. In the capital all education - duly reviewed - is regarded as unnecessary, while a premium is placed on trivial social graces. When Jeannot's parents fall, still more rapidly than they had risen, the fashionable promptly desert him. By chance he is found by Colin, still a provincial but now a wealthy manufacturer, who takes in the family and associates them with his enterprise. The moral - Happiness Lies Not in Vanity. This is the first *conte* set entirely in France. It is the first to deal in social mobility and questions of class rather than geographical displacement and 'universal' human behaviour. It is almost the first (we must not forget *Zadig*) to end in collective happiness. It is realist, satirical then sentimental, and optimistic: the new bourgeois mode.

The narration shows complementary, and striking, innovations. The incipit:

> Plusieurs personnes dignes de foi ont vu Jeannot et Colin à l'école dans la ville d'Issoire en Auvergne, ville fameuse dans tout l'univers par son collège, et par ses chaudrons.

The latter part of this sentence mocks Issoire, but the tone is patronising and even affectionate rather than hostile. The first part establishes a immediacy that we have not encountered before. It invokes witnesses to the truth of the tale (apparently without irony). It uses the perfect tense, implying conversation with a listener, and temporal proximity to the events. The realist detail of town and province will be followed in the second sentence by detail as to the social status of the two young men. There are some realist elements in the Parisian portion of the tale, such as the textual citation of fragments of songs. Immediacy is also maintained throughout by reducing the mediating role of the narration, in ways we shall look at now.

Narration - in the *Contes* or elsewhere - normally uses the preterite or imperfect tenses. *Jeannot et Colin* follows the rule. However, within its eight pages, the historic present is used in six sequences. (For comparison, I observe only one use in the fourteen pages of *Le Monde comme il va*.) Here, contextualised, is the first.

> Jeannot n'étudia plus, se regarda au miroir, et méprisa tout le monde. Quelque temps après un valet de chambre apporte une seconde lettre à M. le marquis de la Jeannotière; c'était un ordre ... (p.269)

The historic present functions to suppress the temporal gap between story and reader, giving the events narrated a more immediate or 'dramatic' impact.

Another rhetorical device which has a similar effect is the suppression, when direct speech is reported, of the subject and verb of presentation. In *Jeannot et Colin* the two devices may be used together.

> Il retourne donc chez sa maîtresse, il la trouve tête à tête avec un jeune officier fort aimable. 'Quoi! c'est vous M. de la Jeannotière ...' (p.275)

Another example of the combination: 'A ce nom, le marquis lève les yeux, la voiture s'arrête: "C'est Jeannot lui-même, c'est Jeannot"' (p.276). But there are also three cases where the presentative mediation is dropped from a whole series of speeches, resulting in an almost theatrical effect. The first is:

> - ... une chose dont j'ai oublié le nom, mais qui commence par un *B*. - Par un *B*, madame? ne serait-ce pas la botanique? - Non, ce n'était point de botanique qu'il me parlait; elle commençait vous dis-je, par un *B*, et finissait par un *on*. - Ah! j'entends, madame; c'est le blason ... (p.273)

The other cases are the sequences beginning 'Eh! mon Dieu! monsieur le marquis ...' (p.275) and 'Qu'est-ce donc ...?' (p.276). This stylistic effect is not absent from earlier *contes*. (One example is *Le Monde comme il va*, p.48). But, again, we have here a new concentration.

The quotation of direct speech also has more immediacy when there is more mimetic realism in its representation. This kind of realism is contrary to classical norms, and especially to those of Voltaire. Even in the *Contes* such mimetic effects are few in number and limited in degree. They are usually just emblematic, offered less as idiolect than as a touch of local colour ('Il parla en ces termes: "Étoiles de justice, ..."': *Zadig*, ch.iii) or as moral portrait ('"Par tous les dieux", dit le soldat, ...': *Le Monde comme il va*, ch.i). But here we have some suggestion of the irregularity of a real conversation, as in the example quoted above. We have modest use of spoken idiom: 'je n'en sais pas un mot, répondit le bel esprit, et bien m'en a pris'. We have more pointed imitation of the languid speech of the fashionable fop: ' - Voyons un peu, dit le marquis, ce que c'est que ça, ce que c'est que cette aventure-là' (p.274).

This mimesis is part of a notable development in the treatment of language and discourse in the *Contes*. It recognises some of the specific features of oral - as distinct from written - register. It presents, briefly, a plurality of different oral registers. And it shows them engaged with each other. Social engagement and struggle is indicated in the conversation quoted above. This offers a nice representation of the rhetorical and social subleties of the exchange: the presumption and irritation of the wife of the parvenu; the deference and pedantry of the hired tutor. The dialogism in this instance is doubled by the carnivalising of the word. Attention is drawn to its phonetic and orthographic body, which is comically fragmented. We are given its head ('un *B*'), invited to add a trunk ('la botanique') which is then discarded, given its feet ('un *on*'), and we end with a quite different body ('le blason'). *Jeannot et Colin* also presents other kinds of discursive engagement. These - free indirect style, and what one might call cultural quotation - are quite complex. We look at them now.

Early in the text we have a puzzling case of fragmented utterance embedded in utterance. 'Colin, toujours tendre, écrivit une lettre de compliments à son ancien camarade, *et lui fit ces lignes pour le congratuler*' [sic] (p.270). The italicised clause appears to be a quotation from Colin's letter, transposed in tense and person to fit the narrator's discourse. This cannot properly be called free indirect style, because the quoted portion is clearly marked off, by the italics. It is however a form of elision. We approach genuine *style indirect libre* with the following sequence.

> Monsieur, ébloui de ces raisons, passa condamnation, et il fut conclu que le jeune marquis ne perdrait point son temps à connaître Cicéron, Horace et Virgile. Mais qu'apprendra-t-il donc? car encore faut-il qu'il sache quelque chose; ne pourrait-on pas lui montrer un peu de géographie? 'A quoi cela lui servira-t-il?['] répondit le gouverneur. (p.271)

We should probably read 'ne perdrait point son temps' as free indirect style rather than narratorial antiphrasis. It leads to a remarkable integration of narratorial and diegetic voices. 'Mais ... géographie' must be the utterance of the father - by its informal register and the diegetic reply it receives - taken over by the narrator.

Italics in the *Contes* are usually used not only for titles of other works, or as emphasis ('*Sauve qui peut!*': *Aventure indienne*, exurgit, p.283), but as the equivalent of quotation marks to draw attention to the code ('un banc qu'on nommait un *tribunal*': *Aventure indienne*, p.282). Jeannot's tutor says 'S'il sait *les moyens de plaire*, il saura tout'. The italicised words are the abbreviated title of a well-known contemporary book. However, the absence of capital letters suggests that we should read it not as an allusion to a particular work but as quotation of a phrase in general currency. It is not clear whether the phrase is marked off by the speaker or solely by the narrator. Ambiguity as to 'who is speaking' arises also when the tutor says 'les gens de qualité (*j'entends ceux qui sont très riches*) savent tout sans avoir rien appris' (p.272). The italics are presumably for emphasis (especially given that the clause qualifies a main clause whose last part is familiar quotation, a phrase from Molière which had entered general currency). But whose emphasis? Ambiguity as to whether we have titular or general quotational italicisation arises again when the narrator tells us that Jeannot 'fit [des chansons] pour ses maîtresses. Il pillait *Bacchus et l'Amour* dans un vaudeville, *La Nuit et le Jour* dans un autre, *Les Charmes et les Alarmes* dans un troisième' (p.273). Jeannot's improper appropriation of fragments from other discourse is playfully paralleled by the narrator. Notable again is the new social specificity and level of the quotation. Relatively 'everyday' registers are mirrored by relatively popular cultural quotation; both are closely engaged with the narratorial voice.

There are several other new features in the narration. After the primal couple here have been presented and the story of their separation told, a new paragraph opens.

> Les lecteurs qui aiment à s'instruire doivent savoir que M. Jeannot le père avait acquis assez rapidement des biens immenses dans les affaires. Vous demandez comment on fait ces grandes fortunes? C'est parce qu'on est heureux. M.Jeannot était bien fait, sa femme aussi ... . Ils allèrent à Paris pour un procès ... . Jeannot [le père] plut ... . Dès qu'on est dans le fil de l'eau ... on fait sans peine une fortune immense. Les gredins du rivage vous regardent voguer à pleines voiles ... . C'est ce qui arriva à Jeannot le père, qui ... retira de l'école monsieur le marquis son fils, pour

le mettre à Paris dans le beau monde. (p.270)

The account of how Jeannot's parents rose to wealth constitutes a flashback. It analeptic character is the more marked by its contrast with the incipit of the tale which places the main story close to the present time. The linear narration of the earlier *Contes*, like their fable time, is replaced by something more complex and dramatic. The second notable feature in this paragraph is the interpellation of the reader, to whom a question is assigned: 'Vous demandez ...'. This too is a new device. We note another 'vous'. 'On est dans le fil de l'eau' becomes 'les gredins vous regardent ...'. This 'on/vous' representing the type of the parvenu bridges the gap between reader and Jeannot *père*. More fully, the gap is bridged by narratorial 'other-voicing'. This is - again - not quite free indirect style, but rather dramatic monologue. 'Les gredins du rivage vous regardent ...' offers us the dismissive vocabulary and tone of the parvenu in the voice of the narrator.

Along with innovation at the levels of story and narration, we seem to have in *Jeannot et Colin* a new meaning. The ending is sentimental, moral and optimistic. Tears are much in evidence, friendship and family are restored, social utility and hard work and provincial simplicity are vindicated. All ends for the best. This is the new bourgeois ethos. We find it circa 1760 in the 'drame bourgeois', such as Sedaine's *Le Philosophe sans le savoir*, and in short fiction such as some of the *Contes moraux* of Marmontel.[1] Story, narration and meaning in Voltaire's tale thus appear to be of a piece. But his *Contes* as a whole are characterised by pastiche and parody. Do we have here the new bourgeois mode, or the

---

[1] The story and moral of *Jeannot et Colin* resemble quite closely those of Marmontel's *La Mauvaise mère*: see W.E. Roberts, *Morality and Social Class in Eighteenth-century French Literature and Painting* (Toronto, 1974), pp.82-85. There may also be a stylistic influence. The omission of verbs of presentation when reporting rapid dialogue is a device much used by Marmontel. He claims it as his own invention, but this is incorrect: see Vivienne Mylne, 'Literary techniques and methods in Voltaire's *contes philosophiques*', *SVEC* 57 (1967), pp.1055-80 (pp.1075-76). Like the increased use of the historic present, these new effects of immediacy can be found in other contemporary writing such as Diderot's *La Religieuse*. They are a sign of the times.

old irony directed at that new mode? The former assumption has long
prevailed - as demonstrated by the numerous moralising adaptations of
Voltaire's tale in the last two centuries. But the only substantial critical
studies of this tale, published in the 1980s, have argued for the ironic
reading.[2] Certainly provincialism is treated with a degree of mockery.
The new rhetorical effects are compromised not only by the ironic tone in
the greater part of the tale, but by the emphasis on quotation. 'Les lecteurs
qui aiment à s'instruire doivent savoir ...' is ironic not just because the
instruction that follows is so unedifying, but because in a context of
pointed quotation it reads like not 'itself' but pastiche. Other conventional
sentiments then become suspect too. 'La fortune, qui élève et qui abaisse
les hommes à son gré ...' (p.270), 'la nature qui fait tout ...' (p.273),
become double-voiced. Expanding this reading to the maximum, one
would place the whole text between quotation marks.

However, it seems to me more clever than entirely honest (more
Parisian than provincial?) to argue that meaning is never free from
narratorial irony. Consider the following, from the first crisis of the tale:

Sa mère était seule, sans secours, sans consolation, noyée dans ses larmes;
il ne lui restait rien que le souvenir de sa fortune, de sa beauté, de ses
fautes et de ses folles dépenses. (p.274)

This is cliché, but there is no indication that its pathos and its lesson are
not to be accepted at face value. The factual account fits with previous
narrative information; the moral judgement ('ses folles dépenses') is her
own and that of the narrator as one voice. 'Le marquis ... apprit mieux à

---

[2]   Roy S. Wolper, 'The toppling of Jeannot', *SVEC* 183 (1980), pp.69-82,
essentially repeats his revisionist readings of other tales. Against the traditional habit
of identifying the protagonist's final views with those of Voltaire, he argues that the
protagonist remains part of the total *conte*, in which injustice and folly are endemic,
inconsistency the rule and narrative irony the mode. (There is a short critique of this
reading in Vivienne Mylne, 'Wolper's view of Voltaire's tales', *SVEC* 212 (1982),
pp.318-27 (pp.325-26).)   Christiane Mervaud, *'Jeannot et Colin*:   illustration et
subversion du conte moral', *Revue d'Histoire Littéraire de la France* 85 (1985),
pp.596-620, establishes first this tale's progeny, and its affiliations to the subgenre
established by Marmontel.   She then identifies what she sees as its subversive
differences: belated Moral, focus on Parisian follies, laconic narration, ludic invention
and allusion.   She concludes that in Voltaire's tale 'l'ironie dénonce les fictions
innocentes'.

connaître le monde dans une demi-journée que dans tout le reste de sa vie' (p.275). This turnaround is likewise cliché, but likewise confirmed by the story, and monologic. If there is any sure ground, it is provided here in the voice of the narrator. But these statements in turn prepare and authorise the 'instruction' which Jeannot in his own voice will draw from his experience. Colin, arriving at just the right moment, embraces his long-lost friend. 'Jeannot confus et attendri lui conta en sanglotant une partie de son histoire'. Colin offers to share his enterprise with him. 'Jeannot, éperdu, ... se disait tout bas: 'Tous mes amis du bel air m'ont trahi, et Colin que j'ai méprisé vient seul à mon secours. Quelle instruction!' (p.276). 'Quels poncifs', we might add. But nothing in the passage suggests that we are not to take this tearful didacticism straight.

Colin is 'grossièrement vêtu; c'était un visage rond et frais qui respirait la douceur et la gaieté'. Ahead of four large wagons, in their old-fashioned coach, 'sa petite femme, brune, assez grossièrement agréable, était cahotée à côté de lui. La voiture n'allait pas comme le char d'un petit-maître' (pp.275-76). The rescue-party is cheery, clumsy, even coarse. But it functions, precisely, as antithesis to the smooth cynicism of Paris. It is solid, in contrast to the Parisian house of cards. Moreover it, or the writing, is joyous - a burlesque transposition of Caesar's triumphal entry or Cinderella's pumpkin coach to the mode of the petit-bourgeois. Its emphasis on simplicity is affectionate. The narrator maintains a distance from the rescue-party's aesthetics. But we are clearly invited to approve its ethics. Jeannot's feelings are mirrored in the feeling of the passage, with its historic presents, exclamatory and unmediated dialogue, and sentimentality. His lesson is to be ours.

The lesson is initially affective and interpersonal. The new values are implied in description and action.

> Le petit homme rebondi ne fait qu'un saut, et court embrasser son ancien camarade. Jeannot reconnut Colin; la honte et les pleurs couvrirent son visage. ... 'Viens dans l'hôtellerie où je loge ..., lui dit Colin; embrasse ma petite femme, et allons dîner ensemble'. (p.276)

This intimate model prepares us for the social and economic model to come. In parallel, narrative gives way to systematic exposition. Colin confirms that the carts laden with merchandise are his.

> Tout est à moi et à ma femme. Nous arrivons du pays; je suis à la tête d'une bonne manufacture de fer étamé et de cuivre. J'ai épousé la fille

d'un riche négociant en ustensiles nécessaires aux grands et aux petits;
nous travaillons beaucoup; Dieu nous bénit; nous n'avons point changé
d'état, nous sommes heureux, nous aiderons notre ami Jeannot. Ne sois
plus marquis; toutes les grandeurs de ce monde ne valent pas un bon ami.
Tu reviendras avec moi au pays, je t'apprendrai le métier, il n'est pas bien
difficile; je te mettrai de part, et nous vivrons gaiement dans le coin de
terre où nous sommes nés. (p.276)

The latter part of the paragraph unites the intimate and social models. We
can see that the values are the same. Solidarity operates on several levels.
The earlier physical embrace and the meal (two persons, then three)
becomes the joint manufacturing venture (likewise) and the unity of society
('[les] grands et [les] petits'). This new unity is built on the sound basis
of necessity and utility ('ustensiles nécessaires'). It displaces the false
divisions of class and vanity ('marquis', 'grandeurs'). Modesty (literalised
earlier in 'le petit homme' and 'ma petite femme') goes with goodness
both moral ('un bon ami') and material ('une bonne manufacture'). Hard
work ('nous travaillons beaucoup') receives its Providential reward on this
Earth ('Dieu nous bénit'). Fidelity to origins is also proposed at all levels.
The 'ancien camarade' claims that 'nous n'avons point changé d'état' and
tells Jeannot 'tu reviendras avec moi au pays ... où nous sommes nés'.

The final paragraph of the tale begins with Jeannot's reaction, 'la
tendresse et la honte'. Then 'la bonté d'âme de Colin développa dans le
coeur de Jeannot le germe du bon naturel que le monde n'avait pas encore
étouffé'. Natural goodness, opposed in the new ideology to social
corruption, can be recovered. The triumph of feeling introduces perhaps
the key element in the new ideology, the family. 'Il sentit qu'il ne pouvait
abandonner son père et sa mère'. The family is reintegrated, and reverts
to what was. 'Jeannot retourna dans sa patrie avec ses parents, qui
reprenaient leur première profession'. He achieves happiness. 'Il épousa
une soeur de Colin, laquelle, étant de même humeur que le frère, le rendit
très heureux'.

Attaining wealth and happiness, and returning to one's origins, are
common at the end of traditional tales. Here the happy ending functions
too in the new didactic mode to reinforce a set of moral values. There are
however certain problems here. Paradigmatically the attainment should
precede the return, not follow it. One could say that feeling was the real
goal, wealth and happiness simply its reward. But this fits ill with an ethos
of economic utility. If the values to be reinforced are hard work and

education, they are curiously deprecated by Colin's assurance that 'le métier ... n'est pas difficile'. Both he and the narrator lay less stress on either than on the return to origins. 'Nous n'avons point changé d'état' reflects bourgeois dignity, but also bourgeois bad faith. The changes that have occurred, for all concerned, are in effect suppressed. The original innocence, friendship, place and family can be recovered. The only addition is not one, for the wife Jeannot takes is Colin's sister and 'de même humeur que le frère', the same as him.

Jeannot has been saved, we might say, by the recovery of original feeling. We note however that the loving benevolence of his friend from youth arouses in him 'la honte'. Shame or guilt helps bring him back to childhood. An element of guilt and a return to childhood are also implicit in the next stage of the triumph of feeling. 'Il sentit qu'il ne pouvait abandonner son père et sa mère'. Finally he marries Colin's sister. The embrace of the Parisian seductress is replaced by the fraternal embrace of Colin and the innocent embrace of Colin's sibling who is just like him. These substitutions suggest that Jeannot, regressing into the role of child in the family, wants to marry Colin.

Candide excepted, *L'Ingénu* (1767) probably rates with *Zadig* as the most widely-read and critically-discussed of the *Contes*. The two are almost exactly the same length. As it happens, they also stand chronologically in a symmetrical relation to *Candide*. *Zadig* was written and published about a decade earlier, *L'Ingénu* nearly a decade later. The earlier tale is located in an atemporal Orient but, significantly, *L'Ingénu* is set in France in recent times. The latter work exhibits many of the other features that we have just identified in *Jeannot et Colin*. As in *Jeannot*, they are most evident in the ending. My argument that the tearful conclusion of *Jeannot* does not invite a parodic reading is perhaps strengthened when we look at *L'Ingénu*. The last few chapters of the latter work are heavy with sentiment and didacticism. No critic has suggested that the pathos here is not to be taken at face value. Indeed the principal critical debate has been over the work's apparent internal incoherence. Can the comic distance of the early chapters be reconciled with the emotive intensity of the last?[1] Or are we still left with 'la dualité maintes fois signalée de l'oeuvre, qui commence comme un conte satirique et se termine comme un roman sensible'?[2] The link between tone and genre, nicely made here, is important. It is developed by Carol Sherman who more rigorously divides the text into not two but three sections and tabulates various features of the writing.[3]   My own

---

[1] H.T. Mason, 'The unity of *L'Ingénu*', in *The Age of the Enlightenment: Studies Presented to Theodore Besterman* (Edinburgh, 1967), pp.93-106, argues that the change in tone appropriately reflects the development of the protagonist. This position is enlarged by Priscilla P. Clark, '"L'Ingénu": the uses and limitations of naïveté', *French Studies* 27 (1973), pp.278-86, who links development within *L'Ingénu* to the specifically social orientation of the protagonist, the theme and the genre, compared with earlier tales. The binary view is proposed by David E. Highnam, '*L'Ingénu*: flawed masterpiece or masterful innovation', *SVEC* 143 (1975), pp.71-83, and by Zwi Levy, '*L'Ingénu* ou l'anti-*Candide*', *SVEC* 183 (1980), pp.45-67. Jean Starobinski, 'Le fusil à deux coups de Voltaire: ii. L'Ingénu sur la plage', *Le Remède dans le mal* (Paris, 1989), pp.144-63, proposes binarity as a governing principle rather than an incoherence.

[2] Jacques Van den Heuvel in the 'Notice' in the Pléiade edition, p.970.

[3] See Sherman, *op.cit.*, pp.209-25.

examination will complement her study, then point to the ideological aspects of the new bourgeois realism.

L'Ingénu can be divided into three parts, by several different but mutually corroborative criteria. Of its twenty chapters, approximately the first nine could be called Part I, chapters x to xiv Part II, and chapters xv to xx Part III. The first nine chapters concern the adventures of the titular protagonist in Brittany, and his arrival in Versailles. The Huron repeatedly 'fails to understand' French norms, resulting in serial confrontations which are treated comically. Burlesque literalism is exercised on Biblical and other received discourses. This segment, with its argumentative dinners, joyous battles and multivalent baptism, is distinctly carnivalesque. Chapters xi-xii and xiv relate the conversations in the Bastille between the Ingenu and the old Jansenist Gordon. Here nature and high culture communicate more easily, and are progressively integrated. The tone is sober, the treatment of the speakers neutral or approbatory. Chapter xiii brings Mlle de Saint-Yves to Versailles, while the last six chapters relate her sufferings, reunion in Paris with her lover and the rest of the provincial cast, her death and the fate of everyone else. At odds here are moral feeling and the ways of worldly power. The treatment is, increasingly, intensely emotional and harshly ironic.[4]

Treatment can be examined more precisely through specific narratorial features. Monstrative deixis ('*cette* question ...'; '*voici* ce que ...') by the narrator is rare in most of the narrative. But it multiplies in chs x-xii, then still more so in chs xix and xx. Personal deixis (the narratorial 'je', 'nous', 'on') also occurs more in the second and final parts of the text. Value-assigning adjectives ('la *belle et infortunée* Saint-Yves') are few until ch.xiii, then massively present in chs xvi-xx.[5] The innovatory features that we noted in *Jeannot et Colin* are the more evident in this text. One is the repeated use of the historic present tense. Within the sixty-page narrative of *L'Ingénu* there are about a score of sequences in the historic

---

[4] Highnam argues that the ending both emphasises and partially distances us from emotional suffering, through what he calls 'cosmic' irony: *art.cit.*, pp.79-83.

[5] See Carol Sherman's tabulation of these features, *op.cit.*, pp.217-23. Under monstrative deixis should be added 'Voilà le Huron ...' (vii, p.306), and under personal deixis 'Qu'on imagine ...' (xviii, p.333).

present.[6] Mostly, as one might expect, they serve to narrate action or crisis. This may be comic: 'Il appuyait son large genou contre la poitrine de son adverse partie. Le récollet pousse des hurlements' (iii, p.296). It may be pathetic: 'Elle entra ... . On la présente au gouverneur; elle veut lui parler, sa voix expire; elle montre son ordre ...' (xviii, p.334). The greatest concentrations are in chs ix, xiii and xvii-xx. (There is no occurence in chs x-xii or xiv - the conversations in the Bastille - in which there is no action at all.)   However, these statistics ignore the chapter-headings. Of the twenty chapter-headings, eleven contain a verb in the present tense.[7] For example, ch.xiii: 'La Belle Saint-Yves Va A Versailles'.   Remarkably enough, the first chapter uses the preterite: 'Comment ... [X et Y] Rencontrèrent un Huron'. Chs ii-iv employ past participles. Ch.vi is the first to use the present in its heading. Thereafter, most chapters use it.

The omission of the verb of presentation with direct reported speech also occurs in just under a score of sequences.[8] The distribution is similar to that of the historic present. There are only three or four occurrences in the first half of the narrative, over a dozen in the second half. The effect implicit in these last two devices, as we saw in *Jeannot et Colin*, is greater immediacy.   Deixis likewise tends to bring narrator, events and reader closer together.   Direct narratorial evaluation seeks to circumscribe the reader's response.   All these features are more frequent in the later chapters.

In particular instances the devices may be combined.   The historic present may be preceded by monstrative deixis: 'Voilà que la bonne amie de Versailles arrive ...' (xix, p.337). It may be preceded by personal deixis: 'notre confidente lit la lettre ...' (xvii, p.332). (The woman designated in both these phrases is little better than a procuress - thus the effect is enriched and complicated by sharp irony.)   The historic present may be accompanied by a further device, the narratorial exclamation or question. 'On annonce un courrier de la cour. Un courrier! et de qui?

---

[6] In *Zadig*, a text of equal length, I find just six sequences in the historic present: chs viii, ix (twice), xv and xvii (twice).

[7] *Candide* uses the same type of headings for its thirty chapters. Twenty of these chapter-headings contain a verb in the preterite, just three a verb in the present.

[8] In *Zadig* I find three brief occurrences: pp.60, 84, 99.

et pourquoi? C'était de la part de ...' (xx, p.343). As the narrator knows the answer, he must be claiming to voice the urgent reactions of the protagonists, or of the reader. These interjections appear only in chs xiii-xx. 'Que devinrent monsieur le prieur et sa bonne soeur, et la belle recluse Saint-Yves?' (xiii, p.321) manifestly poses the question on behalf of the reader. 'Mais comment se conduire à Versailles?' (xiii, p.324) might be taken to speak for Saint-Yves too, thus identifying the reader with the fraught situation of the character.

By ch.xix the narrator has become specifically directive of the reader: 'Qu'on imagine une âme vertueuse et noble, humiliée de son opprobre, enivrée de tendresse, déchirée ...' (p.333). In ch.xx the voices themselves are joined in monologic pathos. 'Quelle mécanique incompréhensible a soumis les organes au sentiment et à la pensée? comment ... ?' A whole paragraph of such interrogative exclamation ends emotively with the phrase '... un objet d'admiration, ou un sujet de pitié et de larmes?' This set of rhetorical questions, evidently posed on our behalf, we assign to the narrator. But the next paragraph begins 'C'était là ce que disait le bon Gordon'. The second verb underlines the effect of immediacy, by both its continuous aspect and its implication that these exclamations were actually spoken (not 'se disait'). The adjective requires that we approve the speaker. The sentence continues 'et cette réflexion si naturelle, que rarement font les hommes, ne dérobait rien à son attendrissement' (xx, p.342) - multiplying approbation (and including inversion for elevated effect) in the voice of the narrator.

The narrator in the latter half of the text may offer exclamatory utterance on behalf of the character or ourselves. Reciprocally, certain characters may do the same job for him or us. 'Quoi! s'écria l'Ingénu, des édits rendus par ces gens-là!' (xi, p.318). 'Quoi! il y a de pareils monstres sur la terre! ...' (Saint-Yves; xv, p.328). 'Ah! quelle vertu! s'écria la belle Saint-Yves; quel labyrinthe d'iniquités!' (xvii, p.332). Not only their measured judgements (or rather, those of the Ingenu and Gordon from ch.x onwards) but their primary responses are to be ours. The suppression of the verb of presentation with their direct speech comes to serve the same end. The kind of speech that is presented unmediated alters from the earlier to the later part of the text. Earlier cases foreground rapid dialogue. 'Vous aimez donc cette belle demoiselle à la folie? - Oui, mon oncle. - Hélas! mon neveu, il est impossible que vous l'épousiez. - Cela est très possible, mon oncle, ...' (six short utterances; v, p.301). Similarly in ch.viii at Saumur (seven short utterances), and ch.xiii in Paris (eight short utterances). The instances in chs xiv, xv, xvi and xviii however each concern one long speech. All these long utterances are assigned either to the Ingenu or to Saint-Yves; each constitutes a passionate denunciation of the situation they face.

The last two chapters have often been likened by critics to theatre. At the start of ch.xix the narrator strongly suggests the analogy, by referring to the characters as 'personnages' and the events as 'la scène'. Grouped around the dying Saint-Yves in ch.xx are 'tous les assistants'. Present at 'ce spectacle de la mort', they constitute an audience but are deeply involved. They function as a model for our own response.[9] Two of the devices that we have identified are modified to serve the new aesthetic. The historic present is used not only to convey action but, almost on the contrary, to set a scene.

> Au milieu de ce spectacle de la mort, tandis que le corps est exposé à la porte de la maison, que deux prêtres à côté d'un bénitier récitent des prières d'un air distrait, que des passants jettent quelques gouttes d'eau bénite ..., le Saint-Pouange arrive avec l'amie de Versailles.   (p.346)

The omission of the verb of presentation now occurs with a third kind of direct speech - not dialogue, not long harangue, but brief exclamation. More exactly, exclamatory speech is presented instead by expressive gesture.

> Saint-Yves ... entraîne cette femme hors de la chambre dans un petit passage, jette les diamants à terre devant elle. 'Ah! ce ne sont pas eux qui m'ont séduite, vous le savez; mais celui qui les a donnés ne me reverra jamais.'   (p.338)

(Here we note too both the narrator's resort to the historic present, and the suppression of the conjunction 'et', for still greater impact.)   Again: 'L'Ingénu, reprenant son caractère ..., déchira la lettre par morceaux et les jeta au nez du courrier: "Voilà ma réponse"' (p.344). Speech is placed in apposition to gesture. But it is placed after gesture, so that it only

---

[9] Various theatrical elements in the last two chapters are listed by Carol Sherman, *op.cit.*, p.224. One might add the pointedly Aristotelian instruction for tragic response: the Ingenu's aspect aroused in everyone 'ce mélange de compassion et d'effroi ...' (xx, p.345).

confirms what has been first expressed in the unmediated language of nature. This is not merely theatrical. It conveys, as theatre and painting also increasingly conveyed, a new aesthetic and a new ideology of intense moral feeling.

The age of melodrama will also be the age of the gothic. For the first time in the *Contes*, Voltaire seeks to represent persecution not as the rituals of institutions but as the affective experience of the victim. The act of imprisonment of the Ingenu is given expressive physical substance: 'on referma les énormes verrous de la porte épaisse, revêtue de larges barres'. Just before this we have the shift from external ritual to affective image: 'on le porte en silence dans la chambre où il devait être enfermé, comme un mort qu'on porte dans un cimetière' (ix, p.312). The image is the narrator's. But it is soon taken up, and offered not as simile but with the greater immediacy of metaphor, by the characters. Gordon speaks of the 'tombeau' into which the two prisoners have been 'plongés' (x, p.312; xii, p.320). 'Je suis englouti dans ce tombeau des vivants', exclaims the Ingenu (xiv, p.326). 'Mon amant reste enseveli tout vivant', says Saint-Yves (xvi, p.330). Released from prison, the Ingenu demands 'où sont les monstres qui m'y ont plongé?' (xviii, p.334). The figures of burial and immersion are new. They evoke a fear of enclosure and abandonment. Claustration is presented through affect. However, one may find Voltaire's attempt at gothic subjectivity hyperbolic rather than imaginative. Its repetitiveness also reflects the didactic purpose behind it. It is strongly moralised even in its imagery. The persecutors are 'monstres'. That term has already been used by both the Ingenu and Saint-Yves. Respectively: 'Ceux qui persécutent me paraissent des monstres' (xiv, p.326); 'Quoi! il y a de pareils monstres sur la terre!' (xv, p.328).

During the Bastille episode, the narrative turns to follow Mlle de Saint-Yves. This shift from one protagonist to another, on the same diegetic level, is new in the *Contes*. Focalisation, by way of her situation, brings us to her feelings. Repeatedly assigned to Saint-Yves is the sentiment of horror. Loving the absent Ingenu, threatened with a forced marriage, 'les regrets, la tendresse et l'horreur bouleversaient son âme' (xiii, p.323). Herself at Versailles, she feels 'l'horreur de laisser dans une captivité affreuse l'amant qu'elle adorait' (xvi, p.331). The term pervades the final chapter. Having submitted sexually to Saint-Pouange, she recalls the deed 'avec horreur'. Distressed beyond words, 'soudain elle jetait un cri d'horreur'. Then 'elle sentait toute l'horreur de son état'. After her

death, her persecutor arouses in all 'l'horreur'. Again ethical significance
is brought out. At this stage - alas - it is not only underlined but
insistently monologic. The audience within the fiction respond to Saint-
Yves's story as one, and as we too should respond to the whole story.

> Chaque mot fit frémir d'étonnement, de douleur et de pitié tous les
> assistants. Tous se réunissaient à détester l'homme puissant qui n'avait
> réparé une horrible injustice que par un crime, et qui avait forcé la plus
> respectable innocence à être sa complice.

The intention here is to combine intense sensation with moral
instruction. The predominant tone in the latter part of *L'Ingénu*, for
narrator and characters alike, is a kind of shock. This can also be seen as
a development in the *Contes* as a whole. Shock constitutes an internalising
and moralising of what used to be surprise. 'Mon maître,' said Cacambo
to Candide, 'vous êtes toujours étonné de tout'. The narrator too - much
of the time - was apparently unable to make the connections. Both 'failed
to understand'. Here the carapace of innocence is shattered.
Incomprehension, which functioned satirically, becomes shocked
comprehension. The Fool learns to understand. 'L'Ingénu ... n'était plus
l'*ingénu*' (xix, p.337).

The protagonist's consciousness is modified by the world. This new
realist psychology is of a piece with the work's realist setting, plural
protagonists, and causal plot. We are moving from tale to novel. The shift
however causes problems. The *naïf* is no longer a given, but the
contingent product of a particular environment. The Ingenu must be
explained by Huronia. But Voltaire's account during the Bastille sequence
is an absurdity. To be brought up a Huron means, we are told, 'n'a[voir]
rien appris dans son enfance' (ch.xiv). The tribe has no 'monuments' and
no collective memory (though we are promptly told that almost all nations
claim 'des origines fabuleuses'). This Huron is unaware of the stars, as
regular movement or as wondrous mystery, till taught about them in prison
(ch.xi). Thus the comic anthropology in Part I is subordinated to the
philosophical purposes of Part II. The plot, for all its new causality, seems
to be subordinated to the demands of pathos in Part III. The most curious
instance of this is the change in the obstacle to the Ingenu's nuptials. The
prohibition on marriage between godson and godmother - without which
the last two thirds of the narrative would not occur - is simply forgotten
(see xix, p.340). All now is to hang on the malady of Saint-Yves.

The naming of the hero reflects the literal and conceptual confusion throughout. 'L'Ingénu' is initially defined (by himself p.288; by other characters p.291; by the narrator p.304) in terms of his 'naïveté'. This seems to mean frankness as much as innocence. (His strange initial combination of insouciance, violence, self-possession and 'cordialité noble et fière' corresponds to eighteenth-century French stereotypes of the Englishman rather than the natural man.) But it is not easy to reconcile with the insistence upon his 'grand fonds d'esprit' (pp.293, 303, 313). (Candide, on the contrary, was said to have 'l'esprit le plus simple'.) Upon baptism he becomes for the narrator 'Hercule l'Ingénu' (v, p.299; vii, p.306) or 'l'Ingénu Hercule' (vi, p.303). He renames himself, in the proper realist way, 'Hercule de Kerkabon' (ix, p.311). But the mock-heroic forename never appears again. Clearly its roguish suggestion of sexual promiscuity (iv, p.299; vi, p.303) is incompatible with the new absolute of female virginity, just as the comic transgressions of Part I in general must give way to pathos. He remains 'l'Ingénu' even as he acquires sophistication. Strangely, in ch.xviii he still fails to understand 'ce qu'un autre que l'Ingénu, plus accoutumé au monde et plus instruit des usages de la cour, aurait deviné facilement' (p.334). Yet when he does understand - the following day - this is because '[il] s'était formé par un an de réflexions' (xix, p.338). As the mystery is Saint-Yves's fall, one suspects that realist consistency is again being subordinated in order to maximise pathos. We are told that he is entirely 'changé'. 'Ce n'est plus le même homme; ... il est devenu aussi respectable qu'il était naïf et étranger à tout'. He has learned to 'se posséder' and to practise 'la discrétion' (ch.xix). Yet till the end of the narrative 'l'Ingénu, qui n'était plus l'*ingénu*' continues to be designated as 'l'Ingénu'.

The themes of *L'Ingénu* seem to be liberty and suffering. Etymologically the protagonist's name means 'free-born'.[10] His own gloss takes in 'franchise' in two senses: 'on m'a toujours appelé *l'Ingénu*, reprit le Huron, ... , parce que je dis toujours naïvement ce que je pense, comme je fais tout ce que je veux' (i, pp.287-8). His 'natural' freedom functions comically and satirically in confrontation with Catholic Lower

---

[10] The etymological point is made by Clark, *art.cit.*, p.279 (though her argument for a consistent contrast between the *naïf* Candide and the freeborn Ingenu is weakened by the references we noted to the 'naïveté' of the Huron), and by Eglal Henein, 'Hercule ou le pessimisme', *Romanic Review* 72 (1981), pp.149-65 (p.150).

Brittany, then to generate anger and pathos at Versailles. His imprisonment is thematised as illegitimate loss of liberty. 'Je suis né libre ... . Nous voici tous deux dans les fers', he exclaims in an echo of Rousseau (xiv, p.326). Gordon has already denounced the arbitrary civil procedure by which he has been deprived of 'le bien le plus précieux des hommes, la liberté' (x, p.314). Saint-Yves likewise demands that those in power respect 'la liberté des hommes' (xv, p.328). The universalist language and the Ancien Regime context make this a significant piece of pre-Revolutionary propaganda. The convent in which Saint-Yves was confined is described as 'une espèce de prison où l'on tenait les filles renfermées' (vi, p.304). On the story level, her claustration foreshadows that of Gordon and the Ingenu. All three suffer. 'Gordon ... avait été malheureux avec le jeune prisonnier' (xix, p.337). Saint-Yves is 'cette âme désespérée', 'la triste Saint-Yves', etc. All three are changed., 'L'amour et le malheur l'avaient formée', says the narrator of Saint-Yves (xviii, p.333). 'Gordon ... était changé en homme, ainsi que le Huron' (xix, p.337). Humanity is achieved, though 'malheur' is given the last word.

However, we might read here some less obvious messages. The Ingenu is radically compromised, even absorbed, by the system he initially opposes. In Part I he is converted, in religious and to some extent in broader terms, to the 'usages' of Lower Brittany. In Part II he acquires high culture. In Part III he ends by serving Louvois and thus the whole repressive order that we have just heard all three protagonists so strongly denounce. The theme of liberty seems to be forgotten. Like the drily distributional ending to the narrative, we might put this down to irony.[11] But it is less easy to explain the denial of any underlying opposition. Culture and nature, it seems, are not different. Racine's classical tragedies speak nature's language: 'L'Ingénu ... les sut par coeur sans avoir envie de les apprendre' (xii, p.320). Later we are told that he has added discretion to nature's gifts, and 'le sentiment prompt des bienséances commençait à dominer dans lui' (xix, p.341). The latter clause seems to deny the distinction preceding it. Can one gradually acquire an immediate

---

[11] Henein, *art.cit.*, points to the Ingenu's defeat of the invading English and his conversion of the Jansenist as earlier instances of his service to the repressive French state. He sees him as a derisory version of the Hero throughout. Highnam's view is however more persuasive. Irony in *L'Ingénu* is not derisive but, increasingly, cosmic. It balances personal suffering by setting it within an indifferent universe.

sense? Are the social proprieties a matter of feeling? The conflict between nature and culture is suppressed, in favour of a single cultural voice. The single and orderly voice in fact can be heard quite clearly in the first chapter. From the start this Huron not only 'fai[sai]t des politesses' but 'parlait français fort intelligiblement'. With 'la raison' he silenced the table. He had never liked cannibal feasts.

The ethos of this narrative is good feeling. 'Bonté' and sentiment are ubiquitous. In the first Part the bias is comic and petit-bourgeois. The prior is presented as 'un très bon ecclésiastique'; his companion, 'courte et ronde', has 'un caractère bon et sensible'. Their name, indeed, is Kerka-*bon*. The Ingenu, for all his statuesque savagery, is introduced on a similar scale. Wearing 'petites sandales' and 'un petit pourpoint', he carries 'une petite bouteille' and 'de très bon biscuit'. He shares his beverage with them, and they invite him to share their table (a rustic communion implicit already in *kirk*-à-bon?). The three go off together to dine with 'la bonne compagnie du canton'. Learning that he has '*ni père, ni mère*', immediately 'la compagnie s'attendrit'. In fact, family feeling predates his arrival in the narrative. The worthy Kerkabons, the first couple we meet, are brother and sister. 'Ils s'attendrissaient l'un et l'autre' at the memory of their brother and sister-in-law. Chapter ii reveals the Ingenu to be their long-lost nephew.

On his way to Versailles the Ingenu meets 'un petit homme' who speaks for a group of 'bonnes gens' (ch.viii). Forcibly jailed, he is warmly greeted by 'le bonhomme Gordon' - as he himself had greeted the Kerkabons, but now without the material exchange. Sympathy promptly establishes an affectionate relationship between ''le bon vieillard' and the Ingenu's 'bon naturel' (ch.x). The tone of the narrative becomes more elevated. There will be no more comic diminution and no more physical violence. (Part II deals instead in 'la lecture [qui] *agrandit l'âme*': xi; Part III presents 'les *grands* mouvements de *l'âme*': xx.) But the ethos of the good family is re-established in ch.xix, which is subtitled 'L'Ingénu, la Belle Saint-Yves, et Leurs Parents sont Rassemblés'. She is reunited with her brother the abbé, 'le bon prieur' and his sister 'la bonne Kerkabon'. The Ingenu joins them with his ex-Jansenist. 'Gordon devint en peu de moments cher à toute la famille', says the text (p.337). (We may note that the Kerkabons and the Saint-Yves are in fact unrelated.) Aunt Kerkabon, 'en s'extasiant et en pleurant de joie' at the Ingenu's proposed marriage, tells him 'je vous servirai de mère' (p.340). The Ingenu however seems

more concerned about a father. Before this family reunion he has named
Gordon. As he tells Saint-Yves, 'je l'aime comme un père, je ne peux
vivre ni sans vous ni sans lui' (xviii, p.335). In the last chapter 'le bon
Gordon' watches over the dying Saint-Yves 'comme un père' (p.342). The
final paragraph tells us that 'le bon Gordon vécut avec l'Ingénu jusqu'à sa
mort dans la plus intime amitié' (p.347).

The ethos of family feeling also contains less explicit meanings. We
have just seen how, in the last chapters, imaginary bonds of family
proliferate. There seems no legitimate space left for the sexual love
between the Ingenu and Saint-Yves. But of course the interdiction came
much earlier. 'Il n'est pas permis d'épouser sa marraine; les lois divines
et humaines s'y opposent' (v, p.331). The *frisson* of incest - an aspect of
the new cult of the family - is actually offered from the start. Aunt
Kerkabon was attracted by the Ingenu (ch.i). Even after she knows he is
her nephew, she looks upon him with lust, as does Saint-Yves (end of
ch.iii). The equivalence between the women is not hard to make. It is
Mlle de Kerkabon's brother who announces to the Ingenu the interdiction
on Mlle de Saint-Yves. When all are re-united, the interdiction - as we
noted - seems to be forgotten. But of course it has been internalised.
Saint-Yves, having given herself to Saint-Pouange (a name like hers, a man
like the Ingenu) is racked with sexual shame and guilt. 'Déchirée des
remords d'avoir trahi son amant', she exclaims 'je ne suis pas digne d'être
sa femme' (xviii, pp.333-34). The narrator states that 'elle était vertueuse
dans le crime qu'elle se reprochait' (p.335). The Ingenu before he knows
calls her 'divinité' and 'ange' (though such angelism also puts sexuality at
a maximum distance). When they know, both he and Gordon refuse to
condemn her. But, again, they do not need to. She herself is doing the
decent thing. Like Phèdre or Rousseau's Julie, she is dying. Like the
Princesse de Clèves too, she is removing herself from the world. There are
however differences which mark the new bourgeois ethos. Unlike Phèdre
or the Princesse de Clèves, but like Julie, she has actually committed the
sexual act. Unlike *Phèdre* or *La Princesse de Clèves*, but like *Julie*, this
bourgeois fiction kills the heroine and leaves the males to live on together.

The law of the Father is uttered by the Ingenu's uncle. Then it is
uttered - as a broad principle of submission to law - by Saint-Yves's
brother (ch.vi). Both are men civilly *in loco parentis*. Both, furthermore,
are priests. From them the Ingenu is handed on to the priest Gordon. 'Le
bon prêtre janséniste' while civilising the Ingenu learns to value sexual

love (xiv, p.327). He does not interdict Saint-Yves. But he replaces her.
She pledged marriage to the Ingenu by taking his hand. (The prior
emphasises the significance and the illegitimacy of this action: v, p.301.)
But when the Ingenu rejoins her and the family, he is 'tenant par la main
son janséniste' (xix, p.337). He has told her that he cannot live without
her and Gordon, thus placing them on a par. At her death however it turns
out that he can continue living - with Gordon. The priest Gordon has
several important roles in the last two chapters. Surrogate father to both
the Ingenu and Saint-Yves, he empathises, weeps, comforts or wisely
abstains from comforting. He adduces moral parallels to the present action.
He offers philosophical commentary on man's subordination to forms of
necessity. And - instructing another victim for sexual guilt - he brings
Saint-Pouange to repentance.

> Le bon Gordon ... lui parle avec cet empire que donnent la douleur et la
> vertu. Saint-Pouange ... écoutait Gordon les yeux baissés, et en il essuyait
> quelques pleurs qu'il était étonné de répandre: il connut le repentir. (xx,
> pp.346-47)

L'Ingénu, to conclude, in many respects repeats and develops the
characteristics that we first identified in *Jeannot et Colin*. Both narratives
are set wholly in France and at a recent time. Both treat contemporary
social themes: utility (versus class vanity), liberty (versus abuse of power).
Both narratives begin with a degree of internal focalisation (invocation of
Auvergnat witnesses; seeing the Ingenu initially through the eyes of the
Kerkabons). Both make increasing use of the historic present, omission of
the verb of presentation with speech, and dramatic dialogue. Both hint at
free indirect style and both depart slightly from linear narration. The
tripartite division apparent in *L'Ingénu* can be perceived, looking back, in
Jeannot. Both begin with affectionately comic portraits of provincial life,
then take their protagonists into the corruption of the capital.
Conversational reviews of high culture follow. Disaster strikes; provincials
are reunited; affective solidarity brings about reconciliation. Both, in a
word, move from mildly satirical comedy to heavily sentimental
didacticism. Within *Jeannot* however comedy remains the dominant tone,
and fable - albeit contemporary fable - the genre. In *L'Ingénu* the tone
becomes serious, then intensely emotive and harshly ironic. Narration
slows down, and demands that we feel and suffer with the protagonists.
They are changed by their experience; we too must be changed.

Monologic moral instruction replaces philosophical debate. The suppression of oppositions however occurs in both narratives. Jeannot the fashionable, and Colin the manufacturer, are able to return to their original simplicity. The Ingenu does not wish to return. But culture seems to have been present in nature - also a suppression of opposition. Both narratives end by celebrating male friendship: Jeannot and Colin, the Ingenu and Gordon. Sexual difference is suppressed: Jeannot marries Colin's sister, the Ingenu 'marries' Gordon. Guilt, shame, remorse, saved Jeannot. They eliminate Saint-Yves and save Saint-Pouange. In *L'Ingénu* however they are sexual and their rule is established by the father who is also a priest.

The *Histoire de Jenni* (1775) was written and published some six years after *L'Ingénu*. It has a good deal in common with its more famous predecessor. The two narratives are approximately the same length. The events recounted are set in the same concrete and historical context - familiar still to Voltaire's contemporaries - of the Anglo-French wars at the turn of the century. The English and North American connections, important in *L'Ingénu*, become central in *Jenni*. The main protagonists are now English; they travel to the colony of Maryland. The eponymous hero is again of exceptional strength and physical beauty. The wisdom of the Noble Savage is once more displayed.

Evident here are aspects of the new cult of Nature: exoticism, physical power, moral wisdom. The Ingenu united all three in himself; in *Jenni* the distribution is more complex. In both narratives we are also shown, however, that untutored Nature is insufficient. It is to be completed by French culture or English civilisation. Both narratives are educational, for the hero and ourselves. Not in the old ironic mode where the answer fails to come, but in the new didactic and sentimental mode. Both narratives begin with comic satire and transgression, but end with tearful reconciliation and moral instruction. Reading more critically, we can say that both are narratives of order, progressively suppressing the carnivalesque principle, and specifically of the family. As we shall see, the oedipal drama sketched in *L'Ingénu* becomes central in *Jenni*.

There are a number of specific textual parallels. Contestable but interesting is a similarity at the beginning. The arrival of 'saint Dunstan, Irlandais ... sur une petite montagne qui vogua ...' at the start of *L'Ingénu* is perhaps echoed in the arrival of the English, 'venus, par l'air, d'une île inconnue' and exorcised by invoking 'la Sainte Vierge de Manreze' in chapter i of *Jenni*. An incipit (the start of *L'Ingénu*; the start of the account by Las Nalgas in *Jenni*) establishes the naively pious world of peninsular Catholic communities (Brittany, Spain). It is disrupted in both tales by the dramatic arrival of a magnificent but unselfconscious young man. In both the young pagan is spied upon, naked in the water, by two Catholic women. His strength is exhibited in self-defence when, at the behest of the civil and ecclesiastical authorities, he is seized by the civil guard. 'L'Ingénu ... prend à la gorge deux de ses conducteurs, ... les jette

par la portière ...' (ix, p.312). 'Jenni en tua cinq ...' (i, p.600). The Ingenu
is received in prison by 'un vieillard ... qui ... s'avança d'un air ouvert et
compatissant', soon qualified as 'le bonhomme Gordon' (x, pp.312-13).
Jenni's father Freind is received in Maryland by 'un vieillard qui nous
invita à descendre dans sa retraite', 'ce bonhomme nous reçut avec
cordialité' (vii, p.622). The Ingenu is questioned as to his confessional
allegiance. 'Je suis de ma religion, dit-il, comme vous de la vôtre' (i,
p.290). In *Jenni* the noble savage Parouba, asked to identify his religion,
replies likewise. 'Moi! dit-il, je suis de la mienne; pourquoi voulez-vous
que je fusse de la religion d'un autre homme' (vii, p.622).[1]

The narrator of *Jenni* continues 'cette réponse courte et énergique nous
fit rentrer un peu en nous-mêmes'. In *L'Ingénu* the 'fermeté' of a savage's
utterance quietens his interlocutors, and the narrator comments that 'la
raison fait toujours rentrer les hommes en eux-mêmes' (i, p.287). The
Ingenu's wisdom too is hailed in contrast to the elaborations of theology.
Gordon's 'cinquante ans à m'instruire' leaves him inferior to '[le] bon sens
naturel de cet enfant presque sauvage ... [qui] n'écoute que la simple
nature' (xi, p.318). The wisdom of Parouba is appreciated by Freind in
similar terms. 'Cette pure nature ... en sait plus que tous les bacheliers'
(vii, p.623). Back in the story, the scene of the group gathered tearfully
around the sickbed of the mistreated fiancée is repeated (Saint-Yves;
Primerose). Concluding, we are told of the hero of *L'Ingénu* 'il était
changé', 'tout est changé' (xix, pp.336-37). The last paragraph of *Jenni*
tells us that Birton, a very disparate case but nevertheless the hero's *alter
ego*, 'était tout changé'.

Presentation however differs. Two of the rhetorical devices prominent
in *L'Ingénu* (and first in *Jeannot et Colin*) are less in evidence in *Jenni*.

---

[1]   Comparison with *Candide* on several of these topoi is instructive. For
self-defence Candide, like other earlier heroes, is equipped with a sword. The skill to
use it, and the decent distance it maintains from the adversary, are part of his classical
endowment. Brute strength and immediate contact, on the other hand, are marks of
the new Romantic cult of the natural. The *cordial welcome* is offered in *Candide* by
the King of Eldorado. In the two late *contes* however it is not public and not set in
utopia, but private and realist. *Religious belief* is self-evident to the 'vieillard' in
Eldorado, as it is to the Ingenu and Parouba. But the Eldoradan identifies his credo
as 'la religion de tout le monde' (ch.xviii), whereas the latter insist that their beliefs
are personal. Is this to be read as utopian wisdom versus savage naïvety, or as another
shift, in this case from classical universalism towards Romantic individualism?

In *L'Ingénu* there were at least a score of narrative sequences in the historic present. Here we find only about half-a-dozen (in chs ii, v, vi, vii, ix), though several are substantial. Omission of the verb of presentation with direct speech occurs in only four sequences. All are quite short (chs i, iv, vii, x). This pattern of difference is however readily explained by another difference. Over half of *Jenni* is not narrated but presented directly, using theatrical dialogue. Chapters iii and viii-xi (totalling 32 pages out of 58) take the form of debates, announced within the story and marked off within the text. Occasionally the overall narrator intervenes. But essentially our two rhetorical devices can only occur in the portions of the text which are narrated - less than half. Theatrical dialogue can be seen here as a complementary form of immediacy.

Deictics - within the narrated sections - are far more frequent than in any previous *conte*. The 'vous' and 'je' of reader and narrator appear in the first paragraph. 'Ce fils' and 'ce père' appear in the second paragraph, 'voici' in the third. Value-assigning adjectives are also ubiquitous. We are told promptly of 'le respectable Freind' and 'ce jeune et malheureux Jenni'. The narrating style is liable to be perfervid and exclamatory. 'Il arrive, il entre dans la caverne. Quel moment! que de pleurs et que de joie!' (ii, p.601). The emotive, moralising narration which marked the last chapters of *L'Ingénu* appears - if inconsistently - from the start of *Jenni*. *Jenni* however is subtitled 'Par M.Sherloc'. It is told in the first person by this fictional character. Sherloc is further realised because he is also one of the protagonists, having participated in the events he recounts. He provides the immediacy of the eye-witness, along with that of the personal narrating voice. What we are analysing is offered to us as the narration of Sherloc.

The narrator is explicitly not Voltaire. In *L'Ingénu* one assumed that they were equivalent. The mediation of meaning through a diegetic narrator makes *Jenni* a more complex literary artefact. In earlier *contes* which used first-person narration (*Lettre d'un Turc, Scarmentado*), the 'je' was a cipher of the protagonist, denied coherence of feeling or reflective distance. *Amabed* (1769), fairly late in date and epistolary in form, marks a transition. Writing 'to the moment', its protagonist-narrators combine the old disjunction of the eiron with the new style of didactic pathos. Their affectivity however is still without individual consistency. Sherloc is a realised character. The first-person narration which reveals a subjectivity at the same time as a story is the eighteenth-century novel's most successful mode. *Jenni* shows this further shift in the *Contes* towards the novel's particularity and interiority.

Sherloc the narrator is given specificity. His comparison of Freind with 'nos chevaux de race [qui] courent à Neumarket' (ii, p.601) is, as reference and as figure, quite quirkily English. His remark that women were 'pétries originairement d'une de nos côtes' (v, p.617) shows him to be a Christian of rather literal mind. The former distances him from Voltaire as the product of a specific culture, the latter also as an object of satire. The persona however is not consistently maintained. Sherloc is assigned Voltairean shafts of wit. His narration satirically glosses the Jesuit *Lettres curieuses et édifiantes* as 'rarement l'un et l'autre' (vii, p.628). It reflexively mocks its own account of a young woman 'embellie par ses larmes, comme c'est l'usage' (i, p.602). Contained within his narrative is the rather lewd *récit* by Las Nalgas (ch.i). It seems unlikely - as the awkward presentation implies - that the pious Sherloc would include this improper piece. His violent allegations of atheism against Warburton and Needham (ch.iv) are perhaps not out of character. The difficulty here is gross anachronism: these two enemies of Voltaire belong to the mid-century, not to its first decade in which this story is set. Realism, whether external in the story or psychological in the narrator, is still subordinated readily to wider discursive purposes. Its flaws however do not look like devices to undermine the story or its narrator. The perfervid chapters of *L'Ingénu* we did not take to be parodic. There is little evidence that we are to doubt the moral authority of Sherloc.

The internal narrator is complemented by an internal reader. (The latter is almost equally typical of the eighteenth-century novel, and again *Amabed* marks the transition within the *Contes*.) *Jenni* begins: 'Vous me demandez, monsieur, quelques détails sur notre ami le respectable Freind, et sur son étrange fils'. This diegetic reader is repeatedly addressed thereafter. In the first paragraph of chapter ii, for example, successive sentences begin: 'Vous savez quelle admirable conduite ....'; 'Mais vous peindrez-vous bien la surprise, la douleur, ... ?'; 'Vous savez que les têtes les plus froides sont les plus animées ...'; 'Vous eussiez vu ce père ...'. The apostrophes declare or propose shared knowledge and shared feeling. They also insist that the reader sees in his imagination what is being recounted. He is to experience the narrative affectively and visually as if present - another form of immediacy. On every level possible, narrator and reader are to be as one. The first paragraph, introducing the story, affirms 'Vous serez aussi étonné que je l'ai eté, et vous partagerez tous mes

sentiments'. In this and all the other ways we have noted, the fictional
narrator seeks to dominate. Surrogate for Voltaire, he demands the total
adherence of the fictional reader, surrogate for ourselves.

Rhetorical persuasion is not only an effect anxiously pursued by the
narration. It is a theme of the narration, and of the story. Freind addresses
the House of Commons in defence of his patron Peterborou. Sherloc tells
us: 'Je l'y entendis prononcer un discours ferme et serré, sans aucun lieu
commun, sans épithète, sans ce que nous appelons des phrases ...'. This
analysis of his rhetoric continues for another ten lines (iv, p.613). Later
Freind holds forth to a tribe of savages. He speaks against cannibalism.
Sherloc's account begins: 'Jamais le grave Tillotson ne parla avec tant
d'énergie. Jamais l'insinuant Smaldrige n'eut des grâces si touchantes. Le
grand secret est de démontrer avec éloquence' (vii, p.627). Freind's
eloquence is totally successful in both cases. In the first: 'On l'écoutait
en silence; on ne l'interrompait qu'en disant: *"Hear him, hear him*:
écoutez-le, écoutez-le". La Chambre des Communes vota qu'on
remercierait le comte de Peterborou au lieu de le condamner'. In the case
of the savages: 'ils jurèrent par leur grand Manitou qu'ils ne mangeraient
plus ni hommes ni femmes. Freind, dans une seule conversation, fut leur
législateur; c'était Orphée qui apprivoisait les tigres'. Freind's utterance
is assimilated to those of Anglican bishops and the pagan demi-god who
charmed by his voice. It persuades MPs and tribal Indians. Sherloc
emphasises not just its efficacy but its form and the relation of dominance
that it establishes over its hearers.

These two victories however appear to be only secondary. Each occurs
in the middle of a chapter; in neither is Freind's speech reported directly.
Both occur in the middle of the story. Nearer the start and the end occur
the two verbal transactions which are foregrounded as set-piece debates.
We have here a remarkable symmetry. First Freind converts the 'bachelier
de Salamanque' from Catholic excesses to the simple and civil order of
Anglicanism. The 'conversation familière' is marked off by its
presentation in a separate chapter and through theatrical dialogue (ch.iii).
Later, no less than four chapters of theatrical dialogue are assigned to
Freind's debate with the atheist Birton (chs viii-xi). This 'dispute réglée'
ends with the atheist's conversion. In the first dialogue the tone is
somewhat comic, in keeping with other elements in the first part of the
narrative, of which it constitutes the climax. There is little levity in the
second. The dialogue on atheism seems to be proposed to us as the most

important part of the work. It occupies most of its second half. It
constitutes the narrative climax of the whole, because it saves Jenni from
corruption; and the explication of the theme, declared by the work's
subtitle as 'le Sage et l'Athée'. It is the culminating verbal victory of
Freind. Sherloc's eloquence, thus, presents Freind's. In fact *Jenni* can be
said to deal in three levels of eloquence. In the diegesis proper - the story
-. Freind persuades all-comers. On the metadiegetic level, Sherloc directs
his battery of rhetorical devices to his reader. Beyond that, the real author
Voltaire is trying to persuade the real readers, his contemporaries or
ourselves.

What we are to be persuaded of is the wisdom identified with Freind.
An examination of Freind's significance might start by commenting on the
name that is assigned to him. 'Freind' is likely to be a man of friendship.
Quaker connotations - the Society of Friends - will later be reinforced
denotatively by the statement that he is a direct descendant of William
Penn. Implied by his name are amiability, moral rectitude, religious
seriousness. These qualities are closely confirmed by the formula by which
he is presented, in the first sentence of the narrative: 'notre ami le
respectable Freind'. In the second paragraph we learn that he is an army
chaplain - clearly not Quaker, but in Anglican orders. He is a priest. He
is also designated, in the second paragraph, as 'ce père sage'. He is a
father. In the very first sentence the metadiegetic pairing 'vous/me' was
repeated by the diegetic pairing 'fils/Freind'. The adjective links him to
the 'Sage' - a noun or essence - of the work's subtitle.

In the narrative that follows he is repeatedly qualified as 'l'ami Freind',
'notre ami Freind' or 'notre cher ami'. He is also - after 'le respectable
Freind' - 'le vénérable Freind' and 'le digne philosophe Freind'. He is 'le
sage Freind', 'le sage et charitable Freind'. He is 'ce père', 'ce bon père'
and 'le bon père'. His quality of goodness appears in other formulations
too. He is 'notre bon ami', 'le bon Freind', greeted as 'bon Anglais' and
hailed as 'un bien bon homme'. These qualities are manifested in his care
for his son, but also in other spheres. He is merciful, persuading
Peterborou to spare the Inquisitor. 'Tant de clémence toucha le coeur des
Catalans' (ii, p.603). He defends his disgraced patron. He consoles a
victim of Jenni's misbehaviour 'avec tant de tendresse, avec tant de vérité'
(v, pp.615-16). He is 'généreux' in providing financially for those whom
he has converted. 'Toutes ces bonnes actions' (v, p.617) precede his
dissuasion of the savages from cannibalism, and the great work of

converting the atheists to deism and morality.

The term 'bénéficence' was coined - to express a new sentiment and a new ethics - in the early eighteenth century. In *Jenni* the principle is manifested chiefly through Freind, but reinforced through other characters. Peterborou displays an 'admirable conduite' by preventing rapine in Barcelona (ii, p.600). Privately too Peterborou is 'aussi tendre pour ses amis que terrible à ses ennemis. Jamais homme ne fut plus compatissant ...' (vi, p.620). Lord Baltimore senior succoured the savage Parouba. Behind them all is the great figure of Penn. Beneficence in *Jenni* is active and systematic. It is practical, and carried out by those in positions of power. This is the English model: 'sang-froid' and 'sensibilité' conjoined, realised in efficacious beneficence both public and private by the privileged classes. It contrasts in effect with the cynical or thoughtless rule of clerics and bureaucrats in France, exhibited in *L'Ingénu*. Even French and English doctors illustrate the contrast. In *L'Ingénu* the doctors attending Saint-Yves are characterised by their 'pratique aveugle', enslavement to 'la mode' and professional jealousy (xix-xx, pp.341-42). Three English physicians are mentioned in *Jenni*. Their blend of moral and practical excellence is exemplified in Cheselden, 'dont le coeur est aussi bon que son coup d'oeil et sa main sont habiles' (v, p.616).

Emblematically, Freind combines within himself the key institutions of the English model of society. He is not only a priest but 'Membre du Parlement et de la Société Royale' (ch.ii, title). Thus we may say that he represents firstly a civilly-constituted clergy. Secondly, as an MP in the Commons, he is part of a national body for public political debate and legislation. And thirdly he is a member of the Royal Society, which stands for critical enquiry and scientific progress. Personally he is 'tolérant', a virtue associated with England. Morality and pragmatism are happily combined. Both humanity and utility underlie the principle he enunciates to Peterborou: 'il ne faut jamais faire mourir un homme que quand la chose est absolument nécessaire pour le salut du prochain' (iii, p.602). Cannibalism he opposes because it is, *inter alia*, a practice 'destructive du genre humain' (vii, p.627). Religious belief is advocated as 'la croyance la plus utile' (xi, p.653). Religion has an important social function as a regulator of behaviour. The value to which he finally persuades the atheist Birton is that of the 'honnête homme' (x, p. 650; xi, p.654). He sets up Jenni's marriage 'pour remettre son fils dans le chemin des honnêtes gens' (v, p.617). The young woman in question is an heiress. The vulgarities of British commerce are not allowed to intrude in *Jenni*. We may note however that Freind identifies marriage rights with property rights: 'l'adultère est un larcin' (iv, pp.612-13).

Along with his function as representative of certain social values, Freind expounds religious ideas. This occurs notably in the two debates. He argues his religious 'sagesse' successively against the opposed extremes of the Bachelier's Catholicism and Birton's atheism. The latter debate proceeds methodically. The four chapters could be assigned thematic headings. Chapter viii deals with proofs of God and order (the arguments from Design, Final Causes and a variant of First Cause). Chapter ix is on the problem of evil. Chapter x asks how Divine order is relevant to the human world. Chapter xi urges the social utility, if not necessity, of religious belief.

The religious arguments are of course those of Voltaire. This is not only the most systematic and comprehensive treatment of religious ideas in the *Contes*. It is of particular interest as a genuinely open discussion. Freind's voice is clearly authorised. Yet Birton the adversary also enunciates a number of Voltaire's own positions. These include the belief that matter has existed from eternity (viii, pp.634-35); a sense of the quasi-ubiquity of physical and moral evil on Earth (ch.ix); hints of a horror of matter (p.637) and of the concept of a Divine force animating all things (p.648). Freind is required to evade or even contradict some of Voltaire's intellectual convictions. The latter have long included scepticism about human freewill and about the concept of an immortal soul. Both are at least partially admitted here.[2] Belief in human freewill is required in order to exculpate God from responsibility for human evil (see pp.642, 644; Freind nevertheless seems to flirt with a monadic determinism, p.651). Belief in the soul - to receive reward or punishment in an afterlife - is needed as a force for social order (ch.xi). Overall the proofs for Freind's beneficent Divinity are less than satisfactory. Yet Birton repeatedly

---

[2] Voltaire's inconsistencies and self-contradictions are clearly set out in Clifton Cherpack, 'Voltaire's *Histoire de Jenni*: a synthetic creed', *Modern Philology* 54 (1956-7), pp.26-32. See too the Introduction (§IVb) and notes to *'L'Ingénu' and 'Histoire de Jenni'*, ed. J. H. Brumfitt and M. I. Gerard Davis (Oxford, 1970), and - more accessibly but less clearly - the notes to the Pléiade edition, pp.1254-62. On the notion of a Divine force throughout Nature, see E.D. James, 'The Concept of emanation in the later philosophy of Voltaire', *SVEC* 284 (1991), pp.199-209.

concedes and finally submits. It seems that reasons for belief lie deeper. Freind's principal function is not institutional or philosophical. It is to be a father. In the course of the story we meet a second male parent, the savage Parouba. He is also the only other character to be qualified consistently as 'bon'. He is a 'bon viellard'; four times he is 'le bon Parouba' (pp.624, 625, 626, 643). The first time he is designated by the latter formula is in fact when he bows at the name of Penn. Penn is Freind's grandfather, the beneficent English colonist of part of North America, and thus a good father behind them both. Parouba is introduced in the seventh chapter of twelve. The structural symmetry that we noted in the two dialogues and four conversions is also manifest here, in form and theme. Parouba is in effect Freind's double. Freind as the ideal of civilisation is mirrored by Parouba as the ideal of Nature. The latter is a subaltern double. He proclaims Freind (thus doubling Sherloc); he translates Freind's speech. But he too speaks wisdom. He too possesses '[son] Dieu et [sa] loi' (p.622). He too by moral principle and pragmatic wisdom allows his offspring a degree of freedom (pp.612, 623). He and Freind alike are deeply moved by peril to his child, for Freind is 'père aussi' (p.624). Behind all these good fathers is another. To the atheist, Freind affirms the 'bonté' of the Divinity. This, we are told, is 'le fort de la dispute'. Birton the atheist denies God's 'affection paternelle'. Freind's formula is notable: 'Dieu est un père' (pp.635-39).

Jenni strongly proposes to us the ideal of the good father - a bourgeois version of the patriarch. It is exemplified in Freind, Parouba, Penn and God. However, the evident sense of Freind's formula 'Dieu est un père' can be reversed, to express the major meaning underlying *Jenni*. A father is God. We saw how sentimental and familial values were first established in *Jeannot et Colin*. The friendship of the Ingenu and Gordon in *L'Ingénu* became the relation of surrogate son and father. The latter (a priest with an English name) finally replaced the fiancée in the affections of the former. In *Jenni* the father-son relation is made literal and central. Jenni has a false friend in the atheist Birton, and a false fiancée in Clive-Hart. Birton will be converted to belief in the father, and Clive-Hart 'converted' into Primerose the true fiancée, by the paternal Freind. Underlying *Jenni*'s ethos of beneficence is an assertion of the necessity of order.

Indiscrimination and violence must be repressed by the power of the father.[3]

The Father in *Jenni* is superhuman. Freind the Father is priest, MP and scientist all in one. He combines astonishing 'sang-froid' with intense sensibility, as Sherloc repeatedly observes. He is constantly vigilant and active in every sphere, an orator always victorious and a teacher invariably right. He is the grandson of William Penn, who is hailed by the savages as 'notre Dieu' (vii, p.626). They kiss Freind's feet and hands. In fact not only savages but Catholics and atheists prostrate themselves before Freind. Soon after the start the Spanish Inquisitor was 'prosterné à ses pieds'. At the end 'Birton et ses amis ... se jetèrent aux genoux de Freind'. The verbal accompaniment to these gestures is notably ambiguous. The Inquisitor 'se jeta à ses pieds et ... lui criait miséricorde' (ii, p.601). The Bachelier gives Freind best with the formula 'je suis de votre religion' (iii, p.610). Most pointedly, in the final conversion: 'Oui, dit Birton, je crois en Dieu et en vous' (xi, p.654).

The Father is a Name and a Law. These need only be uttered to establish his authority. Freind instructs Parouba how to calm the violence of the savages. 'Vous leur direz ... que je suis le petit-fils de Penn: ce nom seul suffira' (vii, p.625). The name is spoken. 'À ces mots' the savages instantly switch from war to worship. Parouba refers to his daughter as 'ma chère Parouba'. He continues - underlining rather than explaining - 'il faut que tu saches que Parouba est son nom, parce que Parouba est le mien'. This father goes on to assert that his daughter belongs to him. 'S'il [Jenni] m'avait pris ma Parouba, ce serait un vol. ... C'est un grand péché de voler le bien d'autrui' (vii, p.623). Freind's law in favour of the man in possession is enunciated in words almost identical. 'S'il vous a pris votre maîtresse ...; il ne faut jamais prendre le bien d'autrui' (ii, p.602). He will tolerate his son's fornication with a woman who belongs to no-one. But 's'il s'agissait d'un adultère, j'avoue que je serais plus difficile, parce que l'adultère est un larcin'. Boca Vermeja, he tells her brutally, is now unattached and therefore falls outside the law. 'Pour vous, mademoiselle, qui ne faites tort à personne, je n'ai rien à vous dire' (iv, pp.612-13). Parouba's affirmation 'ma loi est

---

[3] The Freudian reading which follows owes a debt to the latter part of the remarkable article by René Démoris, 'Genèse et symbolique de l'*Histoire de Jenni, ou le sage et l'athée* de Voltaire', *SVEC* 199 (1981), pp.87-123.

là-dedans' (vii, p.623) takes on a new meaning. So does the invocation of Penn and Locke as 'grands législateurs' who 'demandent à leurs peuples' that they believe in God (xi, p.653). So does the stress throughout on Freind's eloquence.

The father is an originator and founder. Penn is first presented as 'le premier des tolérants, et le fondateur de Philadelphie'. 'Tolérant et Philadelphie!' cries the Bachelier, 'je n'avais jamais entendu parler de ces sectes-là' (iii, p.611). He offers a burlesque truth, for these are indeed groups adhering to a religious law. (The patriarch is 'tolérant' only of those who believe. 'Toutes les consciences sont libres ... pourvu qu'on adore un Dieu': ix, p.644.) Penn's law - his word - founds a colony (as Locke's historical contribution to the legislation founding Carolina is pressed into the exemplary configuration). It founds - in Sherloc's expression - 'un autre univers'. The universe itself, Freind fervently argues, has a founder and legislator. We must believe in a 'suprême fabricateur' (viii, p.633). God is the 'Etre suprême, nécessaire, incompréhensible, qui nous a faits' (p.634). God the father is the origin of us all. 'Nous sommes, vous et moi, de la même famille', says Freind (iii, p.604). Penn and Locke had 'leurs peuples'. Penn is a grandfather, founder of a literal family. Freind presents hiself as 'le fils de mon grand-père' (p.603). He himself is throughout the narrative a founder and originator of peoples. He begins by converting the people of Barcelona to the Anglican faith, then the savage tribe to Penn's, then the atheists to God's. But all, as we have seen, are also his own. At the end the young people's marriages make him an originator and founder in his own right. 'Freind leur a servi de père à tous'.

The father is the principle of order. God's universe observes a Newtonian order ('les lois d'une profonde mathématique': viii, p.632). More notably, it observes a biological or sexual order. Freind maintains the doctrine of the invariability of species, and the preformation of 'germs'.[4] Here are perhaps his two clearest statements. 'Les germes impalpables des animaux et des végétaux subsistent, se développent et perpétuent les espèces' (xi, p.651). This means in effect that every living thing can be traced back to its origin, to which it still belongs. 'Il est clair

---

[4] These were Voltaire's positions: see Jacques Roger, *Les Sciences de la vie dans la pensée française du xviiiᵉ siècle: la génération des animaux de Descartes à l'Encyclopédie* (Paris, second ed. 'complétée', 1971), pp.732-48.

que Dieu a fait chaque espèce d'animaux et de végétaux pour la place dans laquelle ils se perpétuent' (ix, p.638). Perpetuation is according to Divine order; sexual indiscrimination is against it. Opposed is the atheist position. In the atheist's universe no God is needed. 'Tout s'est fait de soi-même; ... on peut très bien se passer de Dieu; ... il n'y a point de Dieu' (iv. p.614). 'La nature fait tout', says Birton, 'je ne crois qu'à la nature' (viii, p.632). Both the founding and the perpetuation of the universe, for the atheist, are *sui generis*. They are - therefore - indiscriminate. The universe begins, according to Birton, in 'le chaos' (viii, p.634). Life can be perpetuated, according to new scientific theories adopted by the atheists, in the most disorderly ways. '[D]es anguilles en ont produit d'autres, sans accouplement'; 'on peut faire des hommes avec de la farine de froment et du jus de perdrix' (iv, p.614). Atheism, that is, denies the paternal fiat (the founding word) and orderly differentiation (heterosexual coupling within fixed species).

Freind is very keen on sponsoring fixed couples. He sets up three marriages. He weds Boca Vermeja to the Bachelier, Jenni to Primerose, and 'nous avons marié aussi Birton' (exurgit). His proceeding is not just moral or social. He is, each time, imitating the founding act of the Divinity which originated and ordered humankind. 'Dieu lui-même a marié Adam et Eve'. This Freind affirms to the Bachelier in the latter part of his conversion dialogue, which - we can now see why - places great stress on marriage. Marriage, says Freind, is a sacrament. The most holy men - apostles, saints, bishops, priests - have married. The first assertion is not Catholic, nor the second Protestant. Both are religious. It is at this point and in this way that the Bachelier - we can now see the fuller significance of his name - is converted. 'Je suis de votre religion; je me fais anglican. Je veux me marier ...' is his confession (p.610). The first and third articles are the more important.

'Cela vaut mieux que de cuire des hommes et de déshonorer des filles', adds the convert, renouncing his former errors. The alternative to marriage, that is, is violence and indiscrimination. This is manifest in Catholicism. It is represented by the violence of the murderous Inquisition on the one hand, on the other by 'évêques et ... papes concubinaires, adultères, ou pédérastes' (p.610). But this appalling dual alternative is equally manifest in the other groups whom Freind converts. One is the atheists. Under the influence of atheism, Jenni does two bad things. He wounds a creditor; he leads 'une vie débordée' with Mme Clive-Hart (iv, pp.614-15). Once more the threat is violence and adultery. (Note that a 'créancier' is etymologically a believer; 'Clive-Hart' is semantically another wound or blow.) The other group is the savages. Freind converts them from making war (he establishes peace, as did grandfather Penn before him). And he converts them from cannibalism.

In every case, from theories of the universe onwards, we have here the same opposition. Freind advocates closed dualities, against the disorder of too much or too little differentiation. Either God married Adam to Eve, or there was chaos (all the same and all different). Either there are fixed species and systems of perpetuation, or there are inbred eels and adulterated men (too same and too different). Either we practise marriage, or we practise homosexuality and adultery. Either we accept Freind's law, or we make war on our fellows (too much differentiation) and eat them (too little).

Though Freind's formal dialogues denounce Catholicism and atheism, there is a special importance in the episode with the savages. What is described here as 'la pure nature' is radically ambivalent. It is Parouba, father and adherent of God and the law. It is also cannibalism. The New World is thus both the proof of natural order and the heart of darkness. The word 'horreur' is first used in this text in connection with cannibalism. (vii, p.623). Cannibalism nevertheless is associated not only with the savages. It is linked as well to Catholicism and to atheism. The Spanish in their colonial conquest of South America 'font servir sur leur table des gigots d'hommes et de femmes, des fesses, des avant-bras, des mollets en ragoûts' (ix, p.641). The atheist asserts that 'la coutume de mettre son prochain au pot et à la broche était la plus ancienne, et la plus naturelle'. The pious Sherloc notes of this assertion 'le fond pouvait malheureusement être vrai' (vii, p.627). Freind, summarising the dialogues which flank the episode with the savages, concludes: 'Oui, mes amis, l'athéisme et le fanatisme sont les deux pôles d'un univers de confusion et d'horreur' (ix, p.653). Confusion - indiscrimination - arouses horror. It is all around us. Freind struggles to arrest the constant tendency of things back to violence. The alternative to the order of Freind is the cycle of nature, affirmed by Parouba *fils*: 'je veux les tuer, les manger *à mon tour*' (vii, p.624 [my emphasis]). This is precisely the cycle of Clive-Hart. Her fate shows war leading to cannibalism: she kills and is eaten (vii, p.626). Clive-Hart is only assigned one piece of direct speech. In it she invites her lover Jenni to kill her husband (v, p.616). She uses her sole utterance to urge the son to attack the father. Is Freind struggling to repress incest as well as cannibalism and murder?[5]

The one who lives and dies by indiscrimination is a woman. This is not by chance. Women have a bad time of it, in this world of fathers. There is a curious tension here on the level of overt theme. The narrative which proposes the model of marriage idealises single male parents. Freind's wife is never mentioned. Nor is Penn's, nor Parouba's. Were the progeny of these men not born of woman? The suppression of the female bodily principle has its parallel in Freind's affirmation 'il n'y a point de nature ... tout est art' (viii, p.632).[6] We might suspect that this male art is, like that of God engendering in the Christian narrative, the art of speech. But of course matter exists. Freind even accepts that it may be co-eternal with God (viii, pp.634-35). What he insists is that it is ordered. God is 'maître de la matière'. The body of the universe exhibits male order (Divine foundation and Newtonian law). The human body reveals design and purpose (Final Causes). Opposed to this is female disorder. 'Chez les femmes ... toutes les contradictions se rassemblent'. observes Sherloc (v, p.617). Their very names connote corporality and violence. 'Clive-Hart' is a bodily cleft and heart-cleaver. 'Boca Vermeja' is a mouth red with someone's blood. These women draw Jenni into their orifices. It is clear that he has sexual relations with both. But he does not take the sexual initiative. ('C'est moi qui lui ai fait toutes les avances', says Boca Vermeja: ii, p.602). The only woman to whom the narrative gives approval is Primerose. The pale fiancée Primerose is the opposed double of both Boca Vermeja (the scarlet woman) and Clive-Hart (the illegitimate fiancée). But even she feels more sexual desire than he does (v, p.618). Like the other men it seems that, sexually, he does not need women. Primerose is his father's choice for him.

Jenni feels guilty, but not over desire for women. We are told of his sense of shame and remorse on four occasions. He sheds 'quelques

---

[5] 'Civilisation ... began to detach man from his primordial animal condition. ... [But] the instinctual wishes ... are born afresh with every child ... . Among these instinctual wishes are those of incest, cannibalism and lust for killing.' 'The principal task of civilisation, its actual *raison d'être*, is to defend us against nature.' (Freud, *The Future of an Illusion*, ii and iii.)

[6] The parallel is proposed by Démoris, who identifies nature with the pairing *mater/materia*: *art.cit.*, pp.120-21.

larmes' on learning that his father has made reparation for his assault on the creditor (v, p.616). We hear of 'sa honte' when his father, who has followed him to America, saves him again (vii, p.626). The third occasion is during the dialogue on atheism. When Sherloc tells him that he could recognise virtue in his father were his heart not fouled by vice, 'Jenni baissa les yeux, et parut sentir des remords' (ix, p.643). On all three occasions too - alas - Jenni throws himself at his father's feet (v, p.617; vii, p.625; x, p.650). The focus of his sense of guilt is clear. 'Ah! lui dit Jenni, je ne méritais pas d'avoir un père tel que vous' (xii, p.654). In no case, however, did his father rebuke him. Asked by Sherloc why one should not 'lui représenter... ses fautes', Freind replies 'je veux qu'il les sente'. Sherloc confirms that 'il l'abandonna à sa conscience' (v, pp.616-17).

The triumph of sentimental morality is a triumph for the internalising of guilt towards the father. In this case it is God who has spoken the law. 'Nous a-t-il dicté ses lois? Nous a-t-il parlé?' demands Birton. 'Oui, par la voix de votre conscience', replies Freind (x, p.648). The whole dialogue on atheism ends with Freind's evocation of 'les tourments du remords'. 'Voyez comme notre méchant Richard III meurt dans Shakespeare; comme les spectres de tous ceux qu'il a tués viennent épouvanter son imagination' (xi, p.654). This gothic moral tableau is promptly repeated in the story as the experience of Jenni. 'Pour mon supplice, l'image de Primerose est sans cesse devant mes yeux; je la vois, je l'entends; elle me dit: "Je suis morte, parce que je t'aimais"' (xii, p.655). Clearly we are to understand this as an expression of his sense of guilt. (Primerose's words might however be understood as avowing her own sexual disorder and punishment. Like her bodily convulsions earlier, they recall Saint-Yves. This could be read as a male projection of sexual guilt upon the female.) Jenni thinks that he has killed the object of his father's choice. (Worse still, perhaps he knows that he wanted to. It was he who eagerly ushered her into her enemy's house: vi, p.619.) But in a final astonishing display of power, the father brings her back to life. Jenni marries her. Like Birton and the Bachelier, he submits to the new social religion.

5. 2. i   *POT-POURRI*

Pot-pourri, published in 1765, is undoubtedly the strangest in the canon of the *Contes*. It consists of 15 short sections. Some narrate impersonally; others have a first-person narrator but deal principally in conversations. Broadly there seem to be two narratives. The stronger is a burlesque transposition of the history of the Church into the history of the puppets of the *Foire*. The second element, interspersed and eventually taking over entirely, contains the conversations of a Parisian bourgeois with various persons. It is possible however to identify links between the two elements, at several levels. Diegetically the two are related by the bourgeois's occasional reference to the puppet-history as his own reading matter. Most of the conversations allude to contemporary issues of toleration and religious 'abuses', thus linking them thematically to the burlesque history.[1] Structurally one might say that we have a double axis. The diachronic or 'vertical' narrative of the history of the Church/puppet-show runs from origins to the eighteenth century. Intermittently intersecting it, and taking over once it reaches the present, is the synchronic or 'horizontal' narrative of the bourgeois.

Much in *Pot-pourri* lends itself to a carnivalesque reading. The title promises and the work delivers a mixture. Narrative dislocation is reflected in the mocking tone. The history of the Church is creatively degraded. The free burlesque transposition gives to it - better, gives back to it - a concrete and popular dimension. Christ becomes Polichinelle. His father becomes Brioché, the seventeenth-century puppet-master, his ancestors the clowns of popular theatre and the legendary grotesques of the carnival. Polichinelle's act (Christ's preaching, miracles, ...) steals business from the rival showmen and quacks, who denounce him to the magistrate (Pilate). His roadshow is taken over by the puppeteer Bienfait (the Pope), who later quarrels with one of the ticket-sellers (Luther) who launches in

---

[1] The patterns are carefully set out in the 'Notice' to *Pot-pourri* in the Pléiade edition, pp.895-99, and summarised pp.921-22. In the latter however the grouping of the fifteen sections into 'blocs' overemphasises theme at the expense of narrative (notably in the place assigned to §2). This 'Notice', principally genetic, is to my knowledge the only substantial study of *Pot-pourri*.

competition a new simplified product (the Reformation), etc.[2]   Thus
popular theatre itself is the central conceit.   Reference goes beyond
puppetry to the whole subculture of the 'marché', the 'préau' and the
'tréteaux'; shows, medicines and miracle cures; the prophecy, the almanac
and the popular song. Activities evoked include dancing, juggling, trickery
and a good deal of brawling.   We have here metaphors of dynamism,
exchange and plurality, the figural representations of the carnivalesque.
Polichinelle - Mr Punch - is physically a grotesque. 'Bossu par devant et
par derrière' (§3), he is a bulging distortion of *homo erectus*.   He is
accused of having assaulted others with 'cent coups de pied dans le ventre'
(§3).   This is again both referentially accurate to the historical Polichinelle,
an aggressive anti-hero, and figurally carnivalesque.[3]

Carnivalesque violence is also done to the body of the word.   Its
syllables may be reversed or its letters jumbled.   Diegetically we have
'paroles: *nelle chi li po* ... prises à rebours' (§7); from the second narrator
we have anagrammes ('Morfyé', 'Urieju') (§8). Sense is nonsense, again
on both levels.   Bienfait deals in 'galimatias' (§7).   Section 8 begins
'N'ayant rien entendu au précédent chapitre de Merry Hissing ...'.   The
name assigned to this fictional author, 'Merry Hissing', is pure
carnivalesque. Through a foreign-language pun it signifies joy and odium.
Appearing at the start of Section 2, it is promptly followed by its parallel
at the second level. The first words addressed to the bourgeois are 'Mon
ami, vous *riez* de voir les jésuites *vilipendés* ...'.   The avowal of
incomprehension by the bourgeois reminds us that, intratextually,
Pot-pourri is a narrative doubled by its own sceptical commentary.

---

[2] The narrative can be read either as burlesque transposition or as allegory. More
exactly, the history of the Church and that of popular theatre are freely *superimposed*.
Allusion to the first is implicit, to the second explicit. The Pléiade, which calls the
two systems of allusion the 'allégorique' and the 'obvie', provides footnote glosses for
most specific allusions. I would add that the 'crapaud' (p.241) can be identified with
the Devil - on the grounds that Milton is said to 'déguise[r] Lucifer ... en crapaud' in
Candide, chapter xxv.

[3] Like Mr Punch (but unlike their common Italian ancestor Pulcinella) Polichinelle
was characterised by 'une insolence extrême': see Charles Magnin, *Histoire des
marionnettes* (Paris, 1852), p.42. Polichinelle functioned as an emblem of popular
political protest in the mid-seventeenth century, and protean parody in the
mid-eighteenth century: see the Pléiade notes, pp.928-29.

Intertextually this text undermines the authority of other writing. The sarcasm 'si ces deux historiens se contredisent, c'est une preuve de la vérité du fait' (§1) is also an allusion to other commentary, adding further levels of metaliterary gaming. Metaliterary games however are characteristic of the *Contes* generally. It is the presentation of elements of popular culture that is more exceptional within the *Contes*, and more central for this reading.

However, even if we continue to focus on the Polichinelle story, the carnivalesque reading requires considerable qualification. The material references and figures are there, the comic treatment likewise. But the comedy is chiefly satire. The popular and the corporeal are presented with some contempt. Any celebratory quality is, one feels, a victory for the material over the conscious intentions of the writer. The transposition of the history of Christianity into that of the *Foire* is intended negatively. This is evident from the fact that the culture of puppetry and the populace is presented brutally.

Notations in the Polichinelle narrative tend to be brief. Frequently the tone is harsh and the judgements are dismissive. 'Polichinelle ... ne put jamais parvenir à se servir d'une plume' (§3). 'Les compagnons de Polichinelle [étaient] réduits à la mendicité, qui était leur état naturel' (§7). 'La canaille allaient aux marionnettes' (§3). Polichinelle's ambition, regarded by his parents as displaying 'le bon sens', is 'je gagnerai quelque argent' (§3). Bienfait's aims, and his expression of them, are scarcely more refined: 'je veux, dit-il, beaucoup d'honneurs et beaucoup d'argent' (§7). Polichinelle lives by apparently gratuitous violence - the 'cent coups de pied dans le ventre'. He dies by it: 'il fut avalé par un crapaud' (§3). (In the best traditions of religion and carnival, however, he is resuscitated: §7.) His companions too are assigned business with an animal. The Biblical miracles in *The Acts of the Apostles* are debased to 'ils guérirent même de la gale l'épagneul d'une dame' (§7). The populace also readily fall into violence: 'on se battit longtemps à la porte des marionnettes, dans le préau de la Foire' (§9). Popular culture, in this treatment, is stupid and ugly.

The second narrative level is that of the bourgeois and his interlocutors. We find a marked contrast with the story of Polichinelle, but also a strange similarity. From the start of the second narrative, oppositions are implicit. The second narrator presents himself 'dans mon cabinet'. Contrasting with the disorderly life of public spaces, we have the settled indoor life of the bourgeois. He is reading, privately. Polichinelle by contrast is illiterate; his shows are oral and public. 'Mon voisin M. Husson ... est venu chez moi'. (A neighbour, an informal visit, but the propriety of the title is maintained. They address each other as 'mon ami' and 'monsieur'.) 'Je disputai longtemps contre M. Husson' - but they do not fall to blows. They are discussing what the narrator sees and approves when looking out of his window into the street. 'Les syndics des apothicaires ... allaient saisir des drogues et du vert-de-gris que les jésuites de la rue Saint-Antoine vendaient en contrebande' (§2). Polichinelle's companions, the analogues of the clerisy in that narrative, 'se mirent à composer des drogues dont la vente les aida quelque temps à subsister' (§7). The improper use of panaceas is practiced by showmen and Jesuits alike. Happily it is now being prevented by the apothecaries's syndics - the representatives of petty-bourgeois business order.

The Jesuits, notes M. Husson, have also been 'convaincus d'un parricide [= regicide] en Portugal, et d'une rébellion au Paraguay' (§2). The Huguenots are accused by the narrator of involvement in 'neuf guerres civiles' and of 'attroupement ... contre les lois'(§6). Polichinelle too is denounced for disorderly conduct (§3). By contrast with all these, we hear later of a member of the narrator's family 'qui a servi le roi cinquante-deux ans' (§14). The rural equivalent of the two Parisian bourgeois, 'il a une petite terre qu'il cultive'. His labourers however refuse to work on feast days, preferring to 's'enivrer' (§14). Polichinelle too was accused of drunkenness (§3). Another practioner of 'l'oisiveté' is the abbé of Citeaux, whose unearned income is denounced by the narrator's friend M. Evrard (§15). The puppeteer Bienfait too 'devint si riche' (§7). Polichinelle's companions were mendicants (§7), the opposed extreme. That fate seems to threaten the Jesuit 'père La Vallette, marchand banqueroutier d'Amérique' (§8). This is not proper business practice. Overall the pattern is very clear. On one side are the successive bourgeois and respectability. On the other, identified with popular and ecclesiastical collectivities alike, are illegality, civil disorder, drunkenness, laziness, excesses of wealth and poverty.

The narrator claims to find some of the Polichinelle narrative incomprehensible: 'n'ayant rien entendu au précédent chapitre ...'. Yet he goes on retailing it. His neighbour explains - rightly - that the chapter is 'une profonde allégorie'. But he then repudiates Mr Punch's world absolutely. 'Mon ami M. Husson ... me dit ... qu'il n'allait jamais aux marionnettes' (§8). These statements occur precisely at the centre (there are 15 sections) of *Pot-pourri*. They declare not a polemical failure to understand, but a flat refusal. The refusal is not just partial, strategic or critical. It is total. Yet the ugliness and stupidity they repudiate seems to be that of all reality. Brutality is ubiquitous in the world and the language of the respectable bourgeois.

'Les jésuites vilipendés', 'la haine' and 'les opprobres multiples', 'parricide' and 'rébellion', 'féroces', 'fanatiques' and 'fripons', all appear in the twenty-five lines of Section 2. This is the language of the neighbour Husson. '[Les] sots', 'détestable', 'barbouilleurs de papier', 'vole[r] une province', 'condamner aux galères', 'brûler [des hommes]', occur in the twenty lines of Section 4. This vocabulary is shared by the narrator and 'feu M. Dumarsais' whose views he approves. In Section 6 the narrator and M. de Boucacous voice 'guerres civiles', 'massacres', 'cui[re] [des gens] en place publique', 'hurlements', 'écrase[r] les cervelles des petits enfants', 'un peuple que nous abhorrons', 'vous saigner et vous purger', 'malades' and 'fous'. Some of this language of violence is referential, its significance residing partially in its claim to present objective reality. Other elements shade into hyperbole or metaphor, expressive of a state of mind.

Striking in the later bourgeois sections are the repeated allusions to animals. Polichinelle's story, we may recall, offered us a spaniel and a toad. In the second narrator's story we have moles and lynxes (§10), monkeys and ferrets (§12), insects and lions (§15). The last two are metaphors for objective reality. They occur in a conceit by M. Evrard. 'Il me semble que je marche dans les déserts de Libye, où notre sang est sucé par des insectes quand les lions ne nous dévorent pas'. The image of process is as violent as that of 'Polichinelle ... mangé par un crapaud'. But while the latter was still grotesque, this is desolate. The other animals are proposed as the likeness of man. They express both his contradictions and his essential nature. The images are appalling.

> Les singes font des tours extrêmement plaisants, et étouffent leurs petits. Rien n'est plus doux, plus timide qu'une levrette; mais elle déchire un lièvre, et baigne son long museau dans son sang.

The disorderly world of Polichinelle, which the bourgeois condemn, is cheerful and innocent compared with this presentation of mankind.

The names of these bourgeois, decoded, match the harshness of their language. We do not have a name for the second narrator, who is simply 'je'. But 'je' offers us straightaway two proper names, one for each narrative level. '... des cahiers de Merry Hissing ... mon voisin M. Husson'. Between 'Merry Hissing' and 'monsieur Husson' there is a remarkable resemblance. The half of the neighbour's name which actually identifies him, however, is the 'Hissing' part. Odium dominates. Further guidance as to bourgeois dispositions is offered by the name assigned to the narrator's other companion and interlocutor. 'M. Evrard' (§15) surely signifies through another English pun. He is Mr Ever-Hard. Confirmation of this reading is provided if we go back to Husson. He is characterised by the narrator as 'une tête de fer' (§2) and 'un rude homme' (§8). The bourgeois is a hard man. True, 'je' tries to soften him. 'Je tâchai de l'adoucir' (§2); 'j'ai fait ce que j'ai pu pour l'adoucir' (§8). But then his judgements become even more brutal than those of his interlocutor.

> - N'est-ce pas, dis-je à M. Husson, que les hommes sont superstitieux par coutume, et coquins par instinct? - J'y rêverai, me dit-il; cette idée me paraît assez bonne.   (§10)

This reversal of roles illustrates the fact that these bourgeois are interchangeable. We find a similar reversal in the relation between 'je' and Evrard. 'Je' again seems to shift from stoicism to denunciation. But this time the aggression is translated into action by Evrard. The logic of universal knavery is followed through. The narrator first tries to calm Evrard, telling him 'Ayez patience'. But then he instructs him how to 'vous venger ... avec usure'. *Pot-pourri* ends thus:

> M. Evrard me crut: c'est à présent l'homme de France qui vole le roi, l'État et les particuliers de la manière la plus dégagée et la plus noble, qui fait la meilleure chère, et qui juge le plus fièrement d'une pièce nouvelle.

The radical pessimism of the bourgeois world-view furnishes Evrard with his alibi. If all men are knaves, his own thievery from the public purse merely conforms with universal practice. But how then does he differ from the puppeteer/Pope Bienfait, who became likewise 'fort riche et fort insolent' (§9)? (Picking up the bilingual onomastics, how does Mr Ever-Hard differ from Mr *Punch*?) The answer is perhaps supplied in the exurgit just quoted. This ending, in the best traditions of the *Contes*, is a *mise-en-abyme* and a social obesiance. One such 'pièce nouvelle' offered for judgement is also *Pot-pourri* itself. But in this case the diegetic judgement seems to be made by Evrard in arrogant solitude. His arrogance recalls that of Husson dismissing *Polyeucte* (§8). Like Husson, who disparages Corneille's play as 'un peu bourgeois', he is even alienated from his own class. Evrard opines alone. Still more anti-festive, and perhaps unique in the *Contes*, he may eat alone. It is clear that he stands alone. He is the new bourgeois individualist. Presumably he practises systematic fraud. So do the puppeteer and the Pope, according to the burlesque narrative. But there is a difference. The puppeteer and the Pope belong to popular culture and to religion. They deal in show and ritual, opium for the body and opium for the soul. Evrard deals directly in money. They are part of collectivities, they work with audiences and congregations ('coquins ... et superstitieux'?). Evrard, the new economic man, works alone.

Somewhat contrary to their own logic, however, these bourgeois are also reformists. Their aggressive language expresses not just pessimism about mankind but also anger directed at specific historical institutions. The second narrative began with the narrator and Husson anticipating the fall of the Jesuits. Both these bourgeois are pleased. Husson invokes a collective moral norm: 's'ils sont perdus comme tous les honnêtes gens le désirent ...'. His view of history however is not meliorist but cyclical: '... vous n'y gagnerez rien: vous serez accablé par la faction des jansénistes' (§2). Section 4 is less negative. The narrator reports Dumarsais decrying 'le plus grand des abus'. It is, he says, 'un grand malheur pour l'État' that state offices are sold to the wealthy rather than awarded on the basis of 'émulation' to the 'homme de mérite'. Here bourgeois individualist self-interest joins hands with the public interest as a force for reform.

Section 5 offers a fable showing that religious toleration has social and business advantages, and even a certain justice. This theme continues in Section 6, though it is couched as a criticism of Huguenot zeal, and ends with a shrug. In Section 10 Husson evokes 'la philosophie' and 'la raison humaine'. But he does so only in order to demonstrate, as in Section 12, the universality of human vice and folly. Section 13 begins with a ferociously laconic juxtaposition of sexuality, religious law and money. 'On peut ... aimer sa nièce; mais il en coûte ... quatre-vingt mille francs pour coucher avec sa nièce en légitime mariage.' The matter however becomes local and political when the narrator observes that remittances are 'payables à Rome'. He then estimates the number of dispensations from the Catholic consanguinity laws which are required, does a few sums, and reflects. All in all the kingdom of France pays to Rome

> environ huit millions quatre cent mille livres que nous donnons
> libéralement au Saint-Père par chacun an. Le fardeau serait lourd, tandis
> que nous avons des vaisseaux à construire, des armées et des rentiers à
> payer.
>   Je m'étonne que, dans l'énorme quantité de livres dont les auteurs ont
> gouverné l'État depuis vingt ans, aucun n'ait pensé à réformer ces abus.
> (§13)

The formulation remains sarcastic. But we have within it the key words
'abus' and 'réformer'. We have the confrontation of an ecclesiastical
interest with a national interest. This time we have the imbalance in hard
figures, quantified by the new economic science.

The last two sections of *Pot-pourri* repeat the form and the content of
this argument more forcefully. From the tale of his relation whose
farm-labourers refuse to work on Saint Barbe's Day, the narrator proceeds
inductively to an estimate of production lost nationally. Five million
French workers each gain twenty sous a day, but per year thirty working
days are wasted due to religious holidays, which makes ... (§14). From the
case of the massive wealth of the abbaye de Citeaux, M. Evrard explains
to the narrator the 'abus'. The abbé draws revenues of 150,000 livres per
year, while a 'pauvre curé de campagne' receives 100 écus (ie 300 livres).
The abbatial palace costing two millions could house twenty officers with
their families and breed more soldiers for the King's service. 'Les petits
moines ... deviendraient des membres de l'État au lieu qu'ils sont des
chancres qui le rongent' (§15).

The new bourgeois is sceptical yet punitive, cynical yet reformist. But
perhaps we can now construct a model which contains these contradictions.
The bourgeois lives in Paris (Husson; 'je'), presumably as a petty rentier
or a tradesman, with a degree of leisure time which he uses for reading and
discussing public issues privately with his male peers. Alternatively he is
an educated man 'réduit à enseigner le latin' (Dumarsais, §4). Or he is a
longtime servant of the Crown who now has a small farm (the 'parent',
§14). Or he is a nouveau riche who, despairing of seeing reforms enacted,
has joined the exploiters (Evrard, §15). He is respectable (identifies with
'les honnêtes gens'; ignores the puppetshows), and hostile to those who are
not. He works hard (the 'parent'), and objects to rewards for those who
do not (specifically, mendicants, drunken labourers and monks). He is

puritanical yet lewd; he is righteous but very pragmatic; his language is violent but his arguments are carefully quantified, in money terms. His limited income, perhaps also his trade, keep him very aware of material realities and sceptical of whatever is less verifiable. He is a 'have', but also a 'have not'. Seeing unearned wealth around him, he resents both those who have it and his own exclusion from it. He is intelligent and knowledgeable enough to see that public affairs are badly organised. This he blames on secular stupidity and religious exploitation. These in turn he may attribute to universal knavery, or to the specifics of class privilege and ecclesiastical abuse in contemporary France. He is a royalist, though perhaps principally for reasons of social order and national independence. He inclines to religious toleration, though mainly on pragmatic grounds and as a civil issue. He is not simply anti-clerical, for he shows some concern for the lower ranks of the secular clergy. Rather, he is anti-Rome, anti-Jesuit, anti-monacal and perhaps anti-episcopal. His religion is gallican, egalitarian and utilitarian. So, in effect, are his politics. He is not so much hard-hearted as hard-headed.

5. 2. ii.   *L'HOMME AUX QUARANTE ECUS*

This work was published in 1768. We shall consider it first in terms of literary development within the *Contes*. Secondly we shall look at it as a manifesto of the Enlightenment, principally in its latter part. However, it also reveals intense hostility towards new thinking in the natural sciences. Finally we shall try to identify not only philosophical but more intimate reasons for this reaction.

L'Homme aux quarante écus may be likened in various ways to *Pot-pourri*. It is similarly fragmented in form, narrative and theme. It consists of sixteen sections, which are titled (unlike those in *Pot-pourri*) but not numbered. First-person narration and third-person narration are both employed, as in *Pot-pourri*. Here however theatrical dialogue is also used. Shifts in narrative point of view occur. The narrating 'je' of the first five sections is the protagonist, but then 'je' takes on other identities or else vanishes, and the protagonist re-appears as 'il'. There is in fact little narrative action and much conversation. The eponymous protagonist begins as a poor peasant, his annual income of forty écus being precisely the national average. He ends as Parisian bourgeois in comfortable circumstances. But his modest odyssey functions principally as a peg on which analyses and reviews of reality may be hung. Through him - or occasionally without him - the work tackles a great variety of contemporary economic, scientific, political and cultural questions.[1]

The conversations are unbuttoned. The setting is domestic, the tone familiar. The protagonist and many of the other interlocutors are ordinary people, who address each other as 'mon cher monsieur' or 'mon cher

---

[1] There are two substantial studies of this work. Nuçi Kotta, *'L'Homme aux quarante écus': a Study of Voltairean Themes* (The Hague, 1966) deals entirely with content. Each of the many 'themes' is summmarised, and located in the context of Voltaire's other works or the period. Coverage is thorough and well-informed, though a little uncritical. The longest and perhaps the best chapter is on economics, notably the new school of thought known as Physiocracy which is Voltaire's primary target. Robert Ginsberg, 'The Argument of Voltaire's *L'Homme aux quarante écus*: a study in philosophical rhetoric', *SVEC* 56 (1967), pp.611-57, is more concerned with form. Arguing that we should avoid strict generic expectations, it presents the work as a hybrid whose purpose is persuasion. Each section is carefully analysed, and finally tabulated under a number of heads.

voisin'. The classical restraint of the earlier *Contes* has given way to a certain bourgeois informality. All this was true of *Pot-pourri*. *L'Homme aux quarante écus* however is considerably more developed. It is four times as long. Though narration is fragmented, narrative focus is fairly consistent. The title announces a principal protagonist. He is featured in most of the sections, including those at the start and end. In the initial sections, like the protagonists in most of the earlier *Contes*, he or his surrogates take the role of the Fool. Because they do not understand the world, they question it and are victimised by it. But now the questioning is much more systematic, and the world much more closely constraining. The French economic system, tax system and penal system are successively interrogated. Agricultural theories fail in practice; theories of generation leave the protagonist no wiser about his wife's pregnancy than before. Much of the first half of *Quarante écus* is a sort of narrative *Sottisier*, a saga of bourgeois bafflement, Voltaire's *Bouvard et P-écu-chet*.

The carnivalesque of the earlier *Contes* appears here in a new transposition. The world is shown as dislocated, inverted and arbitrary as before. But it is closer to our own world. Its follies are once more reviewed. But they are those of the here and now. Its languages are parodied and dismembered. Its clichés are shown forth in italics, and its beliefs in mocking enumerations. But the discourses and vocabulary are much more concrete. The protagonist is now defined quantitatively. His income, the national average, contrasts ironically with a reality in which income varies wildly. The world's incoherence is marked through the device of repeatedly expressing other financial data as multiples of 'quarante écus'. The joyous reviews, in the earlier part of the text, deal in concrete and even technical data. The sources of agricultural income are 'vins, étangs, bois, métaux, bestiaux, fruits, laines, soies, lait, huiles' (p.420). For ex-Jesuits there are other ways of making one's living. 'L'un est à la tête d'une manufacture d'étoffes, l'autre, de porcelaine; un autre entreprend l'opéra; celui-ci fait la gazette ecclésiastique; ...' (p.424). Tax systems come in many national varieties: 'Les Anglais ... . Les Chinois ...; ... au Japon ...; les Lapons et les Samoyèdes ...' (p.430). The body agricultural, the body ex-Jesuit and the body international are followed by the body human. A genetic theory is caricatured as 'l'oeil droit attire l'oeil gauche ..., mais il en est empêché par le nez ... . Il en est de même des bras, des cuisses et des jambes ...' (p.446). We have here, in the main, the carnivalisation of the new sciences.

We have too the appropriate carnivalesque response. The protagonist reacts with laughter. This is made explicit as early as the third section: 'Je me mis à rire, dans mon malheur' (p.419). Later he is able to generalise the reaction, and to move from rue to mockery: 'Il me prend quelquefois des envies de rire de tout ce qu'on m'a dit' (p.447). He or his surrogates can also perceive that the world is laughing at them. 'Boudot ... s'égaya ... à mes dépens' (p.438); 'votre ami ... a voulu rire' (p.452). The world beats the protagonist down. No less joyously it may raise him up.

> Monsieur le contrôleur général ... fit un grand éclat de rire, et me dit que c'était un tour qu'on m'avait joué [de me mettre en prison]. Il ordonna à ces mauvais plaisants de me donner cent écus de dédommagement, et m'exempta de la taille pour le reste de ma vie. (p.436)

However, in the new transposition there are more differences. It is the protagonist himself who voices the response of rueful laughter. In earlier *Contes* the reader was left to supply it. The realist transposition endows the protagonist with greater awareness. He is more self-conscious, and has the potential to understand. More exactly, in the first and last examples above, we see the awareness of the protagonist as narrator. But first-person narration, and the diegetic narrator, are equally a part of the shift towards literary realism.

Realism integrates the character more closely with circumstance and with experience. This we find in *Quarante écus*. Altered circumstances modify the protagonist. He has been exempted from paying the 'taille'. This happier turn of Fortune's wheel is the turn of his own fortunes. It is repeated when he marries, and later receives two modest inheritances. At the same time he continues to ask questions. But increasingly he has established his own views. He and his situation have changed. Now known as M. André, and living in Paris, he gives dinners. These are festive occasions, the more so through his capacity for bringing together persons of heterogeneous opinion.

> C'est un des bons convives que nous ayons [à Paris]; ... . Il aurait fait souper gaiement ensemble un Corse et un Génois, un représentant de Genève et un négatif, le muphti et un archevêque.

(The references are to the Corsican revolt against Genoa, and the dispute between the tiers of government in Geneva. Again we are dealing with the here and now.) His powers become proverbial. 'Toutes les fois qu'il s'élevait une dispute bien acariâtre ..., on disait aux deux partis: *Messieurs, allez souper chez M. André*' (pp.466-67).

The protagonist is now a master rather than a victim of the disorderly world. He has become one of the privileged. He is presented however as a plain man. His name is without pretension, and so is he. He is convivial - 'un des bons convives'. He has, we are told, 'une physionomie ronde qui est tout à fait persuasive' (p.467). If his sympathetic mien recalls Colin, he can also be as harsh as M. Husson. 'C'est un rude homme que M. André' (p.468). The merely fashionable are not invited to his table. 'Ni M. André ni moi ne soupons jamais avec cette bonne compagnie-là' (p.475), is the closing remark by the final narrator. The protagonist remains a bourgeois.

But the acquisition of a proper name itself marks a change. Essence has become development. 'L'Homme aux quarante écus', the emblematic Everyman, has left behind his essential attribute. Left behind too is the work's title. We noted this pattern in *L'Ingénu* - published just one year earlier. In that work we read of 'l'Ingénu, qui n'était plus l'*ingénu*'. Here we find textually a similar contradiction. 'L'homme aux quarante écus, qui était déjà l'homme aux deux cents écus pour le moins, ...' (p.443). In keeping with our differentiation of the two types of tale, the measure in *L'Ingénu* is qualitative, whereas here it is quantitative. But here quantity and quality go together. 'On ne peut guère tromper M. André. Plus il était simple et naïf quand il a été l'homme aux quarante écus, plus il est devenu avisé quand il a connu les hommes' (p.468). Like the Ingenu, he seems to have developed his capacities in considerable part through books. The advice of his friend, directed to all Frenchmen, is 'Lisez, éclairez-vous' (p.460). Whereas the Ingenu acquired wisdom, this man's characteristic is good sense. The penultimate section begins 'Comme le bon sens de M. André s'est fortifié depuis qu'il a une bibliothèque!'. Its title is 'Le Bon Sens de M. André'.

The latter half of the work affirms a belief in enlightenment and progress. These are the values of M. André. 'Il se félicite d'être né dans un temps où la raison humaine commence à se perfectionner' (p.469). But the formulation clearly implies that the narrator shares these values, and shares the view that they are actually being realised. 'Il [M. André] est aujourd'hui au fait de toutes les affaires de l'Europe, et surtout des progrès de l'esprit humain' (p.469). The latter concept is given the same factual status as the former (one may indeed be 'au fait' with both). It clearly carries narratorial authority. We cannot seriously doubt that the author subscribes to it too. Personification, employed by the narrator, leads to allegory, voiced directly by M. André:

> Il me semble ... que la Raison voyage à petites journées, du nord au midi, avec ses deux intimes amies, l'Expérience et la Tolérance. L'Agriculture et le Commerce l'accompagnent.

Joining the monologic chorus, Reason herself speaks:

> Je suis très bien reçue à Berlin, à Moscou, à Copenhague, à Stockholm. Il y a longtemps que par le crédit de Locke, de Gordon, de Trenchard, de milord Shaftesbury, et de tant d'autres, j'ai reçu mes lettres de naturalité en Angleterre. Vous m'en accorderez un jour. Je suis la fille du Temps, et j'attends tout de mon père. (pp.469-70)

As a model of the bourgeois Enlightenment, this account could hardly be bettered. The advent of Reason occurs in England. Its apostles are Locke and other deist or political writers. Its credo is empiricism and toleration, agricultural improvement and the development of trade. The new gospel has spread to the capital cities of several European states. By implication, thus, its agents are the rulers of those states. First on the list are Frederick of Prussia and Catherine of Russia. Its victory everywhere is only a matter of time.[2] All this is asserted in the section entitled 'Le Bon Sens de M. André'. The bourgeois Enlightenment seeks to pass itself off as plain good sense
    Particular elements of the programme are indicated elsewhere in the work. The final section, 'D'un Bon Souper chez M. André', ranges widely over high culture. Even literary controversies may be measured by Enlightenment values. 'On s'éleva contre ces mauvaises critiques, dictées par la haine nationale et le préjugé' (p.474). Internationalism is part of the credo. So of course is the attack on 'prejudice'. Ancient history is subjected to critical examination, and found to be fable. 'Mais enfin,' protests one of the guests, 'Thèbes, Memphis, Babylone, Ninive, Troie,

---

[2] 1768 is probably the high point of Voltaire's hopes for the establishment of an Enlightenment order by reformist oligarchies throughout Europe. A fuller version of M. André's survey is offered in the form of Amazan's journey in *La Princesse de Babylone* (also published in 1768), chs vi-xi. The *Éloge historique de la raison* (1775) finds further evidence of Reason's progress, but concludes less optimistically.

Séleucie, étaient de grandes villes, et n'existent plus'. The Modern reply is firm:

> Cela est vrai ..., mais Moscou, Constantinople, Londres, Paris, Amsterdam, Lyon, qui vaut mieux que Troie, toutes les villes de France, d'Allemagne, d'Espagne et du Nord, étaient alors des déserts. (p.471)

Human energy has built civilisation where there was nothing (except unimproved agriculture, presumably). The cities of Europe replace the cities of antiquity. Implicit in this parallel is a *translatio imperii*, from there and then to here and now. But mankind has gained more than it has lost. 'Lyon ... vaut mieux que Troie' is a radically progressive statement. It affirms that trade and manufactures are superior to received models of high culture. The nineteenth century will see the *translatio* realised in a new urban and imperialist system based on trade and manufactures.

Voltaire's principal target for reform is - as ever - the Church. But now much of the argument is economic. His protagonist, functioning as Fool, fails to understand the practice of annates. Why do the new incumbents of ecclesiastical benefices in France, awarded by the monarch, pay the first year's income to Rome? His interlocutor, computing the annual loss to French revenues at 40,000 livres, explains how the situation came about. The protagonist now understands, for 'il sait un peu d'histoire; il a du bon sens ... '. As a result, 'il parla longtemps avec énergie contre cet abus'. (We note the clear and insistent approval of the narrator - if not the author - declared by the two nouns.) Not that he is hostile to the clergy:

> Comme il révérait les évêques! comme il leur souhaitait beaucoup de quarante écus, afin qu'ils les dépensassent dans leurs diocèses en bonnes oeuvres! Il voulait aussi que tous les curés de campagne eussent un nombre de quarante écus suffisant pour les faire vivre avec décence.

The constant disputes of impoverished country priests with their parishioners over money 'détruisent la considération qu'on leur doit' (p.454). There is not much indication that this emphasis on the need for respect is ironic. Reverence for the bishops seems a little overstated. The repeated reference to 'quarante écus' as the unit of measurement is comic. But the call for beneficent local action by the episcopacy and a decent salary for the lower clergy is surely authorised. The underlying concern here is the establishment of good order.

The practice of annates was also attacked by the bourgeois in *Pot-pourri* (where the estimate of annual loss was 50% higher!). But there the stress was on satire, and the tone contemptuous. Here we have a positive alternative, which looks towards a new civic ideal. The tone of the speaker in this section is finally dithyrambic, that of the narrator no less so:

> Ce digne homme s'attendrissait en prononçant ces paroles; il aimait sa patrie, et était idolâtre du bien public. Il s'écriait quelquefois: 'Quelle nation que la française, si on voulait!' (pp.454-55)

Whereas the secular clergy should be strengthened, the regulars should be abolished. We can identify three reasons. 'Sont-ils plus utiles que moi à la patrie?', demands the 'Homme'. The reply is evident, for the monks produce nothing. By the suppression of the religious orders, 'leurs maisons deviendraient des hôtels de ville, des hôpitaux, des écoles publiques, ou seraient affectées à des manufactures'. The new values are implicitly defined here: the civic, the charitable, the educational and the industrial. 'La patrie auraient plus d'hommes utiles et moins de malheureux.' Alongside these arguments from patriotism and utility comes the argument from humanity. The third argument is that celibacy would destroy mankind: 'le genre humain serait perdu'. In sum, the contrary position is 'inhumaine, antipatriotique, destructive de la société' (p.451). But is the convent not a necessary refuge for young women? No, for if married they would be 'bien meilleures épouses, bien meilleures mères'. Instead of becoming nuns, the narrator adds, 'elles apprendront à filer, à coudre, à faire de la dentelle, à broder, à se rendre utiles' (p.452). It is not clear whether the second model necessarily comes within the first. To the bourgeois ideal of the woman as domestic wife and mother (we are told that the protagonist's wife breastfeeds their son: p.455), may be added that of the woman as productive seamstress.

The same types of arguments are deployed in the section on legal punishments. Indiscriminate application of the death penalty is simply inefficient. 'On a déjà dit, et il faut répéter, qu'un pendu n'est bon à rien, et que les supplices doivent être utiles' (p.455). It is also ineffective. 'Il faut effrayer le crime; oui, sans doute; mais le travail forcé et la honte durable l'intimident plus que la potence.' (Workhouses and social shame offer another glimpse of the nineteenth century on the horizon.) The essential principle is stated. 'Proportionnez les peines aux délits.' But the

majority of this section is concerned with the practice of judicial torture -
still regular procedure in eighteenth-century France. The matter is
introduced existentially. The narrator tells us how the 'Homme' one day
came to him in tears. As a witness in the case of a suspect, later proved
innocent, he had been required to attend his torture.   He concludes
'J'entends encore ses cris et ses hurlements; ils me poursuivent, je pleure
de pitié, et je tremble d'horreur'. The narrator adds 'Je me mis à pleurer
et à frémir aussi, car je suis extrêmement sensible'.

   This primary response to suffering is later evoked, in practically the
same terms, by a third character.   A provincial judge has written a
denunciation of the cruelty of French procedure.   He demands *'Quel
magistrat, un peu sensible à ses devoirs, à la seule humanité, pourrait
soutenir ces idées ... sans frémir d'horreur et de pitié ... ?'.*
He continues:

> *Ne lui semble-t-il pas entendre des voix gémissantes ... le presser de
> décider du sort d'un citoyen, d'un époux, d'un père, d'une famille? ...
> 'C'est donc moi, dira-t-il, qui retiens dans ce détestable séjour mon
> semblable, peut-être mon égal, mon concitoyen, un homme enfin!'* (p.458)

Prison is no longer a comic ritual; it is a fearful experience. Here is the
shift that we noted in *L'Ingénu*. This time the subjective experience is
generalised, but it is also intensified, and relayed through empathetic
models for ourselves within the fiction.   The pompous language, the
breathless style (rhetorical questions, exclamations, deictics, repetition) and
the recourse to direct speech itself, are general characteristics of the new
writing. Especially typical of the period preceding the Revolution is the
attempt to combine the most immediate and non-verbal appeal - the cries
heard and imagined, the scene witnessed or imagined (*'ici un spectacle
effrayant se présente tout à coup à mes yeux'*), the physiological response
of the subject - with a vocabulary of righteous abstractions. The extracts
from the judge's pamphlet are described as fragments 'que l'éloquence
avait dictés à l'humanité'. No longer is verbal language liable to comic
accidents in transmission.   Truth, feeling, speech and writing are one.
Indeed the successive voices, as with the march of Reason, say the same
thing. Here the watchwords are humanity, citizenship and family.

   Peroration is confined to the latter part of the work. Comic and satiric
elements however also appear there.   On the other hand, reformism is
present in the earlier sections as well. A progressivist ethos can be traced

from the start. In the very first section the 'Homme' tells us how he was launched on his way. 'Le curé de ma paroisse, qui a toujours eu de l'amitié pour moi, m'a enseigné un peu de géométrie et d'histoire, et je commence à réfléchir, ce qui est très rare dans ma province' (p.416). We note the recognition of the primary role - potential if not actual - of the *curé de campagne.* 'Un peu d'histoire' will be used to reveal that current practices, where unsatisfactory, are no more than the survival of earlier barbarity and ignorance. Geometry seems to signify a principle of quantification or scientific analysis. But perhaps it also hints at an immanent order. This text does not mention the Divine Geometer; but the section on appropriate degrees of punishment is entitled 'Des Proportions'.

In the course of the tale, the protagonist will be instructed chiefly by a 'Géomètre'. The topics are economics, statistics and biology. On the social scourge of syphilis, the instruction will be given by an army surgeon. As a doctor, we may suggest, he combines dispassionate science with human commitment. The geometer may be seen as a fuller version of the same. We are told initially that he has produced both an actuarial table of life expectancies and a project for bringing piped water to Paris. Thus he is both a scientific analyst and a practical improver. He is described on his first appearance as 'un citoyen philosophe' (p.419). Both these terms have a particular sense in the eighteenth century. The 'philosophe' seeks to bring knowledge and critical reason into the social domain. The 'citoyen' aims to serve his fellows and his country. The protagonist eventually earns the double accolade. After instruction from the geometer and the surgeon, M. André is described as 'notre nouveau philosophe' (p.465). When he tries to reconcile warring factions he is called 'un excellent citoyen' (p.466).

L'Homme aux quarante écus is the most progressive of all the *Contes.* It advocates a number of concrete social and political reforms. They are argued in terms of Enlightenment liberalism but also of a proto-industrialism (Lyon) and of the new republican values ('citoyen', 'patrie'). At the same time it is, in another way, perhaps the most reactionary of all the *Contes.* Its economic stance is mainly retrograde. So is its position on agricultural innovations. Its science is a disgrace and a puzzle. We shall look now at this other side of 'le bon sens bourgeois'.

The unsatisfactory nature of the long section on economics is generally recognised. On the simplest level critics point to a rudimentary error in calculation, or an internal inconsistency.[3]   In what purports to be a scientific analysis by a geometer these are not trivial flaws.   More fundamentally, although Voltaire justly exposes through satire the illogic of the Physiocratic single tax, he seems to accept the theory of value underlying it. Kotta very usefully observes that he was not alone. Hume, and even Adam Smith, also failed to reject the argument that agricultural production is the primary source of value. Voltaire however, unlike these two, also adopts Mercantilist positions. National wealth resides in specie; capital outflow must be minimised by controlling imports, especially of luxury goods. This results in contradictions within the work. It is also a strange negation of Voltaire's own earlier views. The earlier Voltaire had argued for free trade and maximum consumption. Formerly well ahead of his time, Voltaire in *Quarante écus* is well behind it.[4]

For my own reading, the interest of the section on economics resides not just in the incoherences of 'le bon sens'. It lies in Voltaire's shift from an optimistic to a pessimistic position. In *Quarante écus* the protagonist's first two interlocutors affirm that the good time was in the past. The 'Vieillard' regrets the age of Henri IV, when France did not have to 'payer à nos voisins' for 'toutes ces superfluités' (pp.415-16). The geometer says that man is now living in 'le siècle de fer' (p.424). Trade is no longer a mutually beneficial activity uniting the nations - as in *Zadig*. It is a struggle which some must lose. 'Ainsi ils ne pourront avoir de l'argent sans que d'autres en perdent', concludes the protagonist. 'C'est la loi de toutes les nations; on ne respire qu'à ce prix', affirms the Geometer (p.426). The first of these two quotations harks back to the Mercantilism of the seventeenth century. The second, with its metaphors of law and biology, hints at the economic Darwinism of the nineteenth century.

If such thinking is harsh, at least it is hard-headed. The same cannot be said for the instruction that the protagonist receives in other scientific domains. New agricultural techniques are listed or reviewed mockingly. All, including Jethro Tull's practice of sowing in rows, are dismissed (pp.437-8). A proposition in pure geometry is treated as a question of sincerity. The protagonist rejects it 'dans le fond de son âme'. What he

---

[3] Pléiade edition, p.450, note 1; p.425, note 1.

[4] The changes are clearly demonstrated by Kotta, *op.cit.*, pp.72-82. On Hume and Adam Smith, see *ibid.*, pp.62-67.

calls 'un géomètre de meilleure foi' tells him that the proposition pertains to 'ce qui ne peut être dans la nature, ... des chimères idéales'. He concludes that this is an admission of 'la charlatanerie jusque dans la science' (p.419). The proponents of new agricultural techniques are finally dismissed in the same terms. 'Mon cher monsieur, encore une fois, gardez-vous des charlatans' (p.438). In both these domains it would seem that 'le bon sens' is to be identified with 'la bonne foi'. Its enemies lack both.

The next two sections deal with the natural sciences. Each theory is labelled as a 'système' and caricatured. Most are dismissed. To their progenitors is imputed not so much bad faith as folly. The speculations of Maillet and the experimental results of Needham are rolled up together, while Buffon's support of the latter is also mocked. The latter section offers a review of theories of generation. Ancient and Scholastic thinking (Hippocrates, Sanchez) is of course rejected. Harvey's ovism is treated more sympathetically. 'Deux Hollandais' (Leuwenhoeck and Hartsoeker) and the Frenchman Andry are bracketed together as proponents of what we may call animalculism. But the title of 'maître fou' is reserved for Maupertuis (not named; but the allusion is quite clear). The conclusion in each section favours 'le doute' (pp.442, 447). The Geometer points out that among theologians such differences would result in violence. 'Mais entre des physiciens la paix est bientôt faite.' Each scientist breeds with his wife 'sans demander seulement comment ce mystère s'opère' (p.447).

What precedes this conciliatory conclusion, however, is neither peaceable nor scientific. Its satiric violence is objectionable not just through repetitiveness, or even because most of the targets have our respect. It is objectionable because it blatantly negates the standards of the 'citoyen philosophe' preached elsewhere in the work. Instead of humanity and rationality, we have here personal vendettas and very bad science. The first of the two sections itself invites us to hear in it Voltaire's own voice. Its fictional author is described at the start as 'un vieux solitaire'. At the end he notes 'j'aime quelquefois à répéter mes contes, afin de les inculquer mieux' (p.442). This looks very much like an authorial wink. Given the similar stance taken in the other three 'scientific' sections by their principal fictional speakers (the 'Homme', the Letter-writer and the Geometer), we have internal evidence for assigning the whole assault to Voltaire himself.

How do we explain this assault? Kotta offers a good discussion of 'Voltaire and science' (pp.26-37). Conceding that his attitude had become

'negative and mocking', Kotta weighs several possible reasons. He cites
Grimm on Voltaire: 'jamais il n'aura le flegme nécessaire à un
observateur, jamais il n'aura assez peu d'imagination'. Concurring with
the former assertion, Kotta reverses the latter. But clearly Grimm is right
too. Voltaire had too little imagination to take on board certain new ways
of seeing. But this is partly because he had too much imagination, always
trying to assimilate empirical data into just the kind of metaphysical
systems he claims to deplore. This brings us to a second reason. Voltaire's
own 'esprit de système' (Kotta *dixit*) has not only a positive source in his
Deism. It also has a negative source, in his desire to rebut any scientific
position which appears to favour Judeo-Christianity. Maillet's notion that
man emerged from the sea might seem to support the story of the Flood.
The discovery in the falun of Touraine of the fossils of sea-creatures - an
identification repeatedly mocked by Voltaire in the same section - was
indeed seen as confirming the Biblical tale. A third reason adduces the
other pole of Voltaire's fears. Kotta cites René Pomeau on Voltaire's
perception in the 1760s of a link between the new science and atheism.
The atheists eagerly followed experiments such as those of Needham,
which served to demonstrate the possibility of spontaneous generation.
Floods and fossils imply a dynamism in nature, and fit badly into a theory
of Divine order.

   The third account is the most productive. We shall develop it through
other elements within this particular work. After attacking the genetic
theories of Maupertuis through caricature, Voltaire judges them more
directly.

   Ce grand philosophe n'admet aucun dessein de l'Etre créateur dans la
   formation des animaux. Il est bien loin de croire que le coeur soit fait pour
   recevoir le sang et pour le chasser, l'estomac pour digérer, les yeux pour
   voir, les oreilles pour entendre: cela lui paraît trop vulgaire. (p.446)

Strongly implied here are the argument from Design and the argument
from Final Causes. These are the two proofs of the Divinity most favoured
in this period by Voltaire. (Favoured too, according to him, by 'vulgaire'
thinking - another version of 'le bon sens'.) We should note also that the
two sections on the natural sciences are preceded by an apparently
pointless assertion to the effect that 'Dieux a fait les Caraïbes rouges, ainsi
que les nègres noirs' (p.438). God, that is, has established fixed species.
But we can go further. Throughout Voltaire's treatment of apparently

disparate issues in natural science, certain motifs appear. The first of the two sections juxtaposes Maillet on the paleo-history of men, fossils and mountains, with Needham on the experimental production of live matter. The second is on theories of generation and genetics. All, that is, are concerned with origins. We glimpse what Voltaire sees as the alternative to orderly Deism. It is a world of fragmentation, change and flow.

Voltaire begins his attack on Maillet, Needham and Maupertuis with a sweeping assertion. '[Ils] se sont mis sans façon à la place de Dieu' (p.439). He addresses Maillet sarcastically as 'monsieur le créateur' and 'Votre Providence' (pp.440-41). The question treated throughout the latter section is announced as 'comment les enfants se font' (p.443). 'Faire un enfant' (p.443) is rivalled by the enterprise of Needham who in Voltaire's account 'fit des anguilles'. If flour could engender eels, 'on ne douta pas alors qu'on ne fît des hommes' (p.441). Maillet's paleo-history is another usurpation. '[Il] m'apprit que les montagnes et les hommes sont produits par les eaux de la mer' (p.439). Voltaire's account of Maillet continues

Il y eut d'abord de beaux hommes marins qui ensuite devinrent amphibies. Leur belle queue fourchue se changea en cuisses et en jambes. J'étais encore tout plein des *Métamorphoses* d'Ovide. (p.439)

Later he summarises Maillet's doctrine as 'les poissons changés en hommes, et les eaux changées en montagnes' (p.412). Much of the second section deals with ovist and animalculist theories of generation. The review ends by suggesting that man goes through successive pre-natal stages, similarly to lepidoptera. 'Ensuite, si la chenille devient papillon, nous devenons hommes: voilà nos métamorphoses' (p.446). The motifs of change and metamorphosis are clear. It is no longer so clear, in the last example, that they are to be regarded as entirely nonsensical. Harvey's ovism is the theory of human generation treated most sympathetically. The Newtonian dictum, 'la nature est toujours semblable à elle-même', indicates that this must apply in some sense to all species. The Geometer concludes that 'tout vient d'un oeuf'. He adds 'et notre globe est un grand oeuf qui contient tous les autres'. The 'Homme' opines that 'ce système porte tous les caractères de la vérité' (p.444). But the global egg could be a version of the doctrine of the preformation of germs, or of *deus sive natura*. In any case one cannot tell whether it is serious or satirical. Voltaire's text, perhaps despite his intentions, has become ambivalent.

His own ambivalence is not just intellectual, but evident on a more intimate level. His burlesque now offers a vision of organic change. Engendering is linked to flow. Maillet believes that water once covered the world. He has man emerging from 'les eaux de la mer' as a hybrid. Leuwenhoeck and Hartsoeker, at the other end of the scale, set out to 'examiner la liqueur séminale au microscope'. What they discover is described as 'ces petits animaux qui frétillent', then as 'ces petits hommes qui sont si bons nageurs' (p.445).

Disgust is not far away. It is linked with engendering metonymically when the protagonist asks where within the body the foetus is located. 'Entre la vessie et l'intestin rectum', is the reply. ' - O Dieu paternel, s'écria-t-il, l'âme immortelle de mon fils née et logée entre l'urine et quelque chose de pis!' (p.443). It is aroused, curiously, by a scholastic debate on the engendering of Jesus. Father Sanchez in his *De Matrimonio* 'examine, chapitre xxi du livre second, *utrum virgo Maria semen emiserit in copulatione cum Spiritu Sancto'*. The protagonist duly asks what the Latin means. 'Le Géomètre lui traduisit le texte, et tous deux frémirent d'horreur' (p.443). The references to the soul, and to the Virgin Mary and Sanchez, indicate that these juxtapositions are intended to debase the spiritual pretensions of Christianity. It is evident however that the blasphemy is in the mind not of Sanchez but of Voltaire. It is Voltaire who is so disturbed by the juxtaposition of urine and semen with engendering. Its locus, we might add, is not just the body but the female body. Though this is not specified in the first reply, the 'Homme' in response appeals to a specifically male principle. A 'Dieu paternel' is the Creator. Female corporality cannot create. Random flow - 'les eaux' or 'la liqueur séminale' - cannot be the origin.[5]

Flow is linked at the start of the text with change, and with bodily parts. Again we find in Voltaire's burlesque hints of abhorrence. In his account of the evolution of Maillet's marine creatures, 'leur belle queue fourchue se changea en cuisses et en jambes'. Fishes do indeed have forked tails, but so does the Devil. It is indeed true that a tail, in order to become the lower part of a human being, would have to change at its base into 'cuisses'. But 'les cuisses' have a heavily sexual and female connotation. He also likens the so-called fossils to 'langues' and to 'parties naturelles du beau sexe' (p.440). The lewdness of the latter comparison

---

[5] Our reading of *Jenni* is confirmed in a number of respects, albeit briefly, by indications here.

invites us to interpret the former in the same way. At the end of the review of genetics we have '[l]es bras, [l]es cuisses et [l]es jambes', then '[l]es mamelles et [l]es fesses' (p.446). The grotesque body, in this transposition, is not joyously but violently satiric. It is exhibited with a degree of revulsion.

The response explicitly recommended is a general scepticism. Towards the end of each of the two sections on natural science, the protagonist and the geometer conclude in favour of 'le doute'. The geometer thematises the principle, and extends it very widely.

> Je vous conseille de douter de tout, excepté que les trois angles d'un triangle sont égaux à deux droits, et que les triangles qui ont même base et même hauteur sont égaux entre eux, ou autres propositions pareilles, comme, par exemple, que deux et deux font quatre. (p.447)

Here is 'le bon sens' at its most basic. It seems impossible to reconcile with the 'bon sens' which proposes a programme of civic reform. In *Pot-pourri* scepticism dominated. Here the bias goes the other way. Both texts show the ambivalence of bourgeois good sense. However, neither version of pragmatism suffices. Like Voltaire himself, the protagonist continues to ignore his own wisdom. 'Oui, je crois qu'il est fort sage de douter; mais je sens que je suis curieux ...' (p.447). He wants to understand not only physics but metaphysics. He lists numerous questions which puzzle him, including mind-body relations and human freedom in relation to God's omniscience. In this context he is able to reintegrate the spiritual and the physiological. 'Mes sensations ... m'étonnent ...; j'y trouve du divin, et surtout dans le plaisir' (p.448). Our final *conte* will take up this materialist revelation.

5. 2. iii *LES OREILLES DU COMTE DE CHESTERFIELD*

Les Oreilles du comte de Chesterfield et le chapelain Goudman, probably the last to be published of all the *Contes*, appeared in 1775. Like *Zadig*, nearly forty years earlier, it is concerned with the doctrine of necessity. 'Ah! La fatalité gouverne irrémédiablement toutes les choses de ce monde!' is the incipit of the work. Comparison with *Zadig ou la Destinée* however shows some of the changes in writing that have occurred. Many mark the shift from romance to realism. The mysterious and ancient Orient has become contemporary and local London. Zadig possessed of all the advantages becomes Goudman the penurious ordinand. Zadig is successively slave and hero, whereas Goudman leads the bourgeois life of the everyday. In *Zadig* narration is omniscient, and we open with the traditional fabulation of 'il y avait ...'. *Chesterfield* opens with the new effects of immediacy and authenticity - an exclamation voiced by the protagonist as narrator. In the early tale good and bad are quite clear. Fate simply reverses their consequences; and finally all is set right to inaugurate 'le plus beau siècle de la terre'. In *Chesterfield* the world remains disorderly. Most notably, in *Zadig* the discourse is ethical and humanist. *Chesterfield* calls upon the New World and the new natural sciences. Its discourse is principally physiological.

I shall first summarise this tale, which is among the less well-known. We shall compare it with the other two 'bon sens' tales, and contrast it with its contemporary *Jenni*. Then we shall be concerned principally with two aspects of *Chesterfield*: a religion of human sexual engendering, and - yet - a deeply antipathetic view of humanity and its bodily functions.

Goudman fails to obtain a benefice within the gift of Lord Chesterfield, because his patron has defective hearing. 'Mon plus grand mal est la pauvreté' is misheard as 'un grand mal à la vessie'. Instead of getting the living, and with it his *inamorata* Miss Fidler, Goudman finds himself fending off the surgeon. The latter, M. Sidrac, urges him 'Ne soyez plus prêtre, ..., et faites-vous philosophe' (iii, p.580). The majority of the text then consists of conversations, in which Goudman and Sidrac are soon joined by Dr Grou. The discussions range successively over generation, the soul, necessity, human folly, the sexual religion of Tahiti, venereal disease, the effects of bowel movements on our moral dispositions, and paleo-geology. The trio are then interrupted, and the tale concludes fairly promptly. It transpires that Goudman's successful rival has found Miss Fidler to be suffering from syphilis, has separated from her and been deprived of the living. Goudman gets the benefice. We are told that he enjoys Miss Fidler on the quiet, and when necessary he is cured of the consequences by M. Sidrac. He has become one of the fiercest clerics in England, and is more convinced than ever that fatality is everything.

Within this short text, the modes of presentation greatly vary. The tale begins with Goudman narrating his own story. Chapter iii switches to impersonal narration. The discussions are set out mainly but not entirely in the form of theatrical dialogue. The impersonal narrator takes over again for the last few pages. We noted something of the same contradiction (diegetic narrator, multiple presentation) in *Pot-pourri* and *Quarante écus*. In all three we might say that it mirrors the disorder of the new realist world, and the heterogeneity of the topics discussed.

Conversation nevertheless increasingly dominates. As in *Pot-pourri* there is a certain unity of tone. Within each the discussants, middle-aged bourgeois, are to some extent interchangeable. However, as in *Quarante écus*, the protagonist is clearly designated. Goudman like the putative M. André begins as a 'pauvre'. His income is specified. Though in this case it is clearly unearned (iii, p.581), 'trente guinées' sounds very like 'quarante écus'. Both men are also provincials. Realist versions of the *naïf*, they consciously seek instruction. Both converse lengthily with men of science. Both finish in comfortable circumstances. Goudman is told, as M. André came to realise, that 'nous sommes dans un siècle de raison'. Agreement is possible, for 'nous cherchons le vrai de bonne foi' (iv, p.582). Goudman however has none of the reformist concerns of M. André. In England, perhaps, they are not needed. But he shares with the various bourgeois of *Pot-pourri* a resentment of the wealthy and a desire to join them.

The most obvious comparison is with *Jenni*. Both tales are written and published in 1774-75. Both are 'English'. One might almost say that both are Anglican. Goudman and Freind alike are ministers of the Church of England. Indeed both men are designated as 'chapelain' on the first page of the narrative. Their names, Freind and Goudman, seem to signal a shared ethical quality. The tale however does little to suggest that Goudman is a good man. By temperament and role he seems to function not as 'excellent homme' but as 'bonhomme' or 'goodman'.[1] Freind by contrast extends his friendship from a position of privilege. He is an MP and a Member of the Royal Society. His scientific links moreover are purely emblematic or exemplary. They have no function in the story, and little in the debates. His status as 'docteur en théologie' on the other hand is clearly relevant to his conversion of the Catholic and the atheist.[2] His discourse is ethical and social. Goudman however is instructed by two physicians. Sidrac is a 'chirurgien' - we recall this tutelary role in *Quarante écus*. He is complemented by 'le docteur Grou ... un médecin fort instruit' (iv, p.586). Their discourse is principally of bodies.

'Il n'y a point de nature, tout est art.' This epigrammatic assertion is foregrounded in both tales (*Jenni*, viii, p.632; *Chesterfield*, ii, p.578). But rather different lessons are drawn from it. In *Jenni* it prefaces an exposition of order and finalism.

> Portez ... vos yeux sur vous-même; ... tout y est construit en dedans et en dehors pour tous vos usages ... . Depuis la racine des cheveux jusqu'aux orteils des pieds, tout est art, tout est préparation, moyen et fin. Et en vérité, on ne peut que se sentir de l'indignation contre ceux qui osent nier les véritables causes finales ... . Avouons que chaque animal rend témoignage au suprême fabricateur. (viii, p.633)

Nature's art not only demonstrates a Maker. It evidences a Divine purpose, by proving the doctrine of Final Causes. In *Chesterfield* Final Causes are not mentioned. Both texts affirm the supremacy of the Divinity over all things human. But *Jenni* proclaims both the Divine order, 'sa providence générale', and human freewill, 'la liberté que ce grand Etre leur a donnée' (ix, p.642). *Chesterfield* does not affirm human liberty. On the

---

[1] I am inclined to see an onomastic line of English popular foolery in the protagonists of the three 'bon sens' tales. We noted Mr Punch and Merry Hissing in *Pot-pourri*. In *Quarante écus* 'M. André' seems to offer an echo of Merry Andrew. Here we have Goudman/Goodman and Miss Fid[d]ler. The onomastics of 'Sidrac' and 'Grou', however, leave me baffled.

[2] It is worth noting that the historical Freind was a doctor of medicine: see Pléiade ed., p.1228. Voltaire has in effect suppressed this corporeal dimension, as Freind himself suppresses the female bodily principle represented by Boca Vermeja, Las Nalgas and Clive-Hart. The 'guérison' achieved by Freind, celebrated in the exurgit of *Jenni*, is not medical but moral.

contrary, according to that text we are 'les marionnettes de la Providence' (iv, p.584). Providence here is a principle of determinism. God too is subjected to this principle. 'Dieu est donc esclave tout comme moi?' asks Goudman. 'Il est esclave de sa volonté, de sa sagesse, des propres lois qu'il a faites, de sa nature nécessaire' (pp.585-86). In *Jenni* the emphasis is placed on Divine purpose and human freedom. In *Chesterfield* both the Divine and the human are subordinated to a universal necessity.[3]

In *Jenni* Divine pre-eminence is immediately given an ethical significance. 'Je sais qu'il est notre maître, qu'il fait tout, que nous devons tout attendre de sa bonté' (viii, p.635). In *Chesterfield* this ethical dimension is absent. 'Il est notre maître, voilà tout ce que je sais' (iv, p.583). *Jenni* affirms human access to the ethical order, through 'la voix de votre conscience' (x, p.648). *Chesterfield* says nothing about conscience. *Jenni* demands 'la croyance d'un Dieu rénumérateur des bonnes actions, punisseur des méchantes' (ix, p.653). *Chesterfield* says nothing about a God of rewards and punishments. *Jenni* however also briefly urged ethical conduct on what seems to be a principle of imitation. 'Dieu existe, ..., il est juste. Soyez donc justes' (ix, p.645). *Chesterfield* does not say that God is just. But it echoes the last clause, and glosses it as a religious disposition. 'Faisons notre devoir envers Dieu, adorons-le, soyons justes; voilà nos vraies louanges et nos vraies prières' (iv, p.586). This in fact the only point in *Chesterfield* where a moral obligation is clearly affirmed. The principle underlying it is not utilitarian, not even ethical, but spiritual.

True praise and prayer in *Chesterfield* is constituted by giving a religious sense to the source of life. The focus of religion is not social and ethical order, as in *Jenni*. It is sexuality and engendering. This is the teaching of both Sidrac and Grou. The notion is first suggested by Goudman himself. He has just arrived at the realisation - or revelation - that all nature is art. He proceeds to what is for him its most wondrous instance. The general is linked to the personal:

Ce qui m'étonne, et ce qui me plaît le plus, c'est que, par cet art

---

[3] For a different view, arguing for the similarity of intellectual positions in *Jenni* and *Chesterfield*, see R. Virolle, 'Voltaire et les matérialistes, d'après ses derniers contes', *Dix-huitième Siècle* 11 (1979), pp.63-74.

incompréhensible, deux machines en produisent toujours une troisième; et
je suis bien fâché de n'en avoir pas fait une avec miss Fidler.

Sidrac concurs, but he modifies and develops the general proposition:

Oui, il est fort plaisant que deux êtres en produisent un troisième; mais cela
n'est pas vrai de tous les êtres. Deux roses ne produisent point une
troisième rose en se baisant. .... . Le grand, le beau miracle continuel, est
qu'un garçon et une fille fassent un enfant ensemble, qu'un rossignol fasse
un rossignolet à sa rossignole, et non pas à une fauvette. Il faudrait passer
la moitié de sa vie à les imiter, et l'autre moitié à bénir celui qui inventa
cette méthode. Il y a dans la génération mille secrets tout à fait curieux.
Newton dit que la nature se ressemble partout: *Natura est ubique sibi
consona*. Cela est faux en amour; les poissons, les reptiles, les oiseaux, ne
font point l'amour comme nous: c'est une variété infinie. La fabrique des
êtres sentants et agissants me ravit. (ii, p.579)

Implicit in Sidrac's declaration is the doctrine of fixed species.   His
'continual miracle' is a statement about biological order as much as about
engendering itself.   But he is equally moved by the infinite variety of
modes of engendering - even to the point of contradicting a Newtonian
formula.   Like Goudman, he juxtaposes without difficulty sexual pleasure
and religious awe.   One's own life should be spent engendering and
praising, practising the Divine act and thanking the Divinity.
    Dr Grou has travelled the world. Goudman, still seeking instruction,
asks him which among the many religions he has encountered is the most
pleasing. Grou replies

C'est celle de l'île d'Otaïti, sans aucune comparaison. J'ai parcouru les
deux hémisphères, je n'ai rien vu comme Otaïti et sa religieuse reine.
C'est dans Otaïti que la nature habite.

Tahiti is generously endowed by nature with fertile soil, game, vegetables
and fruits.

Mais il y a un besoin plus naturel, plus doux, plus universel, que la religion
d'Otaïti ordonne de satisfaire en public. C'est de toutes les cérémonies
religieuses la plus respectable sans doute. (v, pp.588-89)

Grou proceeds to tell Goudman and Sidrac of the Tahitian ritual.   A
handsome youth and a pretty girl 'sacrifice' together on an altar.   This
sexual ceremony is directed by the Queen and watched by a thousand
Tahitians 'dans un silence respectueux'. Goudman - now remarkably well

informed - assigns to this 'fête sacrée' universal validity.

> Je suis persuadé que c'est la première fête que les hommes aient jamais
> célébrée; et je ne vois pas pourquoi on ne prierait pas Dieu lorsqu'on va
> faire un être à son image, ... Travailler à faire naître une créature
> raisonnable est l'action la plus noble et la plus sainte. C'est ainsi que
> pensaient les premiers Indiens qui révérèrent le Lingam, symbole de la
> génération; les anciens Egyptiens qui portaient en procession le Phallus; les
> Grecs qui érigèrent des temples à Priape.

He concludes by evoking once more his own motif. 'Plût à Dieu que je
pusse sacrifier avec miss Fidler devant la reine Obéira en tout bien et en
tout honneur! Ce serait assurément le plus beau jour et la plus belle action
de ma vie' (vi, pp.589-90).

The sexual act, says Goudman, is a religious act. It is indeed the
primary act of religion. In spiritual terms it is the most holy undertaking.
Historically it is at the origin of all forms of collective worship. 'Natural
religion', we may observe, acquires a new meaning. This primary religion
is not however indiscriminate. Grou avers that the ritual is 'respectable'.
Goudman insists that 'l'institution est toujours innocente et pure', devoid
of 'libertinage' (p.590). Religion is still normative, thus excluding the
disorderly tendencies in sexual desire. That desire moreover is understood
in terms of a finality. As the act of generation, sexual coupling is
recuperated for finalism. It retains nevertheless its status as the truest
prayer and praise to God. And the finality is life itself.

But this is only part of the thematised meaning of *Chesterfield*. All the
interlocutors revere the act of generation. All however also view man with
contempt and disgust. Goudman characterises human beings as 'pleins de
passions, d'orgueil et de misère' (iv, p.584). Sidrac, having investigated
theories of the soul, delivers his assessment. 'De quelque côté que je me
tourne, je ne trouve qu'obscurité, contradiction, impossibilité, ridicule,
rêveries, impertinence, chimère, absurdité, bêtise, charlatanerie' (iv, p.584).
For Grou, Tahiti contrasts with the rest of humankind.

> Je n'ai vu ailleurs que des masques, je n'ai vu que des fripons qui trompent
> des sots, des charlatans qui escamotent l'argent des autres pour avoir de
> l'autorité, et qui escamotent de l'autorité pour avoir de l'argent
> impunément. (v, p.588)

Sidrac's denunciation recalls the attack on the sciences in *Quarante écus*.
Grou's brutal judgement on humankind recalls the world of M. Evrard and

Polichinelle in *Pot-pourri*. Indeed Grou goes further. Like Birton in *Jenni* (vii, p.627), he claims to find everywhere 'des anthropophages' (v, p.588). Having enjoyed their own meal, the three philosophers shift from anger to amusement. The narrator - now impersonal - seems to share their view.

> Comme ils devenaient un peu plus gais sur la fin du repas, selon la coutume des philosophes qui dînent, on se divertit à parler de toutes les misères, de toutes les sottises, de toutes les horreurs qui affligent le genre animal ... . Cette diversité d'abominations ne laisse pas d'être fort amusant. (v, p.587)

Chapter vi, the celebration of Tahiti, has its pendant in the next chapter. Chapter vii begins: 'Le lendemain les trois philosophes agitèrent la grande question: quel est le premier mobile de toutes les actions des hommes.' Here each takes a different view. According to Goudman - the *naïf* projecting his own concerns upon reality - 'le principe de tout était l'amour et l'ambition'. Grou, more disabused, opines flatly for 'l'argent'. Finally, 'le grand anatomiste Sidrac assura que c'était la chaise percée'. The other two are duly surprised. The rest of the chapter is a long speech by Sidrac, who clearly speaks with professional authority. Detailing the functioning of the human intestinal system, he proceeds to explain why all is determined by the close-stool.

One's moral disposition depends on 'les esprits animaux'. These in turn depend on the circulation of the blood, which depends on the chyle, which depends on the mesentery, which is attached to the intestines. 'Ces intestins, s'il m'est permis de le dire, sont remplis de merde.' The consequence is evident. 'Qu'arrive-t-il donc à un homme constipé? Les éléments les plus ténus, les plus délicats de sa merde ... entrent dans le coeur de l'homme le plus galant, de la femme la plus coquette. C'est une rosée d'étron désseché qui court dans tout son corps.'

Sidrac adduces three distinguished examples of this physiological determinism. Cromwell had been constipated for a week when he had Charles I beheaded. Henri II of France was in similar straits when he assassinated the brothers Guise. Charles IX was totally blocked before that terrible St Bartholomew Day. Those whose bowel movements are easy and regular, however, are affable and kindly. At the other extreme is 'le dévoiement'. Here too 'la garde-robe a tant d'empire'. As constipation makes one ferocious, so diarrhoea often turns its victims into cowards. Thus, contrary to the history-books, the English could not have suffered from dysentry at Agincourt. Here Sidrac turns to a denunciation of the absurdities promulgated by historians. Only natural history provides reliable knowledge. But even there one encounters the follies of Burnet, Whiston, Woodward, Maillet, and sundry 'charlatans'. Sidrac ends his diatribe thus:

> Je fais plus de cas d'un bon régime qui entretient mes humeurs en équilibre, et qui me procure une digestion louable et un sommeil plein. Buvez chaud quand il gèle, buvez frais dans la canicule; rien de trop ni de trop peu en tout genre; digérez, dormez, ayez du plaisir, et moquez-vous du reste. (vii, pp.592-94)

Physiological equilibrium alone is verifiable and thus important. Pleasure here is a prudent indulgence within a sceptical if not cynical world-view.

How serious is the case for defecatory determinism? Sidrac's professional status, and the array of concrete technical language in his account, prompt us to take it seriously. The argument is self-consistent. But its very neatness hints at parody. The lengthy but simple chain of causality, and the wildly simpliste version of history, invite disbelief. Placing the complete argument under the rubric of 'la chaise percée' is burlesque. The tone however is not joyous. The attack on history and theories in natural history is harsh. The repeated use of the word 'merde', even within the new discourse of science and realism, is a striking infraction of the proprieties. The image of the human body irradiated from inside with faeces is not Rabelaisian but Swiftian. As an expression of disgust we cannot doubt the seriousness of the chapter.

It seems impossible to reconcile the excremental vision with the religious view identified previously. In particular there is an evident contrast between the two final *dicta* we have cited. 'Digérez, dormez, ayez du plaisir, et moquez-vous du reste' patently contradicts 'Faisons notre devoir envers Dieu, adorons-le, soyons justes'. Both *dicta*, moreover, are attributed to the same speaker. Sidrac however is not alone in his divided outlook. Grou too is divided, no less radically. He projects his ambivalence upon the world. True nature is found only in Tahiti. 'Je n'ai vu ailleurs que des fripons ... des sots, des charlatans'. But the contradiction is present even in Tahiti. 'Parmi tant de gloire et tant de félicité, il y a un article qui me fait frémir', says Sidrac. He refers to venereal disease. The islanders have been infected by their European visitors. But Sidrac's horror is not anti-colonialist. It is VD itself which puzzles and appals him.

> A quoi pensa ce qu'on appelle *la nature*, quand elle versa ce poison dans les sources de la vie? On l'a dit, et je le répète, c'est la plus énorme et la plus détestable de toutes les contradictions. Quoi! l'homme a été fait, dit-on, à l'image de Dieu, *finxit in effigiem moderantum cuncta deorum*, et c'est dans les vaisseaux spermatiques de cette image qu'on a mis la douleur, l'infection et la mort!

The curious blend of Christian and pagan divinity attributed to man does not seem intended to weaken but rather to emphasise the contradiction.

Syphilis as a contradiction has been a topos in the *Contes* for some time. It first appears in *Candide*. There syphilis is a comic and satiric motif (the principle of Pangloss's physical fragmentation, and of a chain of cause and effect). But its significance as a contradiction, existential and philosophical, is also clearly stated. Pangloss's 'piteux état' is caused by 'l'amour, la consolation du genre humain, le conservateur de l'univers, l'âme de tous les êtres sensibles'. Syphilis is 'cette maladie qui empoisonne la source de la génération, ... et qui est évidemment l'opposé du grand but de la nature' (*Candide*, iv, p.153). In *Quarante écus* the power disabled becomes the power self-negated: 'la nature, se contredisant elle-même'. The opposition is again couched both physiologically and ontologically. The effect of syphilis is to 'rendre la tendresse horrible et le plaisir affreux'. The intellectual contradiction is 'que la nature ait attaché de si épouvantables tourments à un plaisir si nécessaire, tant de honte à tant de gloire'. The latter text in fact specifically invokes *Candide*, the work which proved that 'la vérole' and other evils could not be part of the universe of 'l'homme, ... image de Dieu, auquel on voit bien qu'il ressemble comme deux gouttes d'eau' (*Quarante écus*, pp. 460-61). In *Chesterfield*, Sidrac's 'on l'a dit' suggests the same allusion.

Within these apparently parallel statements there is however a degree of development. One might says that we move from paradox to scandal. *Candide* did not in fact say that man is the spit and image of God. This proposition, and the harshly ironic opposition underlying it, is new in *Quarante écus*. *Candide* designated sexual love in the ways we have just cited. But *Quarante écus* calls it 'tant de gloire'. This too takes us from a secular to a religious view. *Chesterfield* develops these hints into a hymn to generation. But *Chesterfield* also develops the opposed tendency. (Syphilis is now the *greatest* contradiction.) The bodily principle arouses horror. The desirable Miss Fidler is diseased. The ideal society is diseased. The most attractive man and woman are fecal matter. In a (female) word, to 'Otaïti et sa religieuse reine' is opposed 'la garde-robe [qui] a tant d'empire'.

A disturbing physiological emblem of this contradiction is first proposed in *Quarante écus*. The Divine image, it said, is initially lodged in the body 'entre la vessie et l'intestin rectum' (p.443). *Chesterfield* is fascinated by both these entities. Flanking the engendering of the Divine image, they provide the work's principle of unity. Initially Goudman is believed to have 'un grand mal à la vessie'. His putative gallstone mirrors the real blockage in Chesterfield's 'oreilles'. But his 'vessie' is also (as is already hinted at the end of ch.i) his sexual organ. His other motivation is identified with 'la vésicule du fiel' - the vessel of frustrated social aspiration (iii, p.580). The two are united to constitute his story (quest for Miss Fidler and the benefice), and his theory ('l'amour et l'ambition'). Finally he will achieve his quest. But at the expense of catching syphilis, the infection 'dans les vaisseaux spermatiques' (and is 'la vésicule du fiel' implied in his becoming 'terrible'?). Set apart and theorised is the account of the 'intestin rectum'. This is given its own chapter, which treats of the determining effects of constipation and diarrhoea. *Chesterfield* is a text about blockage and flow.

Jenni recognises the bodily principle in order to show why it must be suppressed. The moral and social didacticism of that work limits, and in some cases prevents, the expression of other truths. *Chesterfield*, amoral and more open, allows the direct expression of multiple truths. Arguably those of Voltaire, they appear at a number of different levels. There is the materialist truth of our physiological dependence. Two of the speakers, and the story, offer the interpersonal truth that we are motivated by 'l'amour', 'l'ambition' and 'l'argent'. The speakers agree on the moral truth of human vice and folly. Grou reveals the dream of a harmonious society - Tahiti is a realist version of Zadig's kingdom, Eldorado or the Ganges of *La Princesse de Babylone*. The speakers agree on the philosophical truth of determinism - a universal 'enchaînement' or a burlesque empire of the bowel. They agree on the spiritual truth that to engender life is the primary act of religion. Yet they are haunted by a horror of the body.

CONCLUSION

In the French Enlightenment in general, there are definite limits to the carnivalesque. Some of these limits are illustrated in Voltaire's *Contes*. Centrally deficient in the *Contes* is the representation of the concrete and the popular. Material objects, daily life (especially outside the privileged classes), non-standard or oral registers, tend to be excluded. When they are admitted, the treatment is liable to be negative. Didacticism, and the pathos with which it is later allied, are not negative elements. But they are somewhat restrictive or monologic in that they tell the reader what to think and feel. The discourse tends to the binary - double rather than several. The narratives themselves might be said to be deficient in 'body', being in the main regular in structure and spare in style.

On the other hand, the *Contes* can be said to be profoundly carnivalesque. Their chief characteristic is joyous mockery. A sense of the grotesque shapes the depiction of human bodies, social life, and the workings of the universe. Language and discourses are also mocked. Language is given a body in order to carnivalise it, occasionally but with some consistency. Word-play includes comic naming, multilingual puns, invented forms, anagram, semantic literalism and clashing etymology. Terms are foregrounded by italicisation. Received discourses are second-voiced as quotation marked or unmarked, by pastiche and by parody. Literature is itself a constant target, especially in the forms of romance and fable with their promise of ideal beauty and truth. The romance quest is treated playfully. The truth sought usually fails to come.

The *Contes* are deeply carnivalesque despite the relative absence within them of the popular and the oral. The tale as a genre is popular and oral in its origins. These tales seek the widest readership. Though the narratives themselves generally eschew the demotic, they deal principally in collectivities - groups, social practices and conversations. Though they deprecate the public life of the streets, they or their protagonists are quite promiscuously sociable. They take place on journeys and in cities. They are set in communal arenas - courts, market-places, inns, salons and later parlours. They focus on ritual and exchange - especially in the forms of religion, meals, sex and debate. Pursuing the greatest philosophical questions, they also exhibit a fascination with the base material stratum. They engage with contemporary society and its issues, initially by analogy and allusion, then directly. Depicting the social institution, and invoking the literary system, they satirise and celebrate both. Individually and collectively, they function as a totalising review of reality. The violence which characterises them, expressing Voltaire's anger and joy, figures the dynamic interaction and constant transformation of all things.

The forms of the carnivalesque, in the *Contes*, change over the long period of Voltaire's production. Tracing these successive forms, we shall draw our examples mainly from tales that we have not studied individually. Early *contes* tend to the geometric. Our chapter on *Le Monde comme il va* showed the importance of the line and the circle. *Micromégas* too works on the circle and the line. 'Après avoir raisonné pendant une révolution du soleil [circle], ils résolurent de faire ensemble un petit voyage philosophique [line].' The protagonists travel 'de globe en globe' or 'de lune en lune'. They land on a ring, or ride a parabolic comet. Equipped with 'instruments mathématiques', they meet earthmen flourishing 'quarts de cercle'. Communication is by means of an 'entonnoir' made of 'fibres circulaires'. Most notably of course, the text playfully bombards us with numbers. We have here a comic celebration of the universe of Newton. The universe of Plato is not dissimilar. Globes and numbers are also much featured in *Songe de Platon*. Again we are dealing in almost abstract figure. In these two tales only the Earth - clashing voices in *Micromégas*, clashing ecosystems in *Songe de Platon* - is given any substance. Both tales are literally cosmic, but almost disembodied.

This Cartesian carnivalesque is reflected in the structure of many early tales. We noted in Chapter 1 that *Zadig* and *Memnon* seem to work in triads. We noted the clausal syntax of *Lettre d'un Turc*, which is quite geometric in its balance and distribution: 'les uns ... , et les autres ...', 'plusieurs ... , d'autres ... '. *Les Deux Consolés*, still more simple in its structure, proceeds through a list. Each unit is marked off in parallel: 'souvenez-vous ... ', 'Il faut que je vous conte ... ', 'je vais vous apprendre ... '. The narrative syntax of longer tales may still be that of semi-discrete and parallel units. *Memnon* proceeds one by one through its triple undertakings. *Zadig* offers a succession of quasi-independent episodes, each in its own neatly headed chapter.

Zadig and *Memnon* still feature the line and the circle, but with a little more substance. In *Memnon* the combined figure, circle and line, repeatedly recurs. 'Memnon mit la tête à la fenêtre'; 'cette gorge ronde deviendra plate'; 'un emplâtre sur l'oeil'; 'des cerceaux de vingt-quatre pieds de circonférence'. We return to the abstract with 'il y a un globe où tout cela se trouve; mais ... tout se suit par degrés'. The combined figure also seems to provide a focus for each episode in *Zadig*. In ch.i the key event is 'un coup de flèche reçu près de l'oeil'. In ch.ii it is 'détourner un ruisseau' and its variant. In ch.iii it arises from Zadig 'se promenant auprès d'un petit bois'. In ch.iv he is saved thanks to 'une pêche ... tombée sur un morceau de tablette à écrire'. The narrative climax begins in ch.xvii, in which the setting is 'une grande lice bordée d'amphithéâtres'. The philosophical climax, ch.xviii, ends with the line-circle figure doubled. For the divine Jesrad the axis is vertical: 'l'ange prenait déjà son vol vers la dixième sphère'. For the human Zadig it is horizontal: 'Prends ton chemin vers Babylone'.

The 'dixième sphère' and the cosmos are already becoming marginalised. The human sphere will become the only totality. Collectively, the latter sphere is Babylon or Memnon's Nineveh, the heterogeneous city. In parallel, we can see how the circle is acquiring corporality on the level of the human person. It has become a head, an eye, a breast. The human body presented thus is fragmented. Indeed it is being damaged: an arrow in the eye or a plaster on it. In parallel, discourse is given a body. The written text may be fractured: 'un morceau de tablette à écrire'. Oral disorder is evoked at the start of *Zadig*. 'Ces propos si vagues, si rompus, si tumultueux' are '[ce] qu'on appelait *conversation* dans Babylone.' The human sphere is indeed Babel, the locus of multiple and clashing languages. It is the dialogic sphere. In fact, the grotesque body of speech does not encompass Zadig. His language is monologically pure - 'le style de la raison' (ch.vii). At the end - only gently ironised - he rules over an orderly Babylon. *Memnon* however ends differently. 'Je ne croirai cela, répliqua le pauvre Memnon, que quand je ne serai plus borgne.' Discursive disagreement and corporeal disorder both figure the world out of joint.

The Orient has put a little flesh on the geometry. *Scarmentado* brings the body closer to home. Apart from the Lappland of *Micromégas*, this is the first tale to be set partially in Europe. Time likewise comes nearer. The protagonist is '[né] dans la ville de Candie, en 1600'. Born emblematically with the century, Scarmentado is propelled through some of its more macabre manifestions. Each encounter on his journey is centred on a public ritual. Telling his own story (narration too is brought nearer), Scarmentado 'fails to understand'. Thus his own account breaks up or fragments the coherence of the event. It emphasises the external or formal aspects. It juxtaposes incongruous elements, debasing the elevated by pointing to the material truth. All these are key characteristics of the carnivalesque figure, now rather more filled out.

Each episode in *Scarmentado* constitutes a grotesque body, created by four narrative constituents. First to be established is cultural place: the world tour successively visits Rome, France, England, Holland, ... , ending with China, India and Africa. Within each Scarmentado encounters a festivity: 'processions', public execution, 'quelque carrousel ou quelque fête', 'cérémonie', 'foire'. A ritual gesture, normally religious, is noted. It accompanies an act of extreme violence. In France, Scarmentado is invited to '[manger] un petit morceau du maréchal d'Ancre, dont le peuple avait fait rôtir la chair'. In Spain 'on chanta dévotement de très belles prières, après quoi on brûla à petit feu tous les coupables'. In Turkey 'l'imam vint pour me circoncire; et, comme je fis quelque difficulté, le cadi ... me proposa de m'empaler'. Aureng-Zebe is 'l'homme le plus pieux de tout l'Indoustan. Il est vrai qu'il avait égorgé un de ses frères et empoisonné son père'. Thus in each episode religion is uncrowned, and violence is blessed. The failure to understand reveals the truth. What is truly holy is the universal cycle. The review is ferocious, yet joyous. The significance of the figure is clearest in another version, where sex is substituted for violence. One night in Constantinople Scarmentado joins with his concubine in a ritual cry. '*Alla, Illa, Alla*; ce sont les paroles sacramentales des Turcs; je crus que c'étaient celles de l'amour.' Sexuality uncrowns religion, and religion blesses sexuality. The most savage satire of human processes is also a celebration.

A fuller analysis of the figures of process is provided by our chapter on *Candide*. Chronologically, *Candide* is the next tale after *Scarmentado*. Its basic narrative formula - the youth toured through the world's disasters - is similar. A brief comparison of the two works is instructive, and enables us to say something more about the greatest of the *Contes* in our Conclusion. *Candide*'s triumph is to disperse the figures of process throughout the body of a more ample, complex and human narrative. In *Candide* disasters are less unalleviated. They are even balanced by a comic utopia. They are more varied, and the physical universe is given its due alongside human practices. There is romance, and more sex (of more kinds). There are many collective meals (likewise). Scarmentado is alone; he is a cypher; the events he records are episodic and impersonal; his itinerary has no motivation. Candide at the start is part of a joyous group. Throughout he is furnished with concrete circumstances. His travels are motivated (expulsion, flight, pursuit of the beloved). On his journey he rarely lacks companions, re-encountering old ones who come back from the dead (Pangloss, the young Baron, Paquette) and collecting new ones (Cacambo, Martin, Giroflée). Other stories are inserted (Cunégonde, La Vieille). A web of humanity - both plot and interlocution - embraces the world. Throughout meaning is sought, as the events are interrogated by the protagonists themselves. At the end almost the whole group are brought together in one place. The last chapter offers reprises of the interrogation, and of the story of the group and of humankind. The new garden is a joyous debasement of Eden. It contains a motley and active society, in what must be a temporary stasis.

After *Candide* it is no longer possible to trace a single line of generic development in the *Contes*. We can identify several tendencies. The two lines of 'bourgeois realist' development we traced in detail in our final chapter. A third is a reworking of the oriental tale. In the best-known examples, a freer fabulation is combined with new elements. *La Princesse de Babylone* is of this type. It begins in that favourite Voltairean city. Initially it is a joyous pastiche of the marvels of romance - the influence of Ariosto is evident - and of the wonders of the Old Testament. Making a massive leap, it then takes us on a tour of the eighteenth-century world. Finally it spirals off into literary reflexivity. The other substantial tale in this line is *Le Taureau blanc*. Again it also reflects Voltaire's new fascination with the Bible. The title and the story derive from the statement that Nebuchadnezzar for a time 'did eat grass as oxen' (*Daniel*, iv). Upon this circumstance is built a lyrical fantasy which mixes Old Testament wonders with pagan myths.

Read in terms of the history of ideas, this mixing of Judeo-Christian and pagan stories would be seen as as serving to relativise and undermine the status of Christianity. The carnivalesque reading would put the emphasis a little differently. It would stress the confrontation of discourses - the dialogic process and the hybrid product. It would emphasise the playful rather than negative treatment of sacred narrative. It would assimilate the undermining of the religious stories to the general principle of disrupting any official discourse. It might note in particular the insertion of Satanic prose - the Devil appears here, in the form of a talkative serpent. It would point to the procedures of joyous debasement: literalisation (the bull), corporality, accumulation (the multiplying of mythical animals). To hybridise and to debase is to renew.

Renewal here includes the phenomenon of metamorphosis. This idea appears more strongly in *La Princesse de Babylone*. The heroine is assisted by a phoenix. The latter affirms that change and rebirth are universal. 'Tout est résurrection dans ce monde. ... . Toutes les particules qui composaient les corps sont changées en différents êtres' (iv, p.373). Here again is the world-cycle, but in a new formulation. The idea of metamorphosis is also mentioned in three of the other four oriental tales from the later period: *Histoire d'un bon bramin, Aventure indienne* and *Les Lettres d'Amabed*. New too in these tales is a concern with vegetarianism. Both preoccupations, but especially the latter, are evidently to be linked with Indian settings. Vegetarianism is explicitly advocated in *La Princesse de Babylone* (where the hero hails from near the Ganges). 'Les hommes alimentés de carnage ... [ont] la fureur de verser le sang de leurs frères' (iii, p.365). Similarly in *Aventure indienne* and *Amabed*. In all these tales however it is juxtaposed with extreme violence. In *La Princesse de Babylone* the hero practises both, and the inconsistency is simply ignored. *Aventure indienne* presents the contradiction as a massive irony. 'Cette loi admirable par laquelle il est défendu de manger les animaux nos semblables' is affirmed in the teeth of the unending cycle of violence in nature. *Amabed* however seems to accept, if not approve, that cycle.

Les Lettres d'Amabed is told through a fictional correspondence. In this respect it is unique within the *Contes*. It is unique within the oriental tales by its degree of realism. It is set not in a fabulous past but in specific and fairly recent history. Amabed and Adaté are a young Hindu couple living in a part of India colonised by the Portuguese. They are falsely accused of apostasy, and Adaté is raped, by the missionary Father Fa tutto. He takes them to Rome, where they are corrupted by the pleasures of the Papal court. This appears to be a fairly crude - and predictable - attack on the Catholic Church. But the meaning is more complex. The couple change. The significance of the tale is thematised in Fa tutto's affirmation 'Io la converteró' (pp.487, 489). Once more, joyous debasement reveals the truth. This priest brings about every kind of conversion. The gentle, monogamous and vegetarian couple come to enjoy the aggressive, orgiastic and carnivorous practices of Catholicism. The text is replete with figures of penetration and flow. There remain hints of a horror of corporeal process - in the Roman kitchens 'le sang et la graisse coulaient' (p.514). But the implication of the whole is that violence is the life force.

The fascination with corporeal process and the horror of it are two tendencies identified in our last chapter. They are increasingly evident in the realist tales. On the commonsensical side, *Quarante écus* engages with the new biological sciences. *Chesterfield* seems to subscribe to a materialist determinism. But the ambivalence is evident. On the other side, *L'Ingénu* concludes in favour of moral sentiment. But its advocate, Gordon, is a determinist. In *Jenni* the bourgeois patriarch imposes his law and denies the body. But in the debate with Birton he makes concessions to materialism. Anticipated are the two major cultural preoccupations of the next hundred years - science and bourgeois order. The other development that we identified in the later realist tales is no less important. Increasingly they use personal narration. They show a new concern with subjectivity and pathos. *Amabed* also illustrates these tendencies. The events are conveyed to us through the couple's letters. Voltaire attempts, not very successfully, to represent their terror and confusion. We saw something similar in the latter part of *L'Ingénu*. The conclusion of *L'Ingénu* is not only moralistic. Juxtaposing intense personal suffering and an indifferent cosmos, it anticipates Romanticism. The genius of the *Contes* however is not for alienation but for joyously angry engagement. It is not for the subjective grotesque of the mind but for the grotesque in the world - that of the body, the community and the universe. If it is a little less than fully corporeal, this is more congenial to Voltaire's temperament and enables him to show more clearly its articulations.

BIBLIOGRAPHY: WORKS CITED

EDITIONS OF THE *CONTES*:

Voltaire, *Romans et contes*, ed. Frédéric Deloffre and Jacques Van den Heuvel (Paris: Gallimard [La Pléiade], 1979).
All references, unless otherwise indicated, are to this edition.

Romans et contes, ed. René Pomeau (Paris: Garnier [Flammarion], 1966).

Zadig ou la Destinée: Histoire orientale, ed. Georges Ascoli, revised Jean Fabre (2 vols, Paris: M. Didier, 1962).

'Micromégas': a Study in the Fusion of Science, Myth and Art, ed. Ira O. Wade (Princeton: Princeton University Press, 1950).

'L'Ingénu' and 'Histoire de Jenni', ed. J.H. Brumfitt and M.I. Gerard Davis (Oxford: Basil Blackwell, 1970).

THEORY:

Adam, Jean-Michel, *Le Récit* (Paris: Presses Universitaires de France, 1987).

Bakhtin, Mikhail, *Rabelais and his World* (Cambridge Mass.: M.I.T. Press, 1968).

[=*L'Œuvre de François Rabelais et la culture populaire au moyen âge te sous la renaissance* (Paris: Gallimard, 1970)].

Problems of Dostoevsky's Poetics (Manchester: Manchester University Press, 1984).

'Discourse in the novel', *The Dialogic Imagination*, ed. Michael Holquist (Austin: University of Texas Press, 1981).

[='Du Discours romanesque', *Esthétique et théorie du roman* (Paris: Gallimard, 1978)].

Speech Genres and other Late Essays, ed. Caryl Emerson and Michael Holquist (Austin: University of Texas Press, 1986).

Genette Gérard, *Palimpsestes: la littérature au second degré* (Paris: Seuil, 1982).

Greimas, A.J., *Sémantique structurale* (Paris: Larousse, 1966).

Propp, Vladimir, *Morphology of the Folk-tale* (Austin: University of Texas Press, 1968).

CRITICISM AND SCHOLARSHIP:

Editions of the *Contes* as above.

Andreas, James, '*Candide* as comic *conte*', *Approaches to Teaching Voltaire's 'Candide'*, ed. Renée Waldinger (New York: Modern Language Association of America, 1987), pp.124-33.

Apostolidès, Jean-Marie, 'Le Système des échanges dans *Candide*', *Poétique* 48 (1981), pp.449-58.

Barber, W.H., 'Voltaire's astronauts', *French Studies* 30 (1976), pp.28-42.

Barthes, Roland, *Sur Racine* (Paris: Seuil, 1963).

Betts, C.J., 'Echoes of *Manon Lescaut* in *Candide*', *French Studies Bulletin* 28 (Autumn 1988), pp.14-16.

Bongie, Laurence L., 'Crisis and the birth of the Voltairian *conte*', *Modern Language Quarterly* 23 (1962), pp.53-64.

Bottiglia, William F., *Voltaire's 'Candide': Analysis of a Classic*, Studies on Voltaire and the Eighteeenth Century 7 (1959).

Cherpack, Clifton, 'Voltaire's *Histoire de Jenni*: a synthetic creed', *Modern Philology* 54 (1956-7), pp.26-32.

Clark, Priscilla P., '"L'Ingénu": the uses and limitations of naïveté', *French Studies* 27 (1973), pp.278-86.

Coulet, Henri, 'La Fantaisie dans le conte français du xviiie siècle', *Burlesque et formes parodiques*, ed. Isabelle Landy-Houillon and Maurice Ménard (Paris-Seattle-Tübingen: Biblio 17, 1987), pp.503-25.

Dalnekoff, D.I., '*Le Monde comme il va*: a satire on satire', *Studies on Voltaire and the Eighteenth Century* 106 (1973), pp.85-102.

Delattre, André, *Voltaire l'impétueux* (Paris: Mercure de France, 1957).

Démoris, René, 'Genèse et symbolique de l'*Histoire de Jenni, ou le sage et l'athée* de Voltaire', *Studies on Voltaire and the Eighteenth Century* 199 (1981), pp.87-123.

Francis, R.A., 'Prévost's *Cleveland* and Voltaire's *Candide*', *Studies on Voltaire and the Eighteenth Century* 208 (1982), pp.295-303.

Gilot, Michel, 'Le Cycle des semaines dans *Candide*', *Lettres et réalités: mélanges de littérature générale et de critique romanesque offerts au professeur Henri Coulet par ses amis* (Aix-en-Provence: Université de Provence, 1988), pp.117-29.

Gilroy, James, 'Peace and the pursuit of happiness in the French utopian novel: Fénelon's *Télémaque* and Prévost's *Cleveland*', *Studies on Voltaire and the Eighteenth Century*, 176 (1979), pp.169-87.

Ginsberg, Robert, 'The Argument of Voltaire's *L'Homme aux quarante écus*: a study in philosophical rhetoric', *Studies on Voltaire and the Eighteenth Century* 56 (1967), pp.611-57.

Henein, Eglal, 'Hercule ou le pessimisme. Analyse de *L'Ingénu*', *Romanic Review* 72 (1981), pp.149-65.

Henry, Patrick, 'Sacred and profane gardens in *Candide*', *Studies on Voltaire and the Eighteenth Century* 176 (1979), pp.133-52.

Highnam, David E., '*L'Ingénu*: flawed masterpiece or masterful innovation', *Studies on Voltaire and the Eighteenth Century* 143 (1975), pp.71-83.

Howells, Robin, '*Télémaque* et *Zadig*: apports et rapports', *Studies on Voltaire and the Eighteenth Century* 215 (1982), pp.63-75.

'The Burlesque as a philosophical principle in Voltaire's *Contes'*, *Voltaire and his world*, ed. R.J. Howells, A. Mason, H.T. Mason and D. Williams (Oxford: Voltaire Foundation, 1985), pp.67-84.

'Processing Voltaire's *Amabed*', *British Journal for Eighteenth-Century Studies* 10 (1987), pp.153-62.

'Rococo and carnival', *Studies on Voltaire and the Eighteenth Century* 308 (1993), pp.187-223.

James, E.D., 'The Concept of emanation in the later philosophy of Voltaire', *Studies on Voltaire and the Eighteenth Century* 284 (1991), pp.199-209.

Le Jeu au xviiie siècle (Aix-en-Provence: Edisud, 1976).

Kotta, Nuçi, '*L'Homme aux quarante écus': a Study of Voltairean Themes* (The Hague: Mouton & Co., 1966).

Lanson, Gustave, *L'Art de la prose* (Paris: Arthème Fayard, 1930).

Levy, Zwi, '*L'Ingénu* ou l'anti-*Candide*', *Studies on Voltaire and the Eighteenth Century* 183 (1980), pp.45-67.

Mason, Haydn, 'The Unity of *L'Ingénu*', *The Age of the Enlightement: Studies Presented to Theodore Besterman*, ed. W.H. Barber, J.H. Brumfitt, R.A. Leigh, R. Shackleton and S.S.B. Taylor (Edinburgh: Oliver and Boyd, 1967), pp.93-106.

'Voltaire et le ludique', *Revue d'Histoire Littéraire de la France* 84 (1984), pp.539-52.

'*Zadig* and *Manon Lescaut*', *French Studies Bulletin* 29 (Winter 1988), pp.21-22.

'*Zadig* and the birth of the Voltaire *conte*', *Rousseau and the Eighteenth Century: Essays in Memory of R.A. Leigh*, (Oxford: Voltaire Foundation, 1992), pp.283-294.

Magnin, Charles, *Histoire des marionnettes en Europe depuis l'antiquité jusqu'à nos jours* (Paris: Michel Lévy Frères, 1852).

Mervaud, Christiane, '*Jeannot et Colin*: illustration et subversion du conte moral', *Revue d'Histoire Littéraire de la France* 85 (1985), pp.596-620.

'Du Carnaval au carnavalesque: l'épisode vénétien de *Candide*', *Le Siècle de Voltaire: hommage à René Pomeau*, ed. Christiane Mervaud and Sylvain Menant (2 vols, Oxford: Voltaire Foundation, 1987), ii, pp.651-62.

Mylne, Vivienne, 'Literary techniques and methods in Voltaire's *contes philosophiques*', *Studies on Voltaire and the Eighteenth Century* 57 (1967), pp.1055-80.

'Wolper's view of Voltaire's tales', *Studies on Voltaire and the Eighteenth Century* 212 (1982), pp.318-27.

Pelckmans, Paul, *Le Sacre du père: fictions des Lumières et historicité d'Œdipe 1699-1775* (Amsterdam: Rodopi, 1983).

Pomeau, René, *La Religion de Voltaire* (Paris: Nizet, 1974).

'Le Jeu de Voltaire écrivain', *Le Jeu au xviiie siècle* (Aix-en-Provence: Edisud, 1976), pp.175-6.

Robert, Raymonde, 'La Parodie du conte merveilleux au xviiie siècle', *Dire la parodie: colloque de Cerisy*, ed. Clive Thomson and Alain Pagès (New York-Bern-Frankfurt-Paris: Peter Lang, 1989), pp.183-99.

Roberts, Warren E., *Morality and Social Class in Eighteenth-century French Literature and Painting* (Toronto: University of Toronto Press, 1974).

Roger, Jacques, *Les Sciences de la vie dans la pensée française du xviiie siècle: la génération des animaux de Descartes à l'Encyclopédie* (Paris: Armand Colin, 1971).

Sareil, Jean, 'Le Rythme comique, accélération et ralentissement dans les *Contes de Voltaire*', *Colloque '76: Voltaire*, ed. Robert L. Walters (London Ontario: Department of French, University of Western Ontario, 1983), pp.141-54.

Sermain, Jean-Paul, 'La Parodie dans les contes de fées (1697-1713): une loi du genre?', *Burlesque et formes parodiques*, ed. Isabelle Landy-Houillon and Maurice Ménard (Paris-Seattle-Tübingen: Peter Lang, 1987), pp.541-52.

Sherman, Carol, *Reading Voltaire's 'Contes': a Semiotics of Philosophical Narration* (Chapel Hill: University of North Carolina Department of Romance Languages, 1985).

Starobinski, Jean, *L'Invention de la liberté 1700-1789* (Geneva: Skira, 1964).

'Le Fusil à deux coups de Voltaire. 1. Sur le style philosophique de *Candide*; 2. L'Ingénu sur la plage', *Le Remède dans le mal* (Paris: Gallimard, 1989), pp.122-63.

Stewart, Philip, 'Holding the mirror up to fiction: generic parody in *Candide*', *French Studies* 33 (1979), pp.411-19.

Tanner, Tony, *Adultery in the Novel* (Baltimore: Johns Hopkins Press, 1979).

Taylor, S.S.B., 'Voltaire's humour', *Studies on Voltaire and the Eighteenth Century* 179 (1979), pp.101-16.

Undank, Jack, 'The Status of fiction in Voltaire's *Contes*', *Degré Second* 6 (July 1982), pp.65-88.

Virolle, Roland, 'Voltaire et les matérialistes, d'après ses derniers contes', *Dix-huitième siècle* 11 (1979), pp.63-74.

Wolper, Roy S., 'The Final foolishness of Babouc: the dark centre of *Le Monde comme il va*', *Modern Language Review* 75 (1980), pp.766-73.

'The Toppling of Jeannot', *Studies on Voltaire and the Eighteenth Century* 183 (1980), pp.69-82.

Van den Heuvel, Jacques, *Voltaire dans ses contes* (Paris: Armand Colin, 1967).